POWER, ~~TRADE~~, AND TIME

AN EMPIRICAL INTRODUCTION TO INTERNATIONAL RELATIONS

J. PATRICK RHAMEY JR.

VIRGINIA MILITARY INSTITUTE

TADEUSZ KUGLER

ROGER WILLIAMS UNIVERSITY

ROWMAN & LITTLEFIELD
Lanham ▪ Boulder ▪ New York ▪ London

Executive Editor: Traci Crowell
Assistant Editor: Deni Remsberg
Higher Education Channel Manager: Jonathan Raeder
Interior Designer: Rosanne Schloss

Credits and acknowledgments for material borrowed from other sources, and reproduced with permission, appear on the appropriate page within the text.

Published by Rowman & Littlefield
An imprint of The Rowman & Littlefield Publishing Group, Inc.
4501 Forbes Boulevard, Suite 200, Lanham, Maryland 20706
www.rowman.com

6 Tinworth Street, London SE11 5AL, United Kingdom

British Library Cataloguing in Publication Information Available

Library of Congress Cataloging-in-Publication Data Available

ISBN 9781538127223 (cloth)
ISBN 9781538127230 (paperback)
ISBN 9781538127247 (epub)

♾™ The paper used in this publication meets the minimum requirements of American National Standard for Information Sciences—Permanence of Paper for Printed Library Materials, ANSI/NISO Z39.48-1992.

Brief Contents

PART III Key Issues Confronting the Twenty-First Century

Contents

Figures, Tables, and Boxes

FIGURES

TABLES

BOXES

Foreword

POWER, SPACE, AND TIME is a major work of scholarship and a breakthrough in pedagogy for international relations (IR). On one hand, many textbooks exist already in IR and convey basic curriculum, such as the paradigms of the field and historical information about major events, quite effectively. On the other hand, standard introductory texts tend to leave an important gap that increasingly endangers student learning about international relations in the fast-paced twenty-first century. *Power, Space, and Time* takes seriously the need to convey the results of systematic empirical research to prepare students for the world beyond the classroom. Through this text, it becomes possible to learn about empirical international relations, data sources, and the relevance of research findings to the real world of foreign policy decision-making and action.

J. Patrick Rhamey Jr. and Tadeusz Kugler, the authors, are outstanding scholars who possess a wide range of interests. With excellent abilities in both communication and research methods, Patrick and Tad are an ideal team to have produced this textbook. Among their other areas of knowledge, two stand out in the context of this volume. Patrick is an expert on the study of regions, while Tad is an authority on demographics and economic performance. The interdisciplinary and comprehensive nature of *Power, Space, and Time* reflects the combined talents and gifts of these two rising academic stars. I am well acquainted with Patrick and Tad through the Trans-Research Consortium and can attest to their dedication to the quest for scientific knowledge and its dissemination to students and the general public. Their commitment shines through in the pages of *Power,*

Space, and Time, which clearly is the product of a sustained effort to facilitate learning that will pay off in and beyond an academic setting.

Power, Space, and Time is not only a rigorous but also a quite readable study that conveys scientific explanations and reproducible evidence. Students learn how causal relationships are impacted by both geography and time—something that tends to be peripheral in prior texts on IR. The range of topics covered is impressive. The book begins by introducing a hierarchical approach to international relations, which descends from the path-breaking work of Organski on power transition theory. This perspective helps to balance against the bias encountered throughout much of IR in favor of seeing global and regional systems exclusively from the standpoint of anarchy. Chapters on international conflict, rivalries and alliances, and intrastate conflict reveal that hierarchy and anarchy coexist in both domestic and international politics. A chapter on the Cold War reveals the degree to which the international system can be understood in terms of the dynamics involving a leading and challenging state. The Cold War, with the United States and USSR in those roles, respectively, stands as a completed historical case that can help students to comprehend the evolution of hierarchy in tandem with anarchy that transitioned into the world of today. The academic "forensics" carried out on the Cold War era are excellent; the concepts of hierarchy and anarchy are deployed effectively to explain events.

Power, Space, and Time is also to be commended for its balanced treatment of cooperation and conflict. Topics such as regionalization and trade bring out the importance of geography and temporal effects on prospects for international cooperation. This textbook is very fair and students will see neither idealism nor cynicism in the chapters that pertain to prospects for international cooperation. Like those on conflict, the chapters on cooperation also contain case-oriented illustrations that enhance student learning.

Once students have become familiar with basic concepts and approaches in IR, along with substantial evidence about cooperation and conflict, *Power, Space, and Time* turns more directly to the concerns of today. The chapters in the final phase of the book focus on deterrence and major powers, prospects for a democratic peace, and the United States in its role as a system leader faced with the challenge of a rapidly rising China. All these topics are covered in a rigorous yet accessible manner. One especially interesting feature is the search for lessons for system management from the decline of the British Empire over a century ago. What aspects of the British experience are relevant today? How might lessons be learned from empirical evidence about the evolution of Britain toward peer and eventually subordinate status relative to other states, notably the United States? What arrangements would be most constructive, in both global and regional terms, to promote cooperation and avert war? With the essential tools already in hand, students are prepared to answer these and other pressing questions effectively based on empirical evidence—many steps beyond the endless armchair speculation from television or the internet. The readers of *Power, Space, and Time*, faculty and students alike, will come away with an appreciation for the value of empirical knowledge for both science and citizenship.

Patrick James, Dornsife Dean's Professor of
International Relations, USC, and President,
International Studies Association, 2018–19

Preface

SINCE THE END OF THE COLD WAR, international relations has evolved from a field dominated by theoretical debates between paradigms to heavily empirical research that focuses on mid-range theories that seek to explain specific, observable outcomes. Unfortunately, undergraduate instruction in international relations has not kept up with these developments. In introductory courses, students are presented with the three big paradigms of neorealism, neoliberal institutionalism, and constructivism, which often lack a clear empirical component, and then take a series of topical elective classes as they progress through their college years. However, missing in both many curricula and instructional texts is an attempt to bridge the gap between broad introductory theory and the empirical approaches that characterize much of contemporary international relations research. In part, this disconnect may be due to the absence of statistical knowledge of the student in their introductory coursework, making many quantitative scholarly articles relatively inaccessible to the undergraduate reader.

What we seek to provide in this text is an introduction to the empirical side of doing international relations. We assume students possess no statistical knowledge, introducing some of the data that is most often employed in international relations research and providing descriptive examples through tables and graphs. As the ultimate goal is for students to develop testable hypotheses by the time they graduate, we then heavily reference and provide examples in further readings of research that takes the data we have discussed here and uses it to answer interesting research questions. This text provides an introduction to empirical international relations, a reference of data sources and foundational scholarly publications, and engagement in how to relate academic research to foreign policy. The discussion of the material is broad, not focusing extensively on a single topic. However, we reference in-depth research throughout and provide a list of further readings at the end of each chapter so that readers might delve further into topics of interest.

WHY HIERARCHICAL APPROACHES?

As a theoretical guide to engaging a wide range of questions in international relations, we employ hierarchical approaches as a lens, primarily, power transition, hegemonic stability, and long cycle theories. We do this for two reasons. First, while aspects of these and related approaches are heavily engaged in empirical international relations research and have received increasing attention in popular discussion and the media, they are consistently overlooked in introductory coursework. Therefore, we introduce students to these approaches in this text, contrasting them against the neorealist, neoliberal, and constructivist paradigms.

Second, we want students to think seriously about how observable causal relationships may be affected by both time and geography. By thinking about the causal process as dynamic and interconnected events, rather than as discrete snapshots in time as they are often treated in other approaches, such as neorealism, we believe students can develop a more holistic understanding of international politics. At the same time, as an introductory text to empirical international relations, we also seek to incorporate a systemic focus, driving students to think about what global contextual dynamics may underlie the advancement of democracy, free trade, or normative behaviors frequently the focus of neoliberal and constructivist approaches. The hierarchical theories as presented here provide an introduction to students to think about changes in power over time and geography, granting them broad applicability to the wide variation of outcomes discussed in this text.

STRUCTURE AND FEATURES OF THE TEXT

The text begins with an overview of international relations theory, providing a refresher on the major paradigms and introducing students to hierarchical approaches. In chapter 2, we provide a simple example of how we might engage international relations empirically through a scientific method, including discussion of theory, hypothesis, and testing, with a list of the datasets employed throughout the text. The remainder of the book focuses on outcomes of interest in empirical international relations research, giving the student a descriptive introduction to the data and current findings. Part I (chapters 3–6) focuses on conflictual outcomes: interstate conflict, rivalries and alliances, and intrastate conflict. Part II (chapters 7–10) focuses on cooperative outcomes: organizations, trade, and globalization. Each part concludes with a real-world comparison rooted in recent history to illustrate the empirical dynamics discussed in the preceding chapters. The text concludes with chapters on the most empirically conclusive outcomes in international politics: deterrence and democratic peace. Building on the theoretical and empirical discussions in the preceding chapters, we discuss how hierarchical approaches treat these outcomes as derived from the structure of the international system and follow this discussion with a chapter that relates these findings to what may unfold in the twenty-first century. Concluding the text, we discuss the implications for the future of American foreign policy in the context of a rising China and India or further integrated Europe.

We couple this discussion with a series of pedagogical features designed to both be simple and approachable while also facilitating further engagement by students with the abstract material:

- **Discussion Questions:** Each chapter concludes with a set of discussion questions to both reflect on the chapter's material and promote classroom discussion.
- **Activities:** Parts I and II both conclude with activities designed to help students further understand the causal relationships in the empirical approaches previously discussed and can be used as a foundation for homework assignments or research projects.
- **Key Terms:** Each chapter includes a list of key terms related to both empirical and theoretical material. A glossary at the end of the text provides a list of definitions.
- **Suggested Reading:** Each chapter also concludes with a list of suggested readings related to the chapter's content. In most cases, the readings provide examples executing statistical analysis of the data and theories described and discussed.
- **Sample Syllabi:** Sample syllabi illustrating how the text may be integrated into course work both at the introductory and intermediate levels can be found on the text's webpage: https://textbooks.rowman.com/rhamey-kugler.

ACKNOWLEDGMENTS

Above all else, we are grateful to our better halves, Katie Rhamey and Emily MN Kugler, who have tolerated the long hours spent on this project and always been willing to provide their thoughts. We are also grateful for the research support provided by the Virginia Military Institute, Roger Williams University, and the Charles Koch Foundation without which this project would not have been possible. Our thanks to all those who have given their feedback at various stages in this process, including Alicia Cano, Jorge Capote, Alex Howell, Richard Johnson, Jacek Kugler and Cheryl Kugler, Jennifer Sciubba, Ron Tammen, Aakriti Tandon, Thomas Jefferson Tremmel, and John Vasquez. Finally, we would also like to thank those who reviewed the proposal Michael Slobodchikoff (Troy University), Thomas J. Volgy (University of Arizona), John Linantud (University of Houston Downton), Douglas Lemke (Pennsylvania State University), Gaspare Genna (The University of Texas at El Paso), Kristin Johnson (University of Rhode Island), Boyka Stefanova (University of Texas at San Antonio), and Patrick James (University of Southern California).

We dedicate this text to our students that they might develop an analytical and critical understanding of international politics and use that knowledge to promote a peaceful future.

About the Authors

J. PATRICK RHAMEY JR. is associate professor in the Department of International Studies and Political Science at the Virginia Military Institute and serves on the board of the TransResearch Consortium. He received his PhD in political science from the University of Arizona. His publications include work on the behaviors of major and regional powers, comparative regionalism, and the international politics of sport.

TADEUSZ "TAD" KUGLER is associate professor of political science at Roger Williams University and serves on the board of the TransResearch Consortium. He received his PhD in economics and politics at Claremont Graduate University. His publications focus on the economic and demographic foundations of growth and their connection to international power and the dynamics of recovery after war.

1

A Hierarchical Approach

EMPIRICAL INTERNATIONAL POLITICS AND HIERARCHY

To develop empirical arguments about international politics, we must begin by choosing a lens through which we can organize the enormous amounts of complex information and potential causes we observe. The lens used in this book is an approach to understanding empirical international relations as they relate to hierarchy in the international system. We introduce the reader to hierarchical theories, compare them with the dominant approaches to international relations, and use commonly analyzed data in the areas of both conflict and cooperation to illustrate potential relationships. There is no assumption of statistical knowledge, but, instead, this text merely provides a primer to often-used data in international politics as well as the means to connect it to policy.

Hierarchy is the organization of actors in relationship to one another by some criteria. As an ordering principle, hierarchy explains the relationship between causes and consequences of observed occurrences in international politics both across time (how states change in the hierarchy) and space (how hierarchy changes in different parts of the world). For the most part, the book focuses on hierarchy in terms of power—or the ability to make others do things they otherwise would not do.[1] This ability could be rooted in material capabilities, such as resources a state can use to create military hardware or, alternatively, something less tangible, such as perceptions of threat, strategic geographical location, or how important one state perceives another to be because of specific markers, such as leading organizations, having nuclear weapons, a stable government, or even performing well in an event such as the Olympics.[2] Taking into consideration all these competing pieces of information, states develop ideas about who is "above" and who is "below" them in the international hierarchy. The order of that hierarchy affects both what they *can* do, or what they have the power and resources to accomplish and where, and what they might *wish* to do given the role granted to them or the status they want to receive from others.

Hierarchy and power are heavily rooted in material capabilities, such as military hardware, but these military capabilities on their own are not a sufficient measure. States must also possess what some have called "authority" or what others label "status."[3] A dominant state must not only have the ability to create order and punish those who would seek to challenge that order but also be granted legitimacy and be viewed as a leader by the other actors in the system. Those actors dissatisfied with that leadership are those that may be particularly disruptive and conflictual. This creates the potential for rivalries and wars.

The approaches reviewed in this text examine how states' position in the hierarchy affects both their opportunity to engage in certain behaviors and their willingness to pursue one type of action over another.[4] Hierarchy does not imply that there exists some government of governments but merely a fluctuating order of political authority that has consequences for both those at the top and those within it. Although variations of hierarchy exist across most of the international system most of the time, the system is also anarchic, meaning that there is no one government with complete control over all states. Unlike hierarchical approaches, for some theories, anarchy is an unchanging condition with a fixed effect on state behavior.

Hierarchical approaches suggest that although the system is always anarchic, a significantly powerful state with legitimacy can mitigate the organizational problems of this anarchy over a group of actors. Hierarchy and anarchy are coexistent, where anarchy is always present but its consequences are fluid depending on the extent to which a hierarchy has developed over the system as a whole or some geographic space. Hierarchy can help solve some of the problems of living under anarchy. Likewise, when it breaks down, those problems return with potentially destructive consequences.

Hierarchy and Opportunity

Opportunity is the ability of a state to accomplish some goal, not whether it wishes to do certain things. One key variable that affects hierarchy—and the opportunity of states to use their capabilities—is geography. Geography both restrains states and provides the context for where international politics occur, whether in a region, across a body of water, or over a territorial border. As a constraint, distance creates logistical limitations on opportunity even for the most powerful states, such as the United States today or the British Empire in the nineteenth century. The British, for example, lost conflicts to far less powerful opponents in remote areas of Africa and Central Asia while at the peak of their power. For smaller, less powerful states, however, geography is usually such a significant limit on their ability to pursue foreign policy that they are unable to meaningfully engage their capabilities for or against actors outside their immediate neighborhood.[5] The small island nation of Mauritius, for example, cannot practically go to war with Peru no matter how great its desire might be to do so. Material capabilities provide states with the tools they can use to shape international politics, but geography provides the canvas limiting where they can use those capabilities.

To demonstrate how hierarchy changes across geography, figure 1.1 illustrates a simplified example of the hierarchy of states in the

Figure 1.1   Hierarchy and Geographic Space in Contemporary International Politics

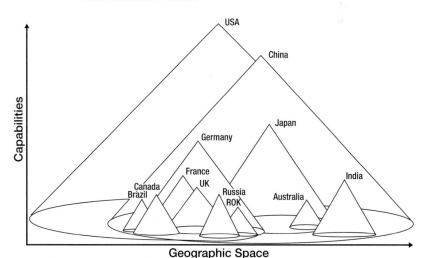

international system today. Chapter 2 discusses various measures of power in greater detail, but for depicting the relative power between states shown in the figure, we use a state's economic size measured by gross domestic product (GDP) as a proxy, or placeholder, for how much power one state has over another.[6] This value is then scaled by how effective a government is at extracting resources from that economy, or its political capacity, for foreign policy use, whether cooperative or conflictual.[7] Airplanes, guns, embassies, and economic aid all require a source of revenue extracted from a domestic population. Governments' effectiveness in extracting resources from their domestic populations varies. They may acquire these resources by taxing industries or citizens' incomes, so each cone represents both how many resources exist in a country and how effective the government of that country is at extracting those resources. As you get geographically farther from a country's border, its ability to use its power degrades as the logistical challenges of crossing distances increase.[8] Thus, the cones, or the relative power of each state, decline slowly over distance as it becomes more difficult for a state to exert its power farther from its borders.

These cones of each state's power overlap in different ways to depict, across geography, the current hierarchy in the international system. Expectedly, the United States is the most powerful. However, as we arrive at Chinese shores, far from the United States, the Chinese become dominant in their immediate surroundings. Beneath these two most powerful states are the other major and regional powers that we typically discuss as important in international politics. Both China and the United States can meaningfully reach most regions of the world with their capabilities and are influential, though the United States is generally the more powerful of the two. In some places, such as Latin America, the United States is clearly dominant even as China attempts to increase its influence in the region. Within Europe, both powers are present as China expands its economic influence, adding to a sophisticated hierarchy of states, manifest in the impressive and dominating importance of the European Union coupled with the increasing belligerence of a Russia that is significantly inferior in its power compared to its Soviet predecessor.

Throughout the text, examples of changes in capabilities, the effect of geographic context on the opportunity of states, and where states reside in the international hierarchy are discussed in detail, both in the contemporary period and from history. Likewise, the ability of states to mitigate the challenges of distance has also changed.

The last clearly dominant power, Britain, may have been relatively more powerful for a period during the nineteenth century compared to its peers than the United States is today; however, combustion engines, airplanes, missiles, and the Internet allow the United States a degree of "reach," or the ability to cross distances, that Britain lacked. Even as we enter a new era of cyber espionage and weaponry, distance remains an insurmountable condition. Just as airplanes and drones help solve the problems of distance but still require places to land and terrestrial forces to provide support, so, too, do cyber-attacks and cyber espionage require bases of support, and they are more threatening weapons in the hands of a neighboring state that is able to use other means of physical intervention than in the hands of a less powerful actor on the other side of the world. In the context of capabilities, we are focusing more on what a state might be able to develop given existing resources rather than the specific use of those capabilities. Decisions about budgets, the distribution of research contracts, the influence of interest groups, and operational tactics occur at an individual decision-making level, although they are likely to be influenced by relative power considerations or security concerns. A state may have a greater willingness to engage in cyber espionage or unconventional conflict if it lacks the physical capabilities to compete with a more powerful state in the development of military hardware.

Hierarchy and Willingness

Your position in the hierarchy may very well affect the types of policies you pursue and how capabilities are expended. Although we do not extensively discuss individual decision-making as it relates to policy choices, we do discuss how hierarchy impacts general foreign policy activity pertaining to conflict and cooperation. For example, a state that others view as important but with declining capabilities is likely to try to lead cooperatively rather than to use conflict to get what it wants, lest confrontation with a more powerful state exposes its weakness, whereas a very powerful state that is not getting its way may not hesitate to flex its muscles.[9] Hierarchy is not just where you stand relative to your peers at the moment but also the trajectory of where you are headed. Two states of the same power and same geographic location will be prone to pursuing different strategies depending on whether they think they might be an up-and-comer on the verge of global dominance or a declining state soon to be relegated to the dustbin of history.[10]

Hierarchy impacts the willingness, meaning preference or desire of a state, to pursue specific actions. The state's own views on where it is and should be in that hierarchy, as well as the role and authority attributed to it by other states in the system, will affect the attractiveness of policy choices. For example, if a state has a significant amount of capabilities but does not believe others are granting it the respect it deserves, it may act in ways that demonstrate that it both is dissatisfied and demands greater respect. As a result, foreign policy actions that demonstrate the state's capabilities as they pertain to power, often of a more conflictual nature, will appear more attractive. The Soviet Union during most of the Cold War captures this foreign policy dynamic. It often pursued policies that showcased military might or tested American resolve by using high-profile military displays to demonstrate its relevance to the system and to instill a belief that it merited equivalent authority to the more powerful United States.

Evidence also suggests that the opposite impact of hierarchy on behaviors may be true. If the international system grants a state greater respect and status than its capabilities merit, that state may pursue more conciliatory and cooperative policy choices that hide or avoid demonstrating its relative weakness. China, for example, was accorded significant importance by the international system immediately following the collapse of the Soviet Union. Although it may have a large infantry force and nuclear weapons, its capabilities are significantly inferior to those of the United States. We might expect, therefore, that China would avoid deploying its relatively technologically unsophisticated military forces given the respect it already receives and the risk of exposing potential military weaknesses. As expected, an empirical observation of foreign policy actions reflects these expectations: China engaged in fewer interventions and conflicts than any major power during the immediate post–Cold War period.

The impact of hierarchy on behaviors is not limited to the jockeying for position among the most powerful states, however. The attribution of status is not only relevant to the dominance of a ruling few but may also take the form of attributing a role or responsibility to a state related to the functioning of the international order. That specialized role may serve to reinforce the authority of the most powerful states and the values its leadership seeks to advance.[11] Countries such as Belgium, Sweden, or Switzerland are not dramatically powerful states at the top of either global or regional hierarchies. However, they perform certain diplomatic functions that accord them a great deal of importance. Likewise, a role as diplomatic negotiator, bureaucratic organizer, or international peacekeeper will shape foreign policy behaviors, serving this specialized function within the hierarchy. The focus of other approaches to international relations is on a narrower subset of outcomes and actors whereas hierarchical methods tend to focus on both conflict and cooperation with insights into the behavior of states both large and small.

COMPETING APPROACHES TO UNDERSTANDING INTERNATIONAL RELATIONS

In international relations, there are three dominant approaches to understanding the behavior of states outside the hierarchical approaches central to this text: neorealism, neoliberalism, and constructivism:

- **Neorealism:** For neorealists, state behavior is determined by their relative power in the international system, not unlike many hierarchical approaches. Unlike hierarchical approaches, states are only ever concerned with preserving their survival in the present and are thus only worried about power. Other considerations, such as human rights, economic growth, or international trade, are subordinate to these security concerns. Furthermore, a state's internal politics are irrelevant, as all states in the ungoverned anarchy of the international system seek survival regardless. Similarly, given preferences are fixed and unchanging due to anarchy, the paradigm usually ignores changes in the system over time or geographic space, as visions of the future are subordinate to survival in the present. This emphasis on preserving security in the present beyond all else may lead to security competition that, in turn, may cause violence unless two actors are evenly matched, leading to tenuous peace in what is labeled a "bipolar" order. Key text: *Theory of International Politics* by Kenneth Waltz (1979).
- **Neoliberalism:** States not only seek security but also seek absolute gains, such as wealth and development. The desire for absolute gains causes states to develop means of governing their interactions despite the anarchic ordering of the international system. They can cooperate under this anarchy through repeated interactions and building trust over time or through the development of international institutions that can share information and punish those that might not abide by their

agreements with other states. Time is an essential component of the evolution of trust between states, but cooperation is evolving and progressive rather than cyclical or temporary, failing to account for the return of disorder and conflict. Neoliberalism is focused on absolute gains in material interests, making the definition of *liberal* used here somewhat different than the term *liberal* that you may encounter in a philosophy or economics course. This original definition comes from the nineteenth-century version of the word meaning free movement of ideas, trade, and people institutionalized domestically by fair legal systems and internationally by agreements between nations. Key text: *Power and Interdependence: World Politics in Transition* by Robert Keohane and Joseph Nye (1977).

- **Constructivism:** The rules and values that govern state behaviors are changeable and depend on the dominant norms, or values, accepted by states in the international system. If states *believe* the world is a threatening, violent place, they are likely to act as realists describe. If they *believe* the world has the potential for cooperation, they will behave like liberals. Either way, there is no one pattern of behaviors that govern international politics as the other approaches suggest. Instead, values change over time, with shifting beliefs and morals. The commonly accepted beliefs about how the world works evolve and change, and therefore, generalizations about how states behave are limited to both place and time. Key text: *Social Theory of International Politics* by Alexander Wendt (1999).

The field of international relations has centered on debates between these three approaches, especially between advocates of neorealism and neoliberalism, since the end of the Cold War. Although they are often simple and easily communicated worldviews useful for explaining specific events, they each lack an accounting for oscillations in order and disorder over both time and geographic space that might be empirically observable. The advantage of all three is the ease of explanation in an undergraduate classroom setting or to policy actors even if empirical evidence is limited. As an alternative, we focus this text's theoretical lens on hierarchical approaches that view capabilities, anarchy, and hierarchy as dynamic, discussing the impact of shifts in capabilities and hierarchy on observable, empirical outcomes, both cooperative and conflictual. Because these approaches focus heavily on capabilities, some characterize them as realist,[12] but they are very different from neorealism because they include shifting preferences of states, the importance of domestic politics and economics, and the ability of hierarchy to overcome the challenges of anarchy.

The Hierarchical Theories

The three main theoretical approaches that emphasize hierarchy in their understanding of empirical international relations are (1) power transition, (2) hegemonic stability, and (3) long-cycle theories.[13] Respectively, the theories capture an empirical understanding of shifting changes in hierarchy, corresponding to politics (1) under parity, or the absence of hierarchy; (2) dominance, or a clear hierarchy; and (3) the evolutionary process between the two. As with the earlier traditional international relations approaches, each has also provided the foundation for offshoots and new theoretical approaches that seek to expand their explanatory ability. Furthermore, some theoretical approaches are related, or similar, albeit assigning importance to different aspects of hierarchical organization, such as David Lake's work on authority. These offshoots and alternatives are discussed where relevant throughout the text. Table 1.1 provides an inventory of the three primary approaches, important theoretical extensions, and similar alternatives.

Each of these approaches emphasizes hierarchy as an ordering principle and offers a different focus on how that hierarchy (or its absence) affects the behaviors we observe in the international system. Alongside hierarchy as an essential concept, these approaches stand apart from neorealism, neoliberalism, and constructivism in international politics by also emphasizing the effect of time and how the distribution in power changes. Notably, hierarchical approaches provide generalizable and empirically testable insights into both periods of cooperation *and* conflict, developing a more comprehensive view of oscillations in stability observed across both space and time.

Relationship to Neorealism

These hierarchical theories share an emphasis on material capabilities and power with realist approaches, but they differ from neorealism because they extend beyond the problem of security under anarchy in their explanations. The hierarchical approaches may be considered partially consistent with foundational realist ideas about political behavior and the importance of power as discussed by the founding father of realism, Hans Morgenthau. Their development has led to

Table 1.1   Hierarchical Approaches to International Politics

Stage of Hierarchy	Theory	Summary	Theoretical Offshoots	Similar Approaches
Parity	Power Transition (Organski and Kugler)	A dominant state and a dissatisfied rising challenger are more likely to engage in conflict with one another as their capabilities become more equal.	Multiple Hierarchy Theory (Lemke) Dominance Vacuum Theory (Rhamey et al.) Parity and Civil War (Cederman) Phoenix Factor (Kugler) Alliance Transitions (Kim)	Leader Time Horizons (David Edelstein) Shatterbelts (Kelly) Power Preference Disparity (Powell) Power Cycle Theory (Doran)
Dominance	Hegemonic Stability (Kindleberger)	Dominant states provide stability to the international system through economic- or security-related public goods, as well as support for normative rules of conduct for others to follow. These public goods benefit most other actors and are provided at a cost to the dominant state so that they might preserve the status quo and thereby their position of dominance.	Hegemonic War (Gilpin) Hegemonic Trade (Krasner) Liberal Leadership (Ikenberry) Financial Order (Drezner and McNamara)	Status Attribution (Volgy) Authority (Lake) Unipolarity (Wohlforth)
Evolution	Long Cycle (Modelski and Thompson)	In their rise and fall, great powers at the core of the international system develop economic and technological innovations that provide order and stability to the international system as they socialize actors. As they decline, the system devolves into conflict as great powers become overextended. War, then, serves as the agent for change for rules and norms by which the international system operates.	Arc of War Theory (Levy and Thompson) Global Leadership (Rasler and Thompson) Comparative World Systems (Chase-Dunn and Hall)	Role Alignment Theory (Lahneman; Thies) World Systems Theory (Wallerstein)

significantly different conclusions from the approaches spawned by *neorealist* founding father Kenneth Waltz, which define states' interests more rigidly in terms of survival under anarchy.

First, for hierarchical approaches, anarchy is not a fixed quality of the international system with a constant, unchanging impact on preferences that leads all states to focus on security. Instead, anarchy exists as a political organization on a spectrum with hierarchical order,[14] shifting in importance where the cause for fear over security depends on the distribution of power in the international system. Anarchy breeds concern for security among states when no one state dominates, and there is a desire to disrupt the existing order by a dissatisfied actor. When a single state dominates, as is more frequently the case in international politics, the strong state's attempts to provide stability mitigate the security problems of anarchy.[15] For these hierarchical approaches, states are not as worried about survival when the problem of anarchy is less prevalent and a dominant state is providing order. This is not because the strong state is benevolent and kind toward others but because the strong state seeks to preserve its position by maintaining the stability of the status quo.

Unlike neorealism, because the relevance of material capabilities is contingent on the means to extract resources, domestic politics do matter, particularly a government's competence and strength. The degree of hierarchy domestically, or the degree of state control over their territory, has a direct impact on its relative power globally and thereby where it falls within the international hierarchy. By incorporating domestic capacity, stability, and time, hierarchical theories provide more nuance for understanding state behavior than do more simplified neorealist approaches. Power must come from somewhere, and the domestic means by which capabilities are extracted and implemented likely have significant consequences for how those capabilities are then used in a state's foreign policy.

Relationship to Neoliberalism and Constructivism

Although the concepts about the importance of power in international politics are similar and broadly realist, the distinctions with respect to neorealism among hierarchical approaches create some dramatically different expectations for the behaviors of states, all of which can be tested empirically. For neoliberalism and constructivism, however, hierarchical approaches may not disagree with some of their empirical claims but suggest hierarchy provides the backdrop for why economic cooperation or normative behaviors develop in the first place. For example, democratic states may not go to war in what is titled the "democratic peace," but is that because of the internal mechanics of democracy or because of a regional or global system developed by a dominant state that values liberal democracies in the creation of cooperating organizations and, for the sake of maintaining the status quo, works to maintain peace among democratic states? Peace, trade, human rights, and progressive values may change, spread, and deepen but only if a dominant power provides stability for those things to proliferate and supports their spread.[16]

One contemporary example of hierarchy influencing the spread of liberal institutions or constructivist values is the European Union. The United States, beginning with the Marshall Plan at the end of World War II, strongly supported European economic integration both for the benefit of American trade and investment and for providing an economic and ideological bulwark against the Soviet Bloc. The idea of European integration, however, was not new and had existed in various permutations for centuries. So what changed that allowed the European integration experiment, and the corresponding values it upholds, to proliferate in a space that only a few years earlier had undergone the bloodiest war in human history? Unlike the previous dominant power, Britain, which sought to keep Europe fragmented and in disarray, the new dominant power sought to promote this integration project. The norms and values prevalent in Europe after 1945, and in Eastern Europe after the collapse of the Soviet Union, have changed dramatically from those in the early twentieth century. And what coincides with that sudden shift from World War II Europe to the peaceful, integrated Europe of today? A dominant state that supported those institutions and norms.

ASSUMPTIONS IN INTERNATIONAL RELATIONS THEORY

One of the assumptions that distinguish approaches to international relations from one another is that of human nature, or, given the absence of government, how might people behave? Given that the international system is anarchic without a clear, single government, how you answer this question will influence which theoretical approach you may think best characterizes state behavior. It is important to remember that states, while composed of and ruling over people, are not unitary actors like individual people, as neorealism and some forms of neoliberalism assume. Hierarchical approaches take a more ambivalent, or at least moderate, view of how states behave under anarchy, not forgetting that a state is a complex political organization.

Although the world lacks a government with complete control over all states, a state that dominates the system more than others, providing rules and structure, would like to remain as such. The best way to achieve that end, however, is not to overextend throughout the globe using force at every opportunity, because as a dominant power, you often lack any obvious interstate threats. As a result, other states in the system are not persistently worried about survival so much as maintenance, or changes, to the current order that may benefit them in more absolute terms. Given the international system as described in figure 1.1, a smaller state such as Brazil is not persistently worried the United States will conquer it but instead is more concerned with how it might improve itself in absolute terms given the hierarchical order the United States created. Hierarchical approaches are, therefore, more about what you are able and interested in doing given the cards you are dealt rather than assuming that preferences, and likewise human nature, are always fixed regardless of your position in the international system. Therefore, under anarchy, or despite it, organic order can arise that reflects the hierarchy among actors, as each seeks to pursue varied interests. This interplay between states, given where they stand in the hierarchy, alongside where they believe themselves to be headed, influences their behavior, and only rarely, particularly during periods of transition, do states fear for their survival.

That states do not always and everywhere fear for their survival is no surprise to liberalism and constructivism. Although liberalism may expect the world to increasingly adopt more liberal values, such as free trade and democracy, like constructivism, most hierarchical approaches are more ambivalent as to what values take root, proliferate, or decline. Human nature is not necessarily "good" any more than it is "bad." Individual liberty, democracy, capitalism, and human rights are not norms that can be simply assumed to persistently grow in the long run but instead are symptoms of the international order created by the dominant power: a reflection of the most powerful state's preferences. Hierarchical approaches, in their added complexity, provide structure and context to the origins of liberal and constructivist theories and improves their empirical testability by incorporating the importance of a uniquely powerful state's capabilities, or opportunity, to pursue specific normative goals. The outcomes pursued by states are not due to the goodness or evil of human nature but are shaped by hierarchy in the status quo.

LEVELS, UNITS, AND LINKAGES

A final key distinction among theories of international politics is the "level" and "unit" of analysis. The level of analysis is the context or area under study. In international relations, the focus is often on the system or state level but, at times, may be a regional space or even individual persons examined in the context of foreign policy decision-making. The unit of analysis is the subject we are studying. It may be individuals, states, nonstate actors, dyads (a pair of states), or the system as a whole. For example, neorealists examine the state as the primary unit of analysis at the international level whereas, for liberals and constructivists, their level of analysis may be individuals, states, domestic groups, or the system, examining a variety of possible units depending on the theory. For hierarchical theories, however, there is an added level of complexity because of an attempt to better reflect the empirical reality we seek to understand. Although for most hierarchical approaches the unit of analysis is most frequently the state, theories are not restricted to a single level of analysis—the system informs the behavior of the state, which is, in turn, affected by capabilities extracted from the domestic sphere. The behavior of the state, then, can be understood as a result of variables from both the international (or regional) and domestic levels of analysis. Some researchers engaging hierarchy may even include the individual level of analysis, such as the research by David Edelstein on how views of the future affect leaders. Hierarchical approaches allow us to begin bridging levels of analysis and integrating domestic hierarchy, perceptions of external hierarchy by individuals or groups, the relative positioning of the state versus others, and the evolving dynamics of the international system at large.

For example, to understand why a state might go to war, we must account for its capabilities that can be used to exert power on others, which requires us to understand domestic resources and extractive capacity given internal politics. Extractive capacity is essentially the authority and control of the state over the domestic system in the same way we might think about the authority and control of a dominant power over the international system. By thinking about capacity, we are including the extent of hierarchy a state has over a domestic population in understanding the behavior of the state in the hierarchy between others within its regional or global order. Thinking across levels in this way, while adding greater complexity, also provides a more empirically accurate depiction of the international system.[17]

Hierarchical approaches may have different emphases, such as the emphasis on the system by long-cycle theory versus the focus on the state in power transition, but in each case the levels of analysis are conceptually interactive.

In contrast, neorealism, with its interest in only states as actors with the sources of power undefined, is far simpler and therefore more easily applied in the abstract or modeled in a board game such as *Risk*. In simplistic terms, states have some pool of capabilities, and they use those capabilities to expand their power as far as possible. However, if we are interested in explanations of politics that empirically capture the reality of the world that we observe, adding complexity by accounting for the source of power becomes a necessity. To be empirically applicable, the theories that explain international politics should reflect the complexity of the world we seek to observe while allowing us to understand that complexity through a parsimonious explanation. A theory of international politics that is simple and easy to understand but does not reflect empirical reality or cannot be tested neither benefits our understanding of international politics nor improves our ability to develop effective foreign policy.

The Relationship between Hierarchical Approaches and Decision-Making

Although we may be interested in better understanding the empirical world in order to have more informed views on foreign policy, it is worth noting that none of these theories is a theory of foreign policymaking but instead is an explanation of observable trends that elucidates why states generally choose to behave according to certain patterns of behavior under specific conditions. No theory explains everything, and although theories such as power transition and neorealism may suggest the types of policies a decision-maker should pursue or the general trajectory of a state's foreign policy, they neither predict individual policies nor generate testable empirical ideas about their specific contents. The reason for this lies in the human element of foreign policymaking that emphasizes the individual level of analysis.

Policymakers are likely to be affected by things such as systemic hierarchy among states, but they are also affected by their own experiences, to whom they are speaking, their own biases or ulterior motives, and limited information. Even with good information, policymakers are prone to making mistakes, just as we all are. We now know, for example, that the Soviet economy and military was far behind that of the United States for much of the Cold War; however, the information available to decision-makers was far less transparent at the time, with members of both the Soviet and American governments inflating the appearance of Soviet power for political purposes. These perceptions (and misperceptions) by decision-makers often influence the particulars of individual foreign policy actions, making theories of international relations inapplicable to these individual decisions even if the general trajectories of states, or the overall policy behavior year over year, reflects the theories we are testing.

This is, in part, what makes our theories of international relations probabilistic. We cannot account for every possible cause behind every single individual action. What we can do is determine how the presence of some variable increases or decreases the probability of some outcome. Therefore, in trying to determine which theory of international politics is most effective in explaining reality, we should evaluate each by how much of the observable world they correctly explain.

The Relationship between Hierarchical Approaches and Geography

The focus of this text is to highlight how both your position and your location in a hierarchy, whether in a time period or over a geographic space, alter both your opportunities and your preferences. Spaces where there is no clear dominant actor, such as Central Asia today, Southeast Asia in the Cold War, or Western Europe at the turn of the twentieth century, tend to be prone to all types of violence, from great wars between major powers to domestic instability or civil conflict. Areas with a clear power structure of states working in concert tend toward the opposite behaviors, such as Europe since the end of the Cold War, constructing a very sophisticated institutional structure ushering in impressive levels of cooperation. As states rise and fall in their capabilities and their areas of influence over geographic space grow and recede, the likelihood of more conflict or more cooperation shifts as well.

MOVING FORWARD

This book begins by first defining key terms, outlining measurements, and discussing the practice of doing empirical international relations research. We then proceed in three parts that examine frequently studied outcomes in international relations through the lens of hierarchical theories: conflict, cooperation, and, finally, based on this discussion, what the future may hold for international politics and the existing global order. Each chapter contains a list of key terms, discussion questions, and suggested further reading. Although hierarchical approaches may not feature as prominently in introductory course work as some others, the relevant research in the field could fill volumes. Therefore, the information contained here is but a primer to some of these theories and their findings, encouraging a thoughtful, empirical approach to understanding international politics as you continue your education.

DISCUSSION QUESTIONS

1. When leaders make decisions about foreign policy, how much do you think they consider the future? How far into the future? How might thinking about the future be different for a leader considering going to war compared to a leader considering a trade agreement?
2. If we try to make foreign policy without empirically understanding how international relations work, what kind of mistakes might we make?
3. Do states only care about their security? Are there other things they worry about more than security at times?

KEY TERMS

anarchy	power
authority	probabilistic
capabilities	proxy
democratic peace	reach
dyad	states
hierarchy	status
norm	theory
political capacity	

FURTHER READING

Kindleberger, Charles P. 1973. *The World in Depression 1929–1939*. Berkeley: University of California Press.

Lake, David A. 2009. *Hierarchies in International Relations*. Ithaca, NY: Cornell University Press, 2009.

Modelski, George. 1987. *Long Cycles in World Politics*. Seattle: University of Washington Press.

Organski, A. F. K. 1968. *World Politics*, 2nd ed. New York: Alfred A. Knopf.

Snyder, Jack. 2004. "One World, Rival Theories." *Foreign Policy* 145 (November/December): 52–62.

2

Concepts and Measures

DOING EMPIRICAL INTERNATIONAL
RELATIONS AND ITS CONSEQUENCES

International relations is the study of political interactions between countries. These countries, or states, are typically the primary relevant actors, but we may also study large corporations, terrorist organizations, international institutions, and other groups that engage across state borders. States are the most frequent actors examined because they are both territorially bound and the most consistently powerful entities, with militaries and comparatively enormous resources. To study the behaviors of these actors empirically means to apply a scientific method to understanding international politics by observing what actors do, analyze those observations, and develop generalizable ideas about how, under certain conditions, these actors are likely to behave. Although the topics and units of study are very different, the approach is no different from how a natural scientist would study particles, bacteria, or chemicals. However, what makes this endeavor challenging is that the objects of our study are complicated and ongoing. We cannot, for example, simply replicate World War II in a laboratory to test our theories.

Furthermore, behind every state and organization in the international system are individual people, with all their quirks, flaws, and experiences. Not only are these objects of study complicated, but unlike particles or chemicals, they can also even react to the scientist studying them. When international relations scholars discover a generalizable finding, such as that democracies do not fight one another, leaders of democracies may hear that theory and respond in their policy decisions, making it very difficult for researchers to avoid influencing the very outcome they are trying to understand.

Because of this complexity, we develop very general theories about how and when states may engage in certain behaviors. These theories are probabilistic, not deterministic, but when evaluating their relative merit, we should determine what theories explain the most about our observable empirical reality: When and why do wars happen? Why do states cooperate? Under what conditions will conflict end and a relationship become peaceful? How does trade change the way a government behaves? When we develop arguments, or theories, about how we might expect states to behave, these are generalizable because we expect them to be generally true, or more likely than just random chance, and not specific to only a single event. It does not, however, mean that our arguments are *always* true. An argument that is always true implies a scientific *law*, such as the laws of motion or thermodynamics. Even the observation in international relations that democracies do not fight one another, what one scholar described to be "as close as anything we have to an empirical law in international relations,"[1] is probabilistic and may have some caveats, as discussed further in chapter 12.

How Empirics May Influence Policy

Investigating international relations empirically means that we seek to observe what countries, groups, and people do internationally, to understand why, and to create general ideas about the patterns we observe. This is particularly important not only to academics and students of international politics but also to practitioners in foreign policy. Just as an engineer uses ideas from physics to build a bridge, so, too, should foreign policymakers rely on what we know of international relations to inform the foreign policy of a state. Much like the bridge, foreign policy is only as effective as the scientific knowledge that it is built upon, and getting it wrong can have deadly serious consequences.

If we want to improve policy, we must not only know empirical international relations but also understand the theoretical explanations behind why those empirical relationships exist. The purpose of this text is to introduce you to a survey of relevant data in international politics that are used by contemporary researchers and foreign policy practitioners and to urge you to think about that data in a rigorous, critical manner. The content is broad, and each chapter merely scratches the surface of extensive research topics. But we provide thorough notation throughout of relevant research so that you may pursue individual subjects in greater depth. We assume that the reader has had no exposure to statistical analysis and so descriptively discuss some commonly analyzed data in the study of conflict, organizations, trade, cooperation, capacity, and other aspects of state behavior typical in international relations research without delving into the mechanics of econometric statistical analysis the research often employs. Theoretically, we focus on hierarchical approaches to contextualize the data and focus our discussion on systemic shifts in international politics. We recognize, however, that these are not the only approaches, nor have we been comprehensive in our review of the data. We aim to provide you with a brief, broad introduction to this area of research while encouraging you to think about international relations as an empirical field with outcomes that are complex and interrelated.

Potential Dangers of Empirics without Theory

Thinking about relationships empirically is relevant to all walks of life, not just the study of international politics. Importantly, you also must be able to contextualize those relationships theoretically. Taking an empirical relationship between a cause and an outcome but having an absent or flawed explanation for the rationale behind that relationship can have truly disastrous policy consequences. For example, members of the George W. Bush administration may have understood that democracies do not go to war. That empirical observation may then have informed a foreign policy designed to promote democracy, forcefully if need be, throughout the world. Although that specific empirical relationship is "true," policymakers may have overlooked other empirical research about democracy and conflict,[2] for example, that transitioning democracies, or states moving slowly toward more free societies from dictatorships, are some of the most violent prone.[3] To solve any problem requires understanding and addressing the causes of that problem, and by misapplying ideas from the democratic peace and ignoring the causes and processes underlying stable democracy, the result of that foreign policy seeking to advance democracy in the Middle East is years of inconclusive conflict, millions dead and displaced, and trillions of dollars spent.

CAUSALITY, THEORY, AND A HYPOTHESIS

This text does not assume that the reader has statistical knowledge but instead has a basic exposure to international relations theory. We illustrate the data that underlie statistical findings in the literature in a direct and an easy-to-understand way, complemented with descriptive graphs and tables, so that you may develop a clear understanding of what the variables important to the study of international politics look like over both time and space. By thinking carefully about the relationship between theory and data, you, too, may develop your own interesting ideas about how these data are related to outcomes of both conflict and cooperation.

So why is a social science a science, and why do we measure concepts? Like the hard sciences, we can use this same method to study humanity and the interactions of international relations. We can measure concepts, such as power, education, class, the influence of international courts, the importance of bilateral investment treaties, and water borders, or more descriptive variables, such as population or landmasses. We can outline the concept of a national economy and then measure that concept via observable constructs, such as GDP, or have disagreements on that measurement and create new ones, such as gross national income. The importance of a concept may be generally agreed upon, but the method of measurement may result in heated disputes. Empirical study requires adherence to definitions with consistency, but as new methods of measurement are devised, fueled by disputes on the current measures, so, too, is the evaluation of the outcome of past studies. Science is never finished and is never done, and a better, more comprehensive way is always around the corner.

Measuring Complex Ideas

Think of something as straightforward as the hypothesis statement that education increases economic growth or even decreases conflict. It is a reasonable statement and one you have likely heard before. First, however, how do we measure education? Total literacy is the easiest, but then how much vocabulary is needed to be literate? Enough to buy a sandwich or what would be required to understand Jane Austin? How about what is necessary for high particle energy physics? Second, most measures of literacy tell us that 95 percent of individuals are literate for the majority of developed and developing countries in the world, and therefore if we have a variable that does not change across countries, it will be shown not to have an effect. Because our proposed cause does not change, it cannot explain changes in the outcome. Observable change is, in this case, a requirement for investigation. A great example from international politics is terrain. Mountains may make certain areas more likely to experience prolonged conflict, but they cannot explain why conflicts vary within the same geographic space over time: the presence of conflict changes, but the presence of mountains does not.

Let's get more complicated. Consider measurements of years of schooling per person. This is a good measure that possesses variability across different aspects of the population, such as gender, wealth, and race. But how do we measure the quality of the schools, or even should we? Do we use standardized tests or access to college? How do we measure learning outcomes? Does it even matter when thinking of the total effects on an economy as a whole? It might be easier to break it down to primary, secondary, and tertiary education: primary being a measurement of basic skills, such as addition and reading; secondary adding the equivalent of American high school; and tertiary being college. What began as a straightforward and direct measurement becomes very complicated very quickly, with a wide range of possible operationalizations. However, the idea that education increases economic growth is a hypothesis statement, not a theory, so what is the rationale behind these ever more complex measurements of education? Why do we think that education is relevant to economic growth? No matter what our measurement or proposed relationship, we must have some reasonable theoretical explanation for why that hypothesis is true over possible alternatives. A good theory should create limitations on your empirical analysis by discounting some parts of what can be measured and emphasizing others. It does not lead to measuring all possible relationships that exist but instead emphasizes relationships that are potentially causal out of the innumerable possibilities. Always keep in mind when reading your own work, the work of others, or even media stories: Are you reading a theory or a hypothesis statement with a correlation and no clear explanation?

Theory in International Relations

In the study of international politics, ideas such as the democratic peace, balance of power, power transition theory, and deterrence will all be referred to as theories. When considering the implications, also consider whether they are actually theories and whether that matters from an empirical standpoint. Do they create consistent definitions of measurements, logical policy points, replicable research, and a suite of testable hypotheses, or are they simply a hypothesis about the relationship between two variables with a limited range of support?

Neorealism is a classic example of a theory. It claims that the key actors on the international stage are states and that they operate in a state of anarchy resulting in mutually conflictual interests. Laws, culture, alliances, and economics are all secondary to security or power. Nations maximize only their security through the acquisition of power. This is a simple theory that can be measured and tested and limits the scope of our examination. Subnational politics, for example, are not important, nor is demography or history, only the *power* of nations relative to each other. The testing is also straightforward. Do the actions of states consistently maximize power and security? Do they live in a state of anarchy focused on capabilities alone with no sense of law or affinity? Although there are many debates over how to measure power, those measurements are often easily applied to hundreds of years and hundreds of countries. This creates a sample size large enough to statistically evaluate the hypotheses from neorealist theory so that we might determine if the theory provides a generally accurate portrayal of state behaviors.

Hypotheses

If neorealism is a theory that can be measured and tested, what is an example of just a hypothesis? Deterrence. In the earliest versions of classical deterrence, the hypothesis is that countries with nuclear weapons past a point of second-strike capability, called mutually assured destruction, will not go to war with each other because the consequences are far beyond the gains.[4] Can we test this hypothesis? We have very few nuclear-armed nations, and none have gone to war with each other or been invaded in their core home territories. Can this be tested when currently we have very few observations but a perfect correlation between nuclear weapons and a lack of conflict between countries that have them? This question is not merely academic but, of course, directly relevant to our unfolding policy concerns surrounding nuclear proliferation with Iran and North Korea. Deterrence may be called a theory, but it is instead a hypothesis statement, which, perhaps thankfully, is difficult to test reliably.

Even once tested, evidence of a correlation does not necessarily imply that two variables are causally related. Discerning such a relationship requires logically derived theory. Correlation, not causation: that is a great challenge to a scientist. Does a variable have an influence, or effect, or is it merely a coincidence that two variables go up or down together? Sometimes this can be farcical. Think about the wonders of trees. In the past twenty years, they have dramatically increased throughout the developed world. Forestland is in many places at a near-hundred-year high. In those same twenty years, income inequality has also gone up, as have deaths due to conflict. So do trees cause the increase in conflict or income inequality? Probably not. What about ice cream consumption? States that consume more ice cream per capita are less likely to experience civil wars. Does ice cream create peace?

Causality is more than a simple correlation. It is the evaluation of what creates the outcome observed. If we provide communities with clean water, this causes infant mortality rates to fall, not correlates because we have an explanation for why access to clean water keeps babies healthy. Now let's consider more complex questions. If we create an international financial system at Bretton Woods, does this cause economic growth among member nations? What then are the direct casual effects of descendant institutions such as the International Monetary Fund or the World Bank both of whom attempt to either create domestic national stability via emergency financing or create economic development assistance. Does increased economic growth, trade relationships, and human development increase peace, as the capitalist peace theory might suggest? As questions get larger and more complex and have a greater degree of possible variable measurements, so, too, does the importance of theory, consistency, metrics, and systematic study.

As you consider the causal relationship between variables in a hypothesis, remember that a null hypothesis is still a hypothesis. One of the greatest limitations of human study is the belief that being "right" is the point. Showing that mountains increase the sustainability of conflict, that differing types of education help an economy, that deserts (or oil) could cause wars to become more likely, or whatever else sounds interesting at the time is an important endeavor, but scientists must be able to look at their data, see the outcome of the study, and then publish the results. A null hypothesis is the opposite of what is expected, meaning your expected cause has no effect! Standing for what is found rather than what you wish to believe or hope for differentiates those that add to our body of knowledge and those who do not. Reality does not care what you want or think, only what *is*.

It is the obligation of researchers to publish what they find, not what confirms their favorite argument.

Measurement

In all the preceding examples, we focus on narrow cases, but trying to apply measurement consistently across nations adds enormous difficulty. Collecting accurate data cross-nationally is both time and resource intensive. Consider the challenge and resources, both in time and in money, required to measure a variable across hundreds of languages, vast differences in culture or style, and massive limitations in accounting. Although generalizing theories across countries is the goal, the practical challenge of achieving it is daunting. Less complicated measurements are more popular not because of greater accuracy but because they are less logistically expensive. Arguably, the perfect measurement of complex concepts, such as power, does not exist. Using the data available is often a necessity, but it is also crucial that you understand your data and what pitfalls it may possess. Know your data!

LIMITATIONS OF EMPIRICAL ANALYSIS

This book focuses on empirical analysis: what data are available and how we might begin to interpret it. However, empirical questions are not necessarily the only questions in studying international politics. If there are questions about politics that are unobservable or ungeneralizable, a scientific and empirical approach will be unhelpful in providing an explanation. For example, we may be interested in understanding the effect of female leaders on a state's foreign policy. Male leaders have dominated the history of state politics across time. Would a change to female leaders, as countries increasingly have powerful female politicians, alter the way that states interact in their foreign policies?[5] The hypothesis is clear, and the research agenda interesting, but the measurement is difficult. In this case, a scientific approach may not be helpful because not only do we have very few female leaders to study but, in most cases, these female leaders also rose to power in otherwise male-dominated societies. Theresa May, Angela Merkel, and Margaret Thatcher all were very successful politicians and were able to rise to leadership positions in their parties and then countries. The issue is that men dominate those parties and governments, and perhaps, these powerful women had to behave "like men" or, at least, adjust their behavior, in order to achieve those positions of leadership.[6]

Would it be different for a female leader rising to power in a party populated by a majority of women or in a country in which female leadership is expected or common? Would that then affect their foreign policy decision-making? Because the few female leaders we have rose to power within the context of male-dominated governments, we might suggest that these empirical observations may not be relevant for explaining how a less male-dominated society may engage in foreign policy. To fully study the effect of female leadership on international politics empirically may require more observations. This does not mean a study should not be conducted, but merely highlights one of empirical analyses' potential limitations.

If we lack quantifiable historical information to answer a question empirically, which we call quantitative analysis, we might seek to uncover answers using a more philosophical or descriptive approach using qualitative analysis. The absence of our ability to employ an empirical, statistical approach does not mean that it is not an important question worth trying to understand and study, nor are the results from nonempirical inquiry invalid. Instead, it merely demonstrates that for different questions, we may need different tools for the job than an empirical approach. Empirical inquiry is a tool that can help us understand certain types of questions depending upon the concepts we wish to explain and the availability of the data. For other questions, that tool might be inappropriate. In these cases, we may try applying examples, such as analyzing historical instances most proximate to our causal relationship, or counterfactual analysis, logically working through a causal process alternative to what is observed to understand better what might occur if observable reality worked out differently.

To this end, a nonempirical approach can be useful when studying an event with a single, unrepeatable cause. For example, although many empirical theories seek to explain the causes of war, if we are interested instead in a unique, unrepeated cause, such as the impact of Adolf Hitler on the occurrence of World War II, using a generalizable approach would be inappropriate because we cannot replicate Adolf Hitler as a possible cause of other conflicts. Adolf Hitler does not exist in multiple wars. We could, however, generalize about the rise of populist-nationalist movements because there are numerous instances of them across countries and across time, but we cannot generalize about the effect of a single person if such an effect exists. In this case, a historical approach may be more effective. Regardless of the type of analysis we seek to employ, we must be clear about the concepts we

BOX 2.1	A Scientific Approach to International Politics

The following outlines in summary form how a research question evolves from a broad theory to a specific empirical finding using power transition theory as an example.

Theory: The distribution of power in the international system has important consequences for the behavior of the most powerful states, where a rising challenger will choose only to contest the dominant state if dissatisfied and will risk war for the chance to alter the status quo.

Hypothesis: As the most powerful state declines in measured national material capabilities to within 10 percent of those of the challenging state, the probability of war between those two states increases if the challenger state is dissatisfied as measured by its degree of dissimilarity in military alliances with the dominant state.

Test: Examine the effect of national material capabilities each year among the most powerful states and alliance portfolio similarity against the onset of war from the Correlates of War data set.

Finding: Based on statistical analysis that includes other possible causes, war is more likely by some percentage.

are trying to explain and, if engaging in empirical analysis, how those concepts will be measured.

MEASURING CONCEPTS

Power is one of the most important concepts in international relations. It is the variable with which many of the most influential theories are focused. Theories such as balance of power, power transition, long cycles, constructivism, neorealism, neoclassical realism, and even neoliberal institutionalism all discuss power as an essential causal variable. So how do you measure it, and what is its definition?

Power
How would you measure the ability of a nation to affect the foreign policy of others? Is it force? Believing military hardware to be of the

utmost importance, the Central Intelligence Agency during the Cold War attempted to measure the capacity to fight the USSR by the total amount of tanks built. They became so obsessed with measuring the number of tanks that they even started to measure ones from World War I captured from the Germans rusting in the middle of Siberia.[7] Should decades-old broken, obsolete tanks count as power? Alternatively, this is an easy measurement to make and sustain. Tanks are not all that easy to hide, and they are reasonably similar cross-nationally. No nation produced more tanks than the USSR. The most famous, the T-54, which means the tank from 1954, was built in such numbers that some believe enough metal was used to circle the Earth or walk halfway to Berlin on the tops of tanks from Moscow.[8] So many of them exist that the USSR ended up practically giving them away as part of its attempts to buy influence. But how much does a tank represent power or the ability to coerce someone on the other side of the world?

Not much, but if you can make a tank, does that also mean you can make whatever military asset you might need to use force on someone far away? If so, we might consider measuring tanks to be an *indirect variable* or a variable that represents, indirectly, the concept we are studying because we otherwise lack a direct measurement. Tanks as a *direct variable*, in this case, would be that tanks are important unto themselves, while the indirect variable is that tanks are important in what they mean for something else, such as power more broadly.

A more common example of this, and one still in use, is total electrical production. Often, countries do not produce accurate information about their economic productivity. But the amount of electricity used by a state may be a useful indirect variable for representing economic size. The researcher may then use a host of methods, such as satellite imagery, to study the scale of electrical facilities, depth of coal mines, transportation networks, rail, and even the amount of heat or pollution produced. Absent measurements of economic activity like GDP, a variable that was not part of the Soviet concept of economics and thereby did not exist, what is available needed to be used. After the fall of the USSR many differing types of indirect measurements were compared to the actual production within the country as the new Russian state allowed for archival work to be conducted. The findings created radical reconsideration of the Cold War with the USSR having a dramatically lower total economic scale, industrial production, and then overall power as originally considered using things like tanks or electricity as a foundation. Powerplants that had scale but did not have connections to factories or tanks that spent decades in storage turned out not to be useful measures of total capabilities. This is also science; better measurements create better understanding. Furthermore, as we observe the rise of green, more electrically efficient technologies, heavy electrical use per capita may signal economic backwardness rather than advancement.

A popular means of measuring power is the total amount of money spent on the military. For many people within the United States, during their entire lives, the United States has spent about half the world's total military expenditure: close to more than all of the countries in the European Union, Russia, China, and every other country you can name combined. Since the end of the Cold War, no country has even gotten close, not even China. The scale of it is staggering. As of the writing of this text, it will be about three-quarters of a trillion dollars in one year, expected to be more than three times China and more than *ten* times Russia. Indeed, even individual states within the United States have greater amounts of military equipment than almost every single country on Earth. California, Texas, Connecticut, Florida, Washington, and Virginia would all be in the top 20, if not top 3, on the world stage in military hardware.[9] Does this measurement mean that the United States is ten times more powerful than Russia and three times more than China? An issue with this as a measurement is that military expenditures represent not capability alone so much as capability combined with policy interests. In other words, using language from chapter 1, military expenditures are a result of both opportunity and willingness, but in measuring power we are likely only interested in identifying opportunity.

Even once we identify a power measurement that we believe to be most accurate, we might wish to further contextualize it by the degree of political capacity possessed by a state. For example, if we measure power using the GDP of a state, how do we account for the institutional ability of a state to extract that GDP for its own use? In other words, can we measure the ability of a state to tax its citizens, given that states do not all have equally effective governments? Regardless of what policies they pursue, states must have the ability to extract resources from their domestic societies to employ that revenue for policy activity. Comparing states' observed tax revenue to what we might expect them to obtain given their population, wealth, and natural resources provides us with a measure of this political capacity that we can then compare to other states.[10]

There are no perfect answers to the issue of measuring power, and in some cases, using a combination of variables may be the most appropriate choice. Upon identifying that measure, however, there are a variety of adaptations we may use to try and adjust power to the context of our analysis. To understand hierarchy as partially a function of capabilities, we may seek to compare one state's amount of power to another, identifying whether the two states are at parity.[11] Alternatively, we may be interested in measuring the concentration of power in certain hands and how many hold how much, in what is known as polarity.[12]

Satisfaction and Reach

But more feeds into the concept of hierarchy than just relative capabilities. For example, if a state has a certain amount of power, how satisfied is it with other powerful states and the status quo? Does it grant powerful states status and authority, or does it hold grievances? How do states use their capacity to reach other geographic spaces? In accounting for such abilities, we might take into consideration states' ability to project power, such as how many miles per day they can reasonably transport military personnel[13] or their economic projection of goods and services.[14]

DATA

Moving forward, it is essential that the reader explore and engage data. Although we provide some general summaries, observations, and illustrations, nothing can replace direct engagement with the raw data. Often, by perusing the numbers, puzzling outcomes are identified that evolve into broader empirical research projects. Furthermore, knowing your data better familiarizes the user with the measurement of concepts, their accuracy, and their potential challenges. To this end, in the following, we list data sources referred to in or relevant to this text and encourage you to explore them. All can be freely accessed online.

Important Data Sources

- Absolute and Relative Political Capacity—Measures of the ability of states to extract resources from their domestic societies. Available from www.transresearchconsortium.com/#data-section.

- Alliance Treaty Obligations and Provisions Project (ATOP)—Details on all forms of alliances, including detailed coding sheets. Available from atopdata.org.
- Correlates of War Data—A repository of multiple data sets that includes the Composite Indicator of National Capabilities (CINC) scores, data on Militarized Interstate Disputes (MIDs), international trade, lists of different types of conflicts, and a host of related variables. Available from www.correlatesofwar.org.
- Diplomatic Contacts Database (DIPCON)—Ambassadorial level diplomatic exchanges between all states. Available from www.volgy.org/projects-and-data.
- Enduring Rivalry Data—List of enduring rivals with start and end dates. Available at www.prio.org/jpr/datasets/#2006.
- Formal Intergovernmental Organizations (FIGO)—List of formal intergovernmental organizations with dates and regional coverage. Available from www.volgy.org/projects-and-data.
- Freedom in the World Data—Codes the personal and political freedoms of people by country. Available from https://freedom house.org/content/freedom-world-data-and-resources.
- Maddison GDP Data—Estimates of state wealth and population dating back thousands of years. Available from www.rug.nl/ggdc/historicaldevelopment/maddison.
- Military Intervention by Powerful States (MIPS)—Data on the interventions by major powers. Available from https://dataverse.harvard.edu/dataset.xhtml?persistentId=hdl:1902.1/15519.
- Polity IV Data—Lists the degree of democracy and autocracy in a state along with other regime characteristics. Available at www.systemicpeace.org/inscrdata.html
- Regions of Opportunity and Willingness (ROW)—Outlines the contours of regions annually and by decade. Available from www.patrickrhamey.com/row.
- Strategic Rivalry Dataset—List of strategic rivalries alongside replication data on their relationship to territorial disputes. Available at https://dataverse.harvard.edu/dataset.xhtml?persistentId=hdl:1902.1/10055.
- Third Party Interventions and the Duration of Intrastate Conflicts—Lists interventions and time periods by third parties in internal conflicts. Available from http://bingweb.bingham ton.edu/~pregan/replicationdata.html.
- United Nations High Commissioner for Refugees (UNHCR)—Data on ongoing human rights crises. Available from https://data2.unhcr.org/en/situations.

- United Nations Population Division—Data on population, including growth projections. Available from www.un.org/en/development/desa/population/index.asp.
- Varieties of Democracy Data—Data on the broad characteristics of democratic states. Available online at www.v-dem.net/en.
- The World Bank—Provides a variety of economic and development indicators. Available from https://data.worldbank.org.

DISCUSSION QUESTIONS

1. If power is the ability to make people do something they otherwise would not, we cannot observe the capacity to do this directly. What are some interesting things we can observe that might tell us how much power a state has? Be creative.
2. What is the difference between a theory and a hypothesis?
3. Imagine you have developed a theory about international politics and successfully tested a hypothesis that shows you are correct. How would you communicate that finding in simple terms to a policymaker?

KEY TERMS

causality
correlation
hypothesis
null hypothesis

operationalization
qualitative
quantifiable
quantitative

FURTHER READING

King, Gary, Robert O. Keohane, and Sidney Verba. 1994. *Designing Social Inquiry: Scientific Inference in Qualitative Research*. Princeton, NJ: Princeton University Press.

Organski, A. F. K., Jacek Kugler, J. Timothy Johnson, and Youssef Cohen. 1984. *Birth, Death, and Taxes: The Demographic and Political Transitions*. Chicago: University of Chicago Press.

Thompson, William R., ed. 2018. *The Oxford Encyclopedia of Empirical International Relations Theory*. Oxford: Oxford University Press.

PART I
Conflict

CONFLICT OCCURS AT ALL LEVELS OF ANALYSIS in political science. Regardless of whether it is in the form of interpersonal fights, group violence, civil wars, clashes between minor powers, or major power war, some form of conflict occurs regularly across time. Politics at any level is a question of how coercion—the ability to use violence—is organized. Who has the tools to use violence? Who has the legitimacy to use violence? And who disagrees with the rules of how politics are organized and might use violence to create change?

In answering each of these questions, we look to hierarchy to better understand political organization. Furthermore, as we see in the world today, the degree to which violence occurs changes across geography. Hierarchy, too, changes across geography, with well-organized spaces, such as Europe; contested spaces, such as the Middle East; and even spaces where no states have meaningful influence over territory, such as parts of Central Africa. The degree and type of violence in each space, then, vary, but in all cases, what unites the observations are disagreements about politics and the use of violence to achieve some political aim.

In popular discussion, people often attribute violence to differences between groups on some level of identity: their religion, their ethnicity, or their history. However, although this may be consistent with some empirical observations or correlations, this attribution ignores how violence changes over time. Fighting between Protestants and Catholics, Turks and Arabs, Hutus and Tutsis, or communists and capitalists all experience changes over time in their frequency and severity, even if their identities do not. For a grievance to have a meaningful effect on the probability of conflict, it must interact with the opportunity to challenge politics either at the international level or at the domestic level.

This section analyzes conflict and its patterns and sources at both the intranational and the global levels. Particular emphasis is placed on how conflict behavior changes with hierarchy and how hierarchy domestically might be challenged in a civil war. Finally, we can use the Cold War, a decades-long series of tensions between two powerful actors, to see how shifting hierarchy influences all of these behaviors during the same time period.

3

International Conflict

HIERARCHY AND CONFLICT AS A POLITICAL PROCESS

Conflicts between states are best understood not as individual events but as political processes that unfold over time. As the capabilities of a state rise and fall, the current and anticipated ability to coerce other states will affect how it interacts in the world.[1] The term *conflict* does not inherently entail violence but could be any activity related to force, including not just the use of force but also the threat of force. Typically, in international relations, the great violent wars we observe and seek to explain begin as a series of political exchanges between states trying to achieve some goal, such as a policy objective, control of a bit of territory, or access to a resource.[2] As the two sides are unable to reconcile their differences, they may resort to violence as a means of pursuing their goal further. The violence may be one-sided, with the other side capitulating to demands, but often, violence is met with violence.

When that violence becomes severe, we label these conflicts wars. In the international relations literature, more than 1,000 battle deaths mark the threshold for when a conflict becomes a war. Nothing is magical about that number, but a threshold must, for measurement purposes, create some point for what constitutes severe and what does not. However, this threshold is not without its pitfalls. Unaccounted for, but certainly related, are non-battlefield casualties, and as with any measure, our operational choices should be kept in mind as we proceed. Although the discussion in this chapter addresses all forms of conflict, these uniquely violent conflicts we call wars are our focus. Although relatively infrequent, the destructive capacity of wars makes them perhaps the most noteworthy and oft-studied phenomenon in international relations and thus worthy of understanding empirically and seeking to prevent.

Hierarchy as Context

As discussed in chapter 1, all political acts are a function of opportunity and willingness. The hierarchy of capabilities in the international system impacts a state's opportunity by determining what and where it may use military force. It also affects a state's willingness to use force, depending upon its satisfaction with the status quo and the status that the state receives from others. If others clearly dominate a state's capabilities, or it merely lacks capabilities to project power beyond its borders, it may not have the opportunity to challenge another within its immediate neighborhood, much less a uniquely powerful state globally. Furthermore, even if it has more power than a state that it would like to use force against, a more powerful state nearby could deter it from doing so with the threat of potentially intervening and punishing the aggressor.

Consider this hypothetical, although unlikely, scenario: the Caribbean island of St. Vincent is convinced that war is necessary against nearby St. Lucia, and it possesses a military that can effectively attack its island neighbor. Even with military opportunity to attack St. Lucia, St. Vincent would need to take into consideration the actions of other nearby states. In this case, it would still likely be unwilling to follow through on such an aggressive act if it viewed the United States as likely to intervene. The United States, similarly, would wish to prevent any destabilizing impacts of a conflict, such as economic chaos or refugee flows, so near its territory. This example illustrates how a powerful state being geographically near other, less powerful states will affect the relationships of these states with one another. A further example can be seen in chapter 6 when discussing the Israeli–Egyptian conflict: two countries in which the United States had a strategic interest in promoting peace.

Distance is not the only factor in measuring how powerful states affect the willingness of less powerful states to go to war. In 1990, Iraqi president Saddam Hussein, who was later overthrown by the United States during the second Iraq War in 2003, was quick to ask the American ambassador what the reaction to an invasion of Kuwait might be given both American capabilities and interests in the region. Although the response from the ambassador was misleading ambivalence, history shows that the dominant state, even in so distant a geographic space, could not tolerate a destabilizing outcome to the maintenance of its existing interests. A state's position in the hierarchy is likely to influence its willingness to engage in conflict. As such, the United States as system leader is undoubtedly more likely to intervene in a conflict to preserve the status quo than in one that does not.

Onset, Escalation, and Termination

To understand the relationship between hierarchy and war, we must keep in mind that war is usually but an escalatory step in a political process far removed from the initial grievance or political act that led to its onset. During war, states are confronted with decisions to continue, escalate, or capitulate against their opponents. The relative capabilities of both the belligerents and other states interested in the conflict's outcome will influence their decision.

Even once violence begins, a large-scale war may still be many steps down the road as small skirmishes and military mobilization precede the types of violent, pitched battles that often come to mind. We can break all conflicts down to their onset, escalation or de-escalation, and termination, seeking to identify unique causes to each of the three components of a conflict's process.

In studying conflict's onset, we seek to understand how a relationship may go from a state of peace to a state of coercion and what observable conditions increase the chances a relationship may turn violent. Escalation, alternatively, examines the conduct of that conflict. Only a small subset of conflicts transition from low-level threats or military maneuvers into violent warfare, so by examining escalation, we seek to explain what observable conditions make low-level conflicts become much larger ones.

Consider studies of the democratic peace. They argue that democracies are less likely to escalate a conflict into war. Note that researchers are not claiming that there is no conflict between democratic states but merely that these conflicts rarely break the threshold of more than 1,000 battle deaths. Democratic peace scholar Bill Dixon suggests that the reason for the ability of two democracies to de-escalate their disagreements lies in their shared norms of peaceful dispute resolution. Because they solve their domestic differences peacefully through democratic processes, such as elections, courts of law, or legislative procedures, they are likely to do the same with other democracies in the international system with which they disagree rather than allow those disagreements to escalate.[3]

Finally, the study of conflict termination involves an analysis of how conflicts end. In other words, crucial to the study of war is how states obtain peace. Many people might picture wars ending with unconditional surrender when asked to imagine the resolution of a violent conflict, such as the demise of the Axis powers in World War II. Yet most conflicts are resolved without the total capitulation of either side. These conclusions usually involve some negotiation process between the two sides, frequently involving third parties, such as mutually trusted actors or powerful major powers who are interested in seeing the war's conclusion. Some conflicts may be very short, while others may last years, such as the engagement by the North Atlantic Treaty Organization (NATO) states against Serbia in the 1990s or American intervention in Vietnam during the Cold War. In studying why conflicts terminate, we might seek to understand how conflicts may be abbreviated and what might keep a conflict that has stopped from erupting again in the future.

CONFLICT IN THE INTERNATIONAL SYSTEM

Despite the attention researchers often grant violent conflicts, they are relatively rare. Figure 3.1 shows the number of conflicts recorded in the Militarized Interstate Dispute data from the Correlates of War Project where there is at least some use of force, with or without casualties. True, there are some significant peaks in violent conflicts surrounding sudden cataclysmic events in the international system, such as the collapse of the Soviet Union or World War II. Typically the number of violent conflicts is low with large-scale wars becoming increasingly rare. If we were to focus only on violent conflicts that qualify as wars, this number falls even more, with a maximum of seven in 1940 but, most commonly, zero annually across the past two hundred years. If we examine the raw count of conflicts, it seems to increase over time, but there does seem to be a slow decline since the end of the Cold War.

But if we are to illustrate conflict's presence among states accurately, we must also account for the number of states in the system, the population of which has risen dramatically from only 23 states in 1816 to 194 in 2010. Once we control for the number of states available to engage in disputes, we see that the prevalence of conflict, as illustrated in figure 3.1, has declined steadily since World War II.

Figure 3.1   Conflict Onset by Year

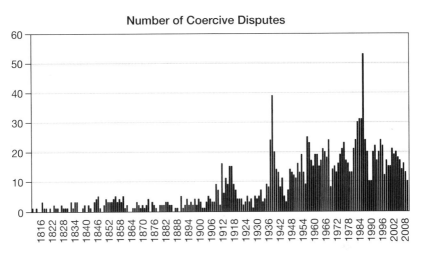

Number of Coercive Disputes

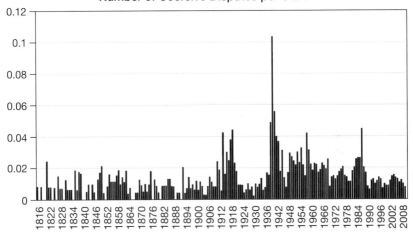

Number of Coercive Disputes per State

Source: Disputes are from Glenn Palmer, Vito D'Orazio, Michael R. Kenwick, and Roseanne W. McManus, "Updating the Militarized Interstate Dispute Data: A Response to Gibler, Miller, and Little," *International Studies Quarterly* (Forthcoming), last accessed July 31, 2019, https://doi.org/10.1093/isq/sqz045. Number of states from Correlates of War Project, "State System Membership List, v 2016" (2017), last accessed August 17, 2019, http://correlatesofwar.org.

There is a brief spike at the end of the Cold War in 1989, but it is not nearly as drastic as that which occurred following World War II. Then the degree of conflict between states in the international system reaches a particularly low point that begins to mirror the nineteenth century. History is not progressively more peaceful or conflictual. Periods of conflict can arise after decades of peaceful interactions among states.

Despite its rarity, however, conflict and war remain a key focus of the international relations literature. Perhaps this is because, as rare as it might be, the cost in lives and its effects on multiple states are so great. For example, in World War II, the number of combatants perished approaches almost 100 million depending upon the estimate. More recently, although only a few thousand U.S. service members have lost their lives in Iraq, hundreds of thousands, or more than a million civilians, have died as a result of that conflict.[4] Because both the human and the associated material costs are so high in war, understanding how conflict begins and how to prevent it from turning violent may grant policymakers the ability to prevent its destruction.

Regardless of the motivating cause of conflict between two states, to meaningfully escalate beyond threats to actual violence requires military resources. Those resources must come from within the domestic society, whether funds, material goods, or population. States use a variety of means to acquire these resources, such as conscripting soldiers, taxing the population to obtain the funds necessary to build military hardware, or, in many cases, buying it from other states. The ability and strength of the state to extract resources from the population is therefore essential to its ability to use force. It is worth noting that a state's decision to go to war may be related to several causes across levels of analysis including the psychology of a leader,[5] whether its domestic institutions be democratic or autocratic, or their history of grievances with an opponent.

BALANCE OF POWER VERSUS POWER TRANSITION

In this section, we focus on state capabilities, or their opportunity to engage in conflict, and how the hierarchy that results from capabilities conditions conflict behaviors. Perhaps the most significant debate in international politics surrounding the effect of capabilities on conflict behavior among the most powerful and therefore destructive states is the dispute between balance of power theory out of the neorealist school of international politics and power transition theory.

Both theories heavily emphasize the importance of capabilities in determining states' conflict behaviors, yet they represent opposites when it comes to their understanding of how capabilities affect the probability of conflict. The root of this debate lies in how states react when confronted with an opponent possessing relatively equal capabilities to their own and whether, as they look toward the future, they are rising or declining in their power. Although neorealists claim that similar capabilities lead to peace, power transition expects the opposite. The end point is two testable hypothesis statements that contradict one another.

Parity and Polarity

Two concepts are essential to this debate. The first is polarity. How many uniquely powerful states exist within the system? Is it unipolar, where there is a single dominant state; bipolar, with two; or multipolar, with three or more? Second, are these powerful actors at or approaching parity, meaning relatively equivalent capability, or are they moving apart? If they are approaching parity, how satisfied are they with the international system?

For neorealism, the expectation is that when there is a balance of power between the two most powerful states, or bipolarity, war is *least* likely to occur. At the core of this theory is the assumption that all states are primarily worried about their survival, and the only truly effective means of securing survival is possessing more power than others. As a result, because two states with equal abilities to harm one another would be particularly destructive in their resulting conflict, their fear of those costs will keep them in check, and they will avoid circumstances that could result in a violent conflict between them. In other words, their competing, equally strong desire to ensure their survival restrains both sides, particularly with the development of nuclear weapons, as discussed further in chapter 11.

If there is but one state that is uniquely powerful, or a system of unipolarity, that actor will be unchecked and, according to neorealism, will employ conflict without restraint. If there are three or more uniquely powerful actors, or multipolarity, the potential for violent conflict becomes particularly treacherous because, under bipolarity, there are only two sides and each side is opposed to the other. This absence of confusion in conjunction with their mutual ability to harm one another prevents conflict. However, when there are three or more actors, although the two most powerful actors may oppose one another, the third-, fourth-, or fifth-most powerful state could swing balance of power to one side's favor. This actor is what Hans Morgenthau calls "the holder of the balance" as they can meaningfully sway balance of power in favor of one side over the other.[6] Uncertainty about balance of power between these opposing sides may cause the actors to initiate a conflict to either prevent an opposing side of allies from growing too powerful or swaying the actions of other powerful states. This confusion when there are more than two is the most dangerous configuration of power.

BOX 3.1	Measuring Polarity and World War

Neorealists expect unipolar arrangements to be quite dangerous due to the absence of a coequal check on the most powerful state. If we look at the 1990s, which all sides agree to be unipolar, we can then determine whether unipolarity offers such instability or if hierarchical approaches are correct that dominant states will seek to preserve the status quo and thereby provide relatively peaceful stability. This was the decade in which possible challengers to the United States such as the USSR disappeared, when China had not yet risen, when Europe was peaceful, and Japan was economically stagnant and no longer growing. Only the United States enjoyed substantial economic dominance and unparalleled military might.

One hypothesis on which both balance of power and hegemonic approaches agree is that multipolarity, or a system dominated by three or more great powers, tends to be particularly conflictual. The case most frequently cited as a prime example of multipolarity leading to war is the onset of World War I. Germany, Britain, and Russia dominated in capabilities within Europe, with France, Austria, and Italy all not far behind. This dispersion of capabilities in the hands of many great powers gave smaller powers, such as the Ottomans, Belgians, the Dutch, and Romanians, the ability to impact relations among these powers through the perceived ability to tip the scales in favor of one side or the other. The result was the most violent war in Western history until World War II just over two decades later, which could also be considered a case of multipolarity when that war began in 1939.

World War I, however, also demonstrates the importance of geography. According to most measures of capabilities, the most powerful country in the world at the time was the United States, but due to distance and the technological logistics of travel, the power of the United States was not particularly relevant. Instead, the dividing lines of the war, the trenches, the greatest battles, and the bulk of the destruction fell among the powers concentrated on the European continent.

For power transition theory, however, there is not necessarily disagreement about the dangers of multipolarity, but great conflicts are about the expected trajectory of capabilities. Is the strength of the most powerful states growing or shrinking? If the system is unipolar, where a single state dominates, that state seeks to preserve the status quo: a status quo in which it is in control. Thus, under unipolarity, it will avoid creating disorder through conflict and instead create stability, leading to assertions of hegemonic stability theory that the most powerful state creates order, or provides public goods, that benefit all other states in the system. However, if a rising state seeks to alter that system, or what we call a challenger, a war may ensue over who will control the rules and conventions that govern the international system in the future. Unlike balance of power, power transition is more interested in the direction capabilities of states are headed over time than the difference between them at any one moment. If one state is dominant and unchallenged, why would anyone initiate a war with that state? Weaker states will generally acquiesce to that strong state's demands while the strong state will maintain stability to preserve its position. However, when the capabilities of a rising state begin to approach those of the strongest state, that rising state has an opportunity to challenge the dominant state and remake the system according to its preferences.

BOX 3.2	Polarity and Parity: Balancing What Power?

There are many ways to define *power* and, thus, many ways to go about measuring when states are relatively equal in capabilities in a way that will impact the order or disorder in the international system. When we talk about polarity, we are talking about both the number of uniquely powerful states as well as the concentration of power in very few hands. If the system is unipolar, then "it contains one state whose share of capabilities places it in a class by itself compared to all other states."[7] Parity, on the other hand, is dyadic in its measurement, meaning strictly relational. Two states are at parity when their capabilities are about equal.

Table 3.1 illustrates how we might measure these two concepts by comparing three ways of measuring power relationally. For the sake of simplicity, we have clustered the years into longer

(Continued)

BOX 3.2	Continued

Table 3.1 Polarity and Parity

Time Period	Polarity (naval)	Parity (capabilities)	Parity (military expenditures)	Relevant Powers
1816–1860	Unipolar	No	Yes	United Kingdom (France & Russia)
1861–1870	Bipolar	No	No	United Kingdom (France)
1871–1880	Multipolar	No	Yes	United Kingdom (France & Russia)
1881–1890	Bipolar	No	Yes	United Kingdom (France)
1891–1914	Multipolar	No	No	United Kingdom (France, United States, Russia, & Germany)
1920–1938	Bipolar	No	No	United Kingdom (United States, Russia, & Germany)
1945–1970	Unipolar	No	No	United States
1971–1990	Bipolar	Yes	No	United States (Soviet Union)
1991–	Unipolar	No	No	United States

Source: This table is adapted from the list from William R. Thompson, "Polarity, the Long Cycle, and Global Power Warfare," *Journal of Conflict Resolution* 30 (1986): 587–615. Rather than list changes annually, we create broader time periods and list the polarity at the most typical state that Thompson gives in a given time period. Parity in capabilities and military spending are from the Correlates of War Composite Indicator of National Capability: J. David Singer, Stuart Bremer, and John Stuckey, "Capability, Distribution, Uncertainty, and Major Power War, 1820–1965," in *Peace, War, and Numbers*, ed. Bruce Russett (Beverly Hills, CA: Sage, 1972), 19–48.

BOX 3.2	Continued

periods that are generally somewhat similar. The first column is an indicator of polarity from William Thompson's measurement of proportional capabilities, defined as the number of states with significant amounts of power that comprise a majority of power in the international system, or, phrased differently, in totaling the power of the most powerful states, how many does it take to equal or exceed 50 percent of global capabilities? In this instance, the capabilities that matter are surface naval vessels. So a system is bipolar if two states combined control more than 50 percent of capabilities and each state possesses at least 25 percent. The other two columns are more straightforward, defined as whether the top two states are within 20 percent of one another on the Correlates of War Composite Indicator of National Capability (CINC) score and their military expenditures, respectively. Comparing this table to the figures of conflicts' rise and decline reveals some interesting patterns and differing conclusions. The polarity measure seems to align with unipolarity being more peaceful and multipolarity being more conflictual, as parity in CINC score capabilities also aligns with greater conflict. However, parity in military expenditures does not demonstrate a similar trend, only consistently present in the relatively more peaceful nineteenth century.

What are other ways we might measure polarity and parity in international politics? What might these alternatives' relationship be with the prevalence of international conflict?

Security and Dissatisfaction

It takes at least two belligerents for a conflict to occur. For power transition theory, conflict initiation and a violent reciprocation by the other state require both sides to believe it to be in their best interests. This can only effectively occur when a state believes that there is a threat to its interests *and* it thinks it has a chance to sufficiently defeat the opposition and achieve its goal, which, in this case, is to hold the position of the most powerful state in the world. These conditions occur under bipolarity, meaning that balance creates conflict. Being evenly matched does not provide a check on conflict behavior because the war may be uniquely destructive, as neorealists suggest. Instead, equity in capabilities gives both sides a chance to win, vanquish the opposition, and create a new world that favors its interests. Power transition theorists would undoubtedly agree with neorealists that a war would be costly, as wars between major powers usually are, but only when there is a chance that both sides might win will both in turn risk that violence to achieve their goals.

Given the costliness of war, the dissatisfaction of a challenger with the current international system must be so great that they are willing to endure those costs for the possibility of victory. As a result, power transition theory adds an additional condition to the preferences of states. Not only must the hierarchy in capabilities have broken down, but the rising challenger must also be dissatisfied with the status quo, or the rules and conventions by which the current system operates, if that challenger will be willing to endure war's costs. This additional caveat is essential, as it makes little sense for a challenger to provoke a war if it is also satisfied with the world as it is. For balance of power theory, however, the preferences of states are fixed toward maximizing power because they only fear for their survival and can only guarantee that survival by acquiring ever more power. Hence, it necessitates an equally powerful state equally desirous of ever more power to present a viable check on another state.

Testing these two theories empirically from a capabilities perspective is reasonably straightforward, but measuring preferences by either approach may present some challenges. First, to determine the distribution of power in the international system, we need to measure power and determine whether one, two, or more states are relatively coequal in their capabilities globally. In the literature, the threshold for "parity" is often when two states are within 20 percent of one another in their measured power.[8] We can measure this distribution in power for individual countries or entire alliance blocs. Alternatively, we might explore the concentration of many different forms of capabilities measures to gauge "polarity" rather than "parity."[9] Whatever our measure, these states do not need to be perfectly equal, just sufficiently comparable in power to perceive one another as peers. In testing, it is often best to do a combination of approaches to build the robustness of a case. After defining our independent variable, or cause, we then would test its significance to the outcome of interest or dependent variable, in this case, conflict.

If a state has military resources, it must then evaluate whether the use of those resources carries with it an acceptable chance of achieving its aims. This depends heavily on both the goal being pursued, as well as the relative capabilities the state believes its opponent may possess. If a state finds its opponent so sufficiently outmatches it that achieving its aims is impossible, the state would be unlikely to initiate a conflict no matter how badly it seeks to achieve its goals.[10] The hierarchy in the international system both provides the opportunity for states to achieve their goals and operates as a restraining force on smaller powers. However, in the absence of clarity surrounding the hierarchy, there may be opportunities for all states, big or small, to use conflict to achieve their aims effectively. As was often the case during the Cold War, a confusion of hierarchy in a geographic space may allow smaller powers to play competing larger powers against one another, creating geographic spaces uniquely prone to conflict.

POWER AND GEOGRAPHY

Although the previous section compares explanations of global war between the most powerful states, World War II is the only conflict where severe theatres of war were globally present. Even in that single instance, the violence was heavily concentrated in Europe. However, applying geography to both balance of power and power transitions theories has consequences for our understanding of state behavior throughout the international system. Distance limits the ability of states to use power. As noted earlier, no matter how badly Mauritius may want to attack Peru, it lacks the opportunity because of the distance that would have to be crossed by its limited military. For most states, then, the relevant group, when it comes to possible conflict, is limited to their immediate neighbors. For power transition theory, neighbors or states in the same region may seek to challenge one another for the position of regional power. In a regional space where there is a dominant actor, it may provide stability for others, in accordance with hegemonic stability theory, making violence less attractive. Proxies for the major power may extend its authority to a regional space,[11] such as Germany and Japan did in their regional spaces as part of the American order.[12]

For balance of power theory, two equally matched neighbors or regional actors may alternatively hold one another in check.[13] In either case, the context of the international system outside a region or dyad, whether unipolar, bipolar, or multipolar, and the region's geographic location relative to the most powerful states will have clear consequences for all states' behavior.

Regional Multipolarity in Europe

From World War II to the end of the Cold War in the 1990s, two major powers dominated international politics: the Soviet Union and the United States. This, as both theories discussed agree, was at least partially an era of bipolarity. Both theories also agree that the post–Cold War order was a unipolar system dominated by the United States. The significance of this shift and the predictions about what would follow is where the two theories diverge. Neorealist thinker John Mearsheimer, adhering to balance of power theory, worried at the Cold War's end that removing the threat presented by the Soviet Union would *eliminate* the bipolar stability of the post–World War II era, resulting in instability on the European subcontinent.[14] The removal of the Cold War balance of power would cause the most powerful European actors, Britain, France, Russia, and Germany, to engage in a sudden arms race. This resulting multipolarity on the continent would lead to a war that resembled the most violent moments of the first half of the twentieth century. In other words, through a balance of power lens, he believed that the conflict between the United States and USSR, although it did involve violent conflicts in multiple states as well as the escalating threat of nuclear war, had prevented yet another world war. When that conflict ended, so would the restraining force that maintained peace in Europe.

From power transition and hegemonic stability perspectives, however, the increased hierarchy resulting from the dominance of the United States would decrease European tensions. As we now know, not only did those tensions decrease, but the European Union was also formed. States not only did not engage in an arms race but also surrendered significant sovereignty and resource control by joining the euro common currency. This does not mean that everyone in Europe was a satisfied regional actor: Russia was and continues to be dissatisfied with the current arrangement. However, the global hierarchy of the United States appears to provide stability alongside the satisfied regional actors of Britain, France, and Germany. One of the challenges to applying either of these theories to regions and lesser states is that, regardless of the region's configuration, regions are nested within a global system with its own structure. Understanding the situation of the region geographically in the context of the international distribution of power can shed further light on which approaches explain more of the conflict we observe in international politics and how regional spaces might shift from spaces of conflict to spaces of relative peace.

Multiple Hierarchies and Dominance Vacuums

Although the evolution of Europe over the past twenty years provides one example of the competing theories constrained to a regional context, to further explore regional orders, we may seek to adjust capabilities across distance, as illustrated in chapter 1. Doing so provides us with geographic spaces where states are both at parity and where only one state is dominant during the same year. We can then test whether the spaces at parity are more peaceful or violent than those dominated by a single state. Furthermore, by dividing the world into spaces where a single power dominates versus those with two or more, we can compare the success of balance of power and power transition theories within the same time periods. Rather than examine the change in power of the two most powerful states over time, we can compare regions with and without parity between their most powerful actors within a single year, providing greater evidence as to the explanatory power of the supported approach.

In applying power transition theory to regions, Douglas Lemke[15] uses the loss of strength gradient[16] to project power across distance among regional actors. Shown in chapter 1, the loss of strength gradient functionally creates a bubble or cone of power that radiates outward from the capital of a state. The farther you get from the state, the less power it can project given the logistical constraints created by distance. He then hypothesizes that within politically relevant regions, which are those where three or more states can reach one another, if one state's power projection dominates all the others, war is less likely. But if the projected power of two states to one another's capital is about equal, and the state is dissatisfied, war will be more likely to ensue. Because, for power transition theory, all states' preferences are not fixed, he uses increases in military spending as a proxy for whether the state is dissatisfied with its regional opponent. Through multiple tests on regions spanning from South America to East Asia, Lemke's results hold, showing parity increases the observance of conflict by up to ten times, depending upon the region, and doubling if the challenging state was also dissatisfied with the status quo.[17]

Dominance vacuum theory applies this same idea to the international system as a whole by using the loss of strength gradient to project the power of the most powerful states.[18] Using the idea of shatterbelts, or geographic spaces that are "inherently more prone to conflict than other areas,"[19] researchers suggest that where the projected capabilities of two major powers are at approximate parity, the probability of conflict triples among not just the competing major powers but among all states in the space as well. By incorporating geography by adjusting power across distance using a power transition framework, we not only explain, in part, why conflicts tend to cluster in particular regions but also how some regions, such as Europe, can oscillate from zones of enormous conflict to places of unprecedented peaceful cooperation.

MEASURING SATISFACTION, STATUS, AND AUTHORITY

The discussion to this point has highlighted empirical examples and tests of the effect of capabilities on the probability that conflict may occur. But, as previously mentioned, satisfaction with the status quo is a crucial variable to the onset of conflict, as a satisfied rising challenger has little reason to initiate a costly war. The capability of states, meaning their power and ability to project it, merely suggests the opportunity of states to engage and maintain conflicts. To understand why conflict happens, we must also understand states' willingness to engage in conflict. For neorealism, preferences are fixed, meaning that the willingness of states to engage in conflict is always the same. The only thing that fluctuates, thus explaining all conflict, is the variation in states' relative power. Power transition theory, however, incorporates the state's views on how the international system functions to gauge its contentedness. The less content or satisfied the state, the more willing it will be to use violent conflict to seek change.

Scholars have measured satisfaction in a variety of ways, although no consensus has developed. Proxies of status measurement include the number of ambassador-level diplomatic missions to a state,[20] the number of state visits received,[21] or the participation of the state in international alliances and agreements.[22] Alternatively, others have looked at measures of domestic values within a state, using survey data to determine its satisfaction. If the internal values of a population align with those of the dominant state, then that government is likely to be satisfied with the international order and pursue similar foreign policies. States with populations that have different values will likely have less trust in the international system and therefore be dissatisfied.[23] This approach shares some similarities with David Lake's concept of authority, where states that participate heavily in the economic and security system created by the most powerful state consent to and are thusly satisfied with the authority of that powerful actor. Relatedly, preferences may be closely tied to institutions, meaning that democracies may be satisfied when the most powerful state is a democracy and nondemocracies less so.[24]

Regardless of how we measure status, we must resort to *proxies* or measures that are not directly representative of the measured concept. It is impossible to know whether a state, its people, and its decision-makers are content with the status quo, as we cannot know their thoughts and desires. We might look toward their actions, but that, too, has complications. For example, we may reasonably expect that a state that initiates conflict is dissatisfied, but to use conflict as a measure of dissatisfaction would render our argument unfalsifiable. Furthermore, not all states that are dissatisfied necessarily engage in conflict. So to generate a useful measure of status quo evaluations by a rising challenger, we must find some measure that is observable but not a part of the actual initiation of conflict that we are trying to explain. However, if preferences are fixed and all states want the same thing, as neorealism suggests, we should not observe the dramatic differences in outcomes that have been discussed throughout this chapter. By incorporating the added nuance of satisfaction (or status or authority), we increase our explanatory capability.

Status and Intervention

Conflicts are processes, not single events, and when we think about conflict escalation or termination as it pertains to changes in hierarchy, we are often thinking about how the hierarchy may have changed during conflict. For example, in the case of both world wars, states entering and leaving the conflict have important consequences for the distribution of power. When the United States entered World War II in 1941, it dramatically tipped the scale of what was, at that point, a close match in the Allies' favor. At that same war's outset, the Axis forces began ahead, but the slow, relative decline in the capacity of the Third Reich to extract available resources for military use caused them to become outpaced by the Allies as early as mid-1940.[25]

Outside conflicts between major powers, where the essential element to their resolution may be the ability to extract capabilities, conflicts between smaller powers can be heavily manipulated in their outcomes and length by the intervention of major powers. In choosing whether to intervene and whose side to join, the *status* or *authority* of a state seems to play an important role. Indeed, when thinking about the impact of hierarchy on conflict behavior, the concepts of status, authority, and satisfaction are likely heavily related not just to conflict onset but also other behaviors, both conflictual and cooperative. States that receive more status than they think they deserve are likely to engage in very pacifistic behavior, both because they are likely to be satisfied given all the status they are accorded and because they want to avoid exposing their relative weakness in capabilities. For example, these status overachievers tend to create and engage in international institutions relatively more extensively than others and avoid conflict.[26] China, for example, in its first decade of major-power status in the 1990s, avoided joining any military conflict whatsoever beyond its immediate borders. By comparison, the United States intervened globally a dozen times.[27] However, states that do not receive the status from other actors in the international system that they think they deserve are likely also dissatisfied and seek to alter the status quo through aggressive foreign policy behavior.

Status and Authority

States operating outside or in contradiction to the authority of the dominant state may likely be targets of a major power intervention. However, the concept of authority is easily understood, although more challenging to measure and apply to conflict behavior. In general, it is the degree to which a state is ingrained in the security and economic architecture of the dominant state, measured as a combination of hosting American military personnel, taking part in alliance structures, and integrating into the monetary and trade regimes the United States promotes.[28] For conflict, the implication would be that an increase in security hierarchy increases the probability that the United States will exercise its authority and intervene as the sole legitimate arbiter on security issues.[29]

In contrast, status is more directly observable as it is attributional rather than participatory. We can measure status by observing the diplomatic behaviors between states as signals of the importance granted from one state to another. Often, this is accomplished by simply tallying the number of ambassadors a state receives.[30] Although the most powerful states, like the United States, send ambassadors almost everywhere, for most states, maintaining and staffing a full embassy is a costly endeavor. Therefore, they limit their diplomatic missions to states that they view as most important: only those they perceive to be uniquely relevant to their foreign policies, such as the powerful and their immediate neighbors. States that receive the status they deserve, such as the United States, we call *status consistent*. Those that receive more are *status consistent overachievers*, such as Belgium, and those that receive less are *status consistent underachievers*, such as the Soviet Union during the Cold War. The presence, excess, or relative lack of status has important implications for state behavior.[31]

These same concepts of status and authority translate to the regional level. Within regional spaces that include a regional power, as opposed to those with no clear leader, the frequency of conflict throughout the region is cut almost in half. If that regional power is also a major power, meaning that it is particularly powerful and globally engaged, then the frequency of conflict is almost reduced to a third. In these regions, conflicts that disrupt the status quo are simply a less attractive means of achieving goals against any opponent, not just against the major regional power, as the strong major regional power is likely to intervene as third party.[32]

Role

There exist many states in the international system that perhaps receive far more status than their capabilities might merit, such as Switzerland or Belgium. They frequently provide functions to the international system, such as peacemaker by facilitating conflict's termination. These states may not be major or regional powers but instead play a "role," meaning that they perform some function in the international system that helps it to operate smoothly and prevents rising levels of violence that may destabilize it. This may also be true of major powers, such as Japan's substantial contributions toward peacekeeping efforts.

AFTER CONFLICT: THE PHOENIX FACTOR

When conflicts do end, often states have endured high costs, and those costs, in the short run, have significantly altered the hierarchy of capabilities among actors. In some cases, those costs may be permanent as the political consequences of the war dismantle a state, such as the collapse of the Austro-Hungarian Empire or the division of Germany. However, in terms of population, resources, and capabilities, most states often recover quickly. This rapid recovery, generally about two decades, is known as the *Phoenix Factor*.[33] States can rapidly return to their previous level of capabilities, even in the face of attempts to keep them held back, such as Germany between World War I and World War II. The development characteristics of the state in question are more important than the damage sustained. Highly educated, technologically advanced, and bureaucratically efficient societies retain those components in most cases after major wars, meaning the key components of recovery remain. If relative capabilities are an important cause of conflict and recover quickly from conflict's consequences, war does not necessarily bring about peace. Instead, we must look to authority, status, and satisfaction as ways for bringing about more peaceful preferences.

DISCUSSION QUESTIONS

1. Why would states that receive less status than they think they deserve be more likely to use conflict?
2. Are most small states satisfied or dissatisfied in the world today? How might the United States make a dissatisfied state more satisfied?
3. At the end of a war, how might the victor prevent its opponent from recovering its capabilities (the Phoenix Factor)?
4. If projecting power across space in the international system allows us to identify shatterbelts of recurring conflict, what policies should the United States pursue to stabilize those spaces, if any?

KEY TERMS

conflict

parity

Phoenix Factor

polarity

shatterbelts

status quo

war

FURTHER READING

Fearon, James. 1995. "Rationalist Explanations for War." *International Organization* 49, no. 3:379–414.

Lemke, Douglas. 2002. *Regions of War and Peace.* Cambridge: Cambridge University Press.

Organski, A. F. K., and Jacek Kugler. 1980. *The War Ledger.* Chicago: University of Chicago Press.

4

Rivalries and Alliances

ORGANIZATION OF PEACE AND CONFLICT

Alliances and rivalries are two observations of states organizing conflict-related behavior. Alliances of all types are forms of managing conflictual behaviors between states by organizing their expectations should conflict occur. They may be offensive, agreeing to attack an opponent or achieve a strategic goal. They may be defensive, promising to protect one another if attacked by an aggressor. Often, they are only consultative, promising to discuss or inform before engaging in some activity. Regardless, alliances can be considered tools of cooperation, at least between their signatories.

In some cases, such as the North Atlantic Treaty Organization (NATO), the alliance may also have a formal organization with rules, leadership, and a headquarters no different from the cooperative organizations discussed in chapter 7. However, in this chapter, we focus on the agreements themselves, their obligations, and how that affects state behavior as it pertains to international conflict. Although alliances are cooperative agreements, this cooperation is focused on the possibility of coercion, either offensively or as a deterrent. We discuss alliances here as one way that states manage the potential for conflict's occurrence and how changes in hierarchy may affect the evolution or demise of these agreements.

States also organize conflictual behavior through rivalries in the form of recurring violence. Rivalries are clusters of actual or potential conflict within a dyad. Analyzing a rivalry is about understanding the evolution of a violent relationship over time as opposed to focusing on a single conflictual event without context. As with many alliances, their relevance goes beyond a single event to more extended periods. This longer period allows us to examine how changes in hierarchy may shape a single alliance or rivalry as they span a more considerable amount of time than individual conflicts.

As processes, rivalries may be openly violent or nonviolent competition over more strategic interests. These interactions are capable of dramatic change not only over time both as interests and issues evolve but also when confronted with shifting hierarchy over the geographic space in which the rivalry resides. Both alliances and rivalries provide an element of empirical predictability to international political behavior. Rivals are consistently more likely to have a conflict with one another than nonrivals, while allies are predictably likely to come to one another's aid.[1] However, in both cases, a dramatic disruption of the hierarchy in the international system could cause those consistent relationships to break down and even reverse: alliance partners may come into conflict with one another or rivalries may end. It is this sudden change, when the predictable behaviors become erratic, that we might seek to understand better when thinking about the influence of hierarchy and its absence on state behaviors.

ALLIANCES: WHY DO THEY FORM AND WHAT DO THEY ACCOMPLISH?

International agreements, such as alliances, may be "just a scrap of paper," as the German chancellor Theobald von Bethmann-Hollweg quipped at the outset of World War I; however, those scraps of paper, even in the anarchic international system, have important consequences for the behavior of states. The value of each agreement lies not in the physical paper or the threat some international government may choose to enforce the agreement as law but instead as a signaling mechanism to other states about preferences and intentions. For a dominant power, they are an articulation of the expected norms of conduct in security-related affairs by which other states must abide. Furthermore, both dominant and challenger states may use alliances as a way to augment their capabilities.

Geographically proximate states within alliances tend to be reliable actors in conflicts and reap benefits from shared borders that enable them to direct their security concerns outside the alliance.[2] As a result, states have the capability that comes from not responding to conflicts individually but instead as an entire alliance group.[3] Similarly, a challenging power may use alliances to bolster its ability to take control of the system from the dominant state, while dominant powers may create security architecture to preserve the status quo.[4]

Alliances, then, are particularly important agreements relating to the obligations of a state in times of conflict. They signal to allies when they are expected to engage in conflict, or come to another's defense, and inform potential enemies to deter them from a conflict initiation.[5] To be effective, these agreements must be public, clear in their terms, and believable in their invocation. For example, the Italians in World War I are often referenced as an example of a state refusing to abide by its alliance, but the explicit terms of the Triple Alliance only committed them to Germany's and Austria's defense. The Italians argued that Austria began the war as an aggressive act against Serbia without any consultation, leaving the Italians to do as they pleased. Furthermore, the Italians stated by ministerial declaration that nothing of the agreement could be considered as "directed against England."[6]

Types of Alliances

When we think about alliances, we often think about agreements providing for mutual defense, such as NATO. However, alliances can take many different forms and have many levels of obligation. Table 4.1 shows how the Alliance Treaty and Obligations (ATOP) data organize these diverse and complex agreements according to the obligations expected of the treaty members: defensive and offensive alliances are those that include "promises to aid a partner in the event of a military conflict" in a protective or aggressive capacity, respectively; neutrality agreements are promises to stay out of conflict; nonaggression pacts are commitments to avoid conflict with one another; and, finally, the weakest form of commitment is consultation pacts that merely serve as agreements to "consult/cooperate" in response to some occurrence.[7] Among the 745 alliances identified across 200 years, many include overlapping forms of commitments.

What relationship might there be among these alliance behaviors, their timing, and hierarchy or its absence? Alliances can be a form of signaling not just of intentions or architecture but also of the combined capabilities of an entire alliance bloc. In some cases, researchers will use the capabilities of an entire alliance to measure relative power, particularly when the allied group is engaged in a conflict or even to measure polarity.[8]

Table 4.1   Alliance Obligations and Their Frequency, 1815–2016

Alliance Type	Number
Defensive	74
Offensive	6
Neutrality	18
Nonaggression	172
Consultation	83
Defensive and Offensive	33
Defensive and Neutrality	8
Defensive and Nonaggression	13
Defensive and Consultation	77
Offensive and Neutrality	3
Offensive and Consultation	5
Neutrality and Nonaggression	33
Neutrality and Consultation	12
Nonaggression and Consultation	100
Defensive, Offensive, and Nonaggression	8
Defensive, Offensive, and Consultation	20
Defensive, Neutrality, and Consultation	2
Defensive, Nonaggression, and Consultation	31
Neutrality, Nonaggression, and Consultation	38
Defensive, Offensive, Neutrality, and Consultation	5
Defensive, Offensive, Nonaggression, and Consultation	1
Defensive, Neutrality, Nonaggression, and Consultation	3

Source: Brett Ashley Leeds, Jeffrey M. Ritter, Sara McLaughlin Mitchell, and Andrew G. Long, "Alliance Treaty Obligations and Provisions, 1815–1944," *International Interactions* 28, no. 3 (2002): 237–260.

Balance of Power and Alliance Transition Theories

For balance of power theorists, alliances function as a way for states to signal their interests and create pacts of two sides. These sides strive to be coequal in capabilities and thereby capable of maintaining peace. Under bipolarity, two countries, or poles, are so dramatically more powerful than everyone else that shifting changes in alliance partners cannot override the balance provided by the two opposing sides. Alliances will form into two, roughly coequal blocs around the two superpowers. In other words, a country joining the Warsaw Pact would not significantly affect the balance between the United States and the Soviet Union because the addition of the alliance partner does not meaningfully alter the already dramatic ability of each side to harm one another.

Under conditions of multipolarity, however, the presence of more than two powerful states threatens the balance. If there are three powerful states, for example, the first and second-most powerful state will supposedly be on opposing sides. This leaves the third state to serve as Morgenthau's "holder of the balance."[9] Whichever side the third-most powerful state joins in a military alliance will tip balance of power and determine the victor. According to neorealists, this instability of alliance politics among the most powerful states leads to conflict rather than the stability of bipolarity, as one side will be necessarily more powerful than the other.

From some hierarchical perspectives, such as Woosang Kim's alliance transition theory, states similarly may use alliances to augment their capabilities. Like power transition theory, changes in power from the internal demography, political capacity, and domestic economic efficiency of states remain the primary source of capabilities; however, states may use alliances to augment those capabilities in reaction to the international context. First, balance of power theory treats the power of a state as a given, leaving it no other course of action to augment its power than alliances. As discussed previously, however, power has its origins in the domestic sphere, and changes within that sphere are the primary source of actual changes to power.[10] But, because manipulating demographic sources such as birth rates can be challenging, states may use alliances as a more immediate and direct means of augmenting their power through combined military capabilities.

Second, balance of power theory assumes that, due to fixed preferences for survival, states will automatically balance in their alliance behaviors and that coequal balance will lead to stability. Hierarchical theories assume that states have other preferences, and therefore, their alliance patterns are likely to mirror those diverse preferences instead of solely balancing with no consideration toward the nature of the state with whom they are allying or opposing. In other words, reflecting their preferences, satisfied states will ally with the dominant power, and unsatisfied states will ally with the challenger. The distribution of power between the two sides, however, will not necessarily be the determining consideration. Then, as with power transition theory, when the satisfied alliance and the dissatisfied alliance are coequal, war will become more likely.

Hierarchy and Alliance Joining

This augmentation of power transition theory to address alliances allows us to use both capabilities and alliance data to examine which approach most accurately describes the behaviors of states. Kim finds war to be more likely as the alliances become coequal,[11] but let us descriptively take a closer look at the ATOP data shown earlier. If balance of power theory is correct, we should expect states to be joining the most powerful state and the second-most powerful state during the Cold War at relatively equal rates but favoring the weaker side. At other points where bipolarity is absent, states should form a bloc in opposition to the strongest power to create that balance. If hierarchical approaches are correct, then alliance patterns should follow satisfaction or dissatisfaction toward the status quo rather than pure power considerations.

Table 4.2 shows the joining behavior of states to alliance agreements that involve some military commitment, offensive or defensive,

Table 4.2   Offensive and Defensive Alliances by Polarity

Period	Polarity	Dominant	Challenger	Both	None	Relevant Powers
1816–1860	Unipolar	1	5	8	13	United Kingdom (France & Russia)
1861–1870	Bipolar	1	0	2	14	United Kingdom (France)
1871–1880	Multipolar	0	1	0	2	United Kingdom (France & Russia)
1881–1890	Bipolar	1	0	0	2	United Kingdom (France)
1891–1914	Multipolar	1	5	0	8	United Kingdom (France, United States, Russia, & Germany)

Period	Polarity	Dominant	Challenger	Both	None	Relevant Powers
1920–1938	Bipolar	2	3	2	12	United Kingdom (United States, Soviet Union, & Germany)
1945–1970	Unipolar	10	15	1	69	United States (Soviet Union)
1971–1990	Bipolar	1	1	0	26	United States (Soviet Union)
1991–	Unipolar	0	0	0	30	United States (China)

Source: Adapted from the list from William R. Thompson, "Polarity, the Long Cycle, and Global Power Warfare," *Journal of Conflict Resolution* 30 (1986): 587–615. Rather than list changes annually, we create broader time periods and list the most typical polarity that Thompson gives in a given time period. Brett Ashley Leeds, Jeffrey M. Ritter, Sara McLaughlin Mitchell, and Andrew G. Long, "Alliance Treaty Obligations and Provisions, 1815–1944," *International Interactions* 28, no. 3 (2002): 237–260.

given the approximate polarity of the system across consistent periods as previously shown in table 3.1.[12] The Dominant column lists alliances that include the most powerful state. The Challenger column includes alliances that involve the challenger(s) listed in parentheses under "Relevant Powers." In some cases, the alliance includes some combination of both. Finally, most alliances involve neither, counted under "None." The years of the two world wars, where hierarchy is in flux and active conflict is occurring between most states and all major powers, are not included.

It is worth noting that most alliances do not involve either the dominant power or potential challengers, but this does not mean that they are unrelated to systemic shifts. Many of these alliances begin immediately following the end of World War II as new governments form, new nations achieve independence, and a dramatic reorganization of international economic and security architecture occurs. With those changes at the global level come changes in regions, and many of these new alliances have much more to do with local security issues rather than global dynamics. For example, states may create geographically stable security complexes within a regional zone to address a local security concern or reduce the costs of security to all members.[13]

In those cases in which alliances involve the globally dominant or challenger states, patterns of behavior appear to depend heavily on the time period. During the majority of the nineteenth century, France, the second-most powerful state, was somewhat satisfied with the order created by Britain after the conclusion of the Napoleonic wars. As such, we see that states most frequently are in agreements with Britain *and* France or Russia, with these joint alliances outnumbering those made discretely with either the dominant or challenger states. However, in the unipolar periods for the United States, only one treaty exists that includes both dominant and challenging power. Where the distribution of alliances favors the challenger in the unipolar period, there are only two offensive or defensive alliances in the 1971–1990 bipolar period, evenly divided between the two states. On the contrary, in the current unipolar period, no new offensive or defensive alliances are found in the data for either the United States or China. This lack of consistency across polarity suggests that alliance behavior may be less about the attempted balancing of power by states in the international system and instead is illustrative of security reorganization following cataclysmic events.

Observe, for example, the number of new alliances across all categories following both World War II and the collapse of the Soviet Union. Thinking about changes over time rather than balancing power might lead us to conclude that sudden shifts in hierarchy result in sudden activity. Who that alliance is with, whether dominant, challenger, or other, may depend on other variables, such as geography. For example, most of the fifteen treaties with the Soviet Union in the first Cold War period are with its immediate neighbors, such as the Warsaw Pact. That arrangement was hardly a voluntary act of balancing or a thoughtful security arrangement by the signatories. Instead, it was a forced arrangement by the puppet governments of Moscow as the Soviet military occupied their streets. Furthermore, satisfaction with the status quo and preferences should heavily influence alliance behaviors just as they influence conflict. Proximity to a powerful state may condition your perceptions of that state's authority and thereby your willingness to play a part in its agreements.

Key to evaluating the balance of power hypothesis, alliance behaviors under bipolarity demonstrate mixed results. We would expect more alliances to occur with the second-most powerful state to balance the power of the most powerful state. However, alliances tend to favor the dominant power in all instances except the last bipolar period, which is even. Opposed to reflecting balancing, this instead likely reflects satisfaction during the period with the existing order. If we account for the capabilities of the alliance partners, the picture skews even more heavily toward the dominant power, as we will see in our discussion of the Cold War in chapter 6.

Geography and Alliance Behaviors

How might we further refine our understanding of alliances given the geography of the international system? Throughout history, alliance partners have tended to cluster together geographically. Is balancing taking place within regions, or instead, are powerful states creating localized security orders? What complicates examinations of alliance politics within regional spaces is the potential for outside actors to intervene, alter behaviors, and change outcomes. A "balanced" or "stable" system can be suddenly thrown into disarray by an external actor interfering, as has often been the case with the interventions of the United States in the Middle East. Alternatively, a strong external power can provide peace and order to a region by allying with region members and creating a shared security architecture, which perhaps accounts for the observed peace between European powers since World War II.[14] Thus, to examine the effectiveness of our theories in predicting alliance behaviors, we would need to focus on regions where outside forces are absent.[15]

Unfortunately, such isolated spaces are somewhat rare today, if they exist at all. Perhaps the closest space relatively absent direct major power engagement is the Central African Great Lakes region. In 2006, states in Central Africa spanning from Zambia in the south to Sudan in the north formed a regional defensive pact. The treaty declares abstinence of military force between signatories and includes provisions to ensure that states do not arm the warlords and rebel groups that plague the more difficult-to-reach geographic spaces.[16] This treaty, like many of the recent agreements in Africa, highlights localized security threats from nonstate actors against the states themselves, serving not as a balancing organization but as an order providing collective security agreement to combat small but destabilizing actors. Although other treaties coincide with former colonial cleavages or economic concerns, there is a remarkable absence of any form of balancing alliance behaviors in this more isolated regional context.

Collective Security

Another outcome we can observe and evaluate is balancing against specific threats. If alliances are merely tools of signaling a balance among particularly powerful actors, then we would expect those alliances to dissolve or become irrelevant following the demise of the threat. Indeed, this is exactly what neorealists suggested would occur to NATO upon the Soviet Union's collapse, followed by a return of conflict on the European continent.[17] However, contrary to their expectations, NATO both expanded its membership and became more active. This evolution of NATO as a *collective security* body providing order to its members coincides with a shift in capabilities across the geographic space. When the Soviet Union collapsed, the United States expanded its influence to provide security order to the space geographically adjacent to existing NATO powers. This expansion allowed new members to focus their resource efforts on domestic development and capacity building instead of on military defense against their neighbors or a new Russian state that was but a shadow of its Soviet predecessor. In this sense, the alliance persists and continues to be a stabilizing force *absent a clear threat*. Contrary to neorealist expectations of threat balancing, NATO expanded to provide stability and a public good, in this case collective security, to a group of states at the direction of the dominant state in the international system.

Indeed, the original intent of NATO, in the words of Lord Ismay, was to "keep the Americans in, the Russians out, and the Germans down."[18] Despite the Soviet Union collapsing from internal pressures and the Germans reunifying, NATO expanded. Although this expansion and continued investment in NATO deters hypothetical future aggressors, it also assures allies of the stability of the American-led status quo.[19] In so doing, the United States facilitates and deepens cooperation on a range of security issues that may arise, as opposed to the traditional view of alliances focused limitedly on targeting a specific country. Absent these specific threats, NATO coordinates on nontraditional security issues, such as transnational terrorism, and monitors stability on its periphery as it has with the recent conflicts in Libya and Syria. This commitment by the United States both mitigates existing security concerns through deepening cooperation between alliance members and prevents smaller threats from expanding into greater ones. Thus, the United States and its allies are effective in maintaining the stability of the status quo of American unipolarity as opposed to merely balancing against an identified opponent.

RIVALRY TYPES AND THEIR CONDUCT

There are several types of rivalries, but perhaps the most frequently studied in the international relations literature are *enduring* and *strategic*. Enduring rivalries are somewhat straightforward, both in their concept and measurement, identified as a pair of states engaged in an observably hostile relationship where there are three or more disputes within ten years.[20] In total, this category covers about 60 percent of all disputes in the Militarized Interstate Disputes data and more than 80 percent of wars where there have been more than 1,000 battlefield deaths.[21] In this case, rivalry is conceptualized as repeated conflict regardless of the substantive cause. By observing the clustering of these militarized conflicts within a single relationship, we can then both control for the fact that conflicts are not randomly distributed among all actors in the international system and highlight that the repeated conflicts within a dyad may create an expectation by the two rivals of continued conflict. Enduring rivalries may be repeatedly violent conflicts, such as India and Pakistan, or repeated instances of lower-level conflict, such as the United States and Peru during the Cold War. Our interest in understanding enduring rivalries lies in the *predictive* value of past events repeating into the future.

Strategic rivalries, on the other hand, are more substantively driven in their identification than their enduring counterparts. Two countries are engaged in a strategic rivalry if they possess some substantive strategic interest over which they may have a dispute: a bit of territory, resource access, or a particular historical grievance.[22] The assumption underlying this alternative coding is not to identify conflicts as they cluster in time but instead to identify the underlying conditions, often geographically driven, that create rivalry and then may eventually lead to significant conflict. So, although enduring rivalries observe the concentrating of actual conflict in time, strategic rivalries highlight when states have conflictual policy goals.

Challenges in Rivalry Measurement

The number of enduring rivalries is far greater than the number of strategic rivalries by almost double. Comparing the enduring and strategic rivalry data sets, we find that there are ninety active enduring rivalries and fifty-five strategic rivalries. The reason for this dramatic difference is in part due to temporal coverage of the two data sets, a phenomenon known as censoring and essential to keep in mind any time we attempt to draw conclusions from data. For example, the enduring rivalries data are coded through 2001. That means that some rivalries are "right-censored" or that they are ongoing at the point the data coverage ends and continue past that point for some unknown amount. A rivalry ongoing in 2001 may continue for some number of years after the fact with the exact number of years uncertain. For the strategic rivalry data set, rivalries are coded through 1999, thus demonstrating a similar issue. We also should keep in mind that data sets can be "left censored," meaning some identified rivalries extend into the past beyond the time period. For example, some rivalries of the nineteenth century, such as England and France, may extend hundreds of years into the past before the data set's start date. Students of international relations should be cautious about these coding rules before drawing conclusions from data lest they should inaccurately assume a rivalry ends in 2001 just because that is when the data stop.

Comparison of the two data sets also offers lessons in how differences in the way we define what a rivalry *is* as a concept can lead us to very different measurements of what rivalries *exist* and why they *begin*, *extend*, and *end*. The enduring rivalry data set lists a far larger number of rivalries given the coding of repeated conflict events over time. Those conflicts may not necessarily be of strategic importance. As an example, featured more frequently in the post–Cold War enduring rivalry data is Serbia. As the conflicts evolved from the breakup of the former Yugoslavia between the many geographically intertwined ethnic groups, rivalries did evolve over territory, historical grievances, and political control, notably between Serbia and newly independent neighbors or old rivals, such as Albania and Hungary, over border disputes or ethnic populations. However, many of the identified rivals with Serbia that are not contiguous to its territory have repeated militarized disputes as part of the NATO intervention in the Kosovo War to stop the genocide that occurred of ethnic Albanians. These repeated disputes fit the enduring definition given their frequency. They mostly would not meet the strategic rivalry definition as they are merely engaging Serbia as allies of the United States and NATO members but not out of their own strategic foreign policy interests.

This measurement issue has important consequences for our findings about rivalries, similar to the importance of defining concepts such as democracy and war. There is, for example, a debate as to whether Finland is at war with the United States and the United Kingdom during World War II. They are usually all considered democracies, and they are technically at war, but are they substantively? In all cases, knowing the measurement of a variable requires careful thought about the concepts and theory you are seeking to explain. No matter what the research question, know your data!

Systemic Hierarchy and Dyadic Rivalry

Regardless of how we code the data, what does the timing of rivalry onset and duration tell us about the effect of hierarchy? Figure 4.1 displays the onset and termination of enduring rivalries across the full range of data from 1816 to 2001, divided by the number of countries in existence as we did for conflict in chapter 3.

An obvious important trend is immediately evident. After periods of sudden system change, such as the consolidation of Germany,

Figure 4.1   Initiation and Termination of Enduring Rivalries

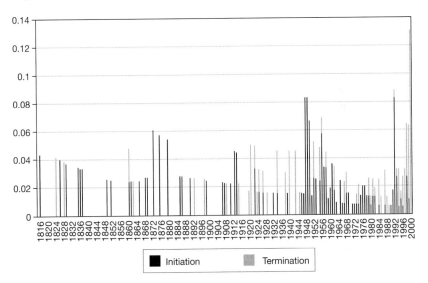

Source: James P. Klein, Gary Goertz, and Paul F. Diehl, "The New Rivalry Data Set: Procedures and Patterns," *Journal of Peace Research* 43, no. 3 (2006): 331–48; and Correlates of War Project, "State System Membership List, v 2016" (2017), last accessed August 17, 2019, http://correlatesofwar.org.

the World Wars, or the collapse of the Soviet Union, rivalries *both* end and begin in greater degrees than at any other period. First, this highlights the instability of the international system during periods in which a challenging major power contests the hierarchy. Rivalries are a form of organized conflict insofar as states direct and anticipate their aggression against a specific target. When the distribution of power in the international system rapidly changes, the resulting shifts in borders or the dominance of a new state over territory where previously none existed can quickly end many rivalries, such as Germany and France after World War II. Similarly, the deterioration of dominance over a geographic space could make relationships that were once held in check by a dominant actor suddenly become violent, as is the case with Afghanistan and the sudden development of rivalries with its northern neighbors following the collapse of the Soviet Union.

Remembering that rivalries will increase as the number of states available to have a rivalry increases, as discussed in chapter 3 with conflicts, the "spikes" in rivalry onset and termination align closely with periods of change. In the nineteenth century, there are relatively few, consistent with the very few states in existence, but the greatest rate of onsets occurs from 1860 to 1880 as Germany consolidates into a single state. Rapid termination of rivalries occurs in the early 1920s as the world is remade, particularly in Europe where borders are redrawn and new countries are created after World War I. Similarly, a sudden shift in rivalries occurs again after the end of World War II. New rivalries form as newly independent states are created and align with one of the two superpowers.

Finally, in the most recent period, new rivalries form suddenly as the Soviet Union collapses following the same trend of new states being created with new disputes. In each case, violent rivalry forms when there is an opportunity to engage in conflict and an issue to fight over. However, in these cases that pivot around cataclysmic systemic events, the redrawing of borders and the elimination of preexisting states likewise terminate old disputes and create new ones.[23] In 2000, near the end of the data set, there is a rapid termination of rivalries. This is a unique batch as it mostly coincides with the end of the conflict in Yugoslavia. However, this set of rivalries also aligns closely with stability ending rivalries and instability creating them in the immediate aftermath of sudden change, such as the breakup of former Yugoslavia.

BOX 4.1	Case of Alliances and Rivalries in Action: World War I

World War I provides an excellent example of decades-old alliances and rivalries both manifesting in violent conflict and in how hierarchy, shifting across geographic space, can influence the expected outcomes of both forms of state behavior. Imagine the distribution of capabilities across geographic space in 1913, on the eve of the war's onset. Three zones of dominance existed, one around Britain, the other around Germany, and the last around Russia.[24] The spaces between them, such as Belgium, the Mediterranean, and much of Western Russia more proximate to Germany, were in a zone of parity, where projected capabilities were evenly matched. Much like the conflict's scope, the spaces of parity cover most of the continent, and the lines where projected capabilities intersect among Britain, Germany, and Russia align closely with the location of many of the war's worst battles.

Three states fail to abide by alliance conditions pertaining to the war: Romania, Greece, and Russia. In each of these cases, the opposing side was dominant over its territory: Austria over Greece at the war's outset, Britain over Romania after Britain entered the war, and Germany over Russia after its capabilities shrink following the Bolshevik Revolution.

Rivalry behaviors tell a similar story of outcomes being influenced by the power projection of the most powerful states, although more globally. At the onset of World War I, there are eleven rivalries among contiguous belligerents to the conflict. In most cases, those rivals end up on opposite sides of the conflict, as we might expect given their history of conflict behaviors. In all cases of rivals fighting each other, their borders lay within a space of contested hierarchy with no clear state dominant over the others. In the cases where this is not true, all in East Asia (China and Russia, China and Japan, and Japan and Russia), the forces of all three end up on the same side despite their rivalry—quite unexpected without keeping in mind the context of hierarchy and geography.

DISCUSSION QUESTIONS

1. Although we just read some of the potential benefits of alliances, what are the possible costs of a state failing to keep its alliance promises?

2. What role do you think rivalry might play in the development of a state's political capacity? Can a rival be used as an internal political tool?
3. Do you think there may be a relationship between rivalry and alliances? How might hierarchy play a role in that relationship?

KEY TERMS

alliances
alliance transition theory
collective security

censored data
enduring rivalries
strategic rivalries

FURTHER READING

Goertz, Gary, and Paul F. Diehl. 1993. "Enduring Rivalries: Theoretical Constructs and Empirical Patterns." *International Studies Quarterly* 37, no. 2:147–71.

Kim, Woosang. 1989. "Power, Alliance, and Major Wars, 1816–1975." *Journal of Conflict Resolution* 33, no. 2:255–73.

Thompson, William R. "Identifying Rivals and Rivalries in World Politics." *International Studies Quarterly* 45, no. 4:557–86.

5

Intrastate Conflicts

EMPIRICAL EXAMINATION OF INTRASTATE CONFLICT

Although there are many types of intrastate conflict, we focus our attention on the two most prominent: civil wars and secessionist conflicts. The onset, duration, and termination of intrastate conflicts are some of the most heavily empirically analyzed fields of recent international relations research.[1] This is, at first, perplexing, as civil wars and secessionist movements are not necessarily international. But they often have international consequences, both increasing the chances of a state using an internal belligerent in a proxy war and offering the potential for internal conflict to spread across borders into neighboring states.[2] Furthermore, consistent with the theoretical purpose of this text, a civil war is, by definition, a challenge to an existing hierarchy. If we observe an internal militarized conflict, we are examining an occurrence of some internal group challenging the political hierarchy of the existing state, either desiring to replace that internal hierarchy by seizing control from the current government or altering the territorial borders of that state in the case of a secessionist movement. Although this chapter focuses on conflicts involving two sides within a state, often the dynamics of the war's start and conduct involve actors from outside the state seeking to influence domestic political outcomes in a proxy war. Those actors may not only be major powers attempting to shape politics within their area of control according to their preferences but may also be neighboring states or even nonstate groups, such as terrorist organizations.

Take the series of conflicts surrounding the breakup of Yugoslavia beginning in 1991. Upon Yugoslavia's demise, political interests within the state quickly coalesced around ethnic lines, with violence erupting within the central part of the former state. That conflict between competing groups within what is now Bosnia, Kosovo, and Serbia eventually led to direct intervention by the United Nations and military operations by the North Atlantic Treaty Organization (NATO). Major power intervention in what began as an internal conflict progressively escalated through the Kosovo War in 1998–1999 when the United States and allied forces directly intervened to stop the Serbian genocide of ethnic Albanians. That intervention, however, was not without risk, as another major power, the Russians, had been allied with the Serbs. Both in the location and in the interests of some key players, the conflict was eerily reminiscent of World War I, when once again an internal conflict, violence between Serbian separatists and the Austro-Hungarian Empire, set off a chain of events that led to global war. Intrastate wars can provide the spark that leads to much larger conflicts as major powers intervene to promote their interests or prevent internal violence from spreading elsewhere. In these cases of conflict expansion, both the external hierarchy of the system and the internal hierarchy of the state play pivotal roles in the war's outcome.

EXTERNAL HIERARCHY AND INTRASTATE CONFLICT

Following their conquest of Ireland in the twelfth century, the English began to refer to the area around Dublin where they were able to exert political and military control as *the Pale*. Outside of this geographic space, local lords challenged the English king's monopoly on power as the Crown had difficulty projecting its will into these more distant spaces. Hence, when something is outside of what we might expect, we use the phrase "beyond the pale." In this section, we're interested in what relationship civil war onsets have with those geographic spaces that are "beyond the pale." As with Ireland in the late medieval period, the area beyond the pale lacks a clear hierarchy, with many competing political actors vying for control and frequently employing violence. Dominant actors may struggle to exert unchallenged control in that space, but they may certainly choose sides, offer support, and intervene to some degree, altering political dynamics and exacerbating violence. Major powers can play a pivotal role in shaping intrastate conflict outcomes *beyond the pale*, or beyond their areas of geographic control where their capabilities are unchallenged, treating the conflict as an opportunity to significantly alter or preserve the politics of a state.[3] Between 1944 and 1999, there were 69 interventions by major powers in civil wars out of a total of 144, or nearly half, and those interventions tend to make those wars more violent and lengthy.[4] Furthermore, these interventions typically occur in the geographic spaces in between major powers where their projected capabilities are evenly matched: the geographic shatterbelts discussed in chapter 3.

Frequency of Intrastate Conflict

Figure 5.1 shows the frequency of intrastate conflict since 1820.[5] What kinds of patterns do we observe from this descriptive graph? First, we immediately notice that the frequency of these internal conflicts seems to be increasing with a peak in the late 1990s. This is in sharp contrast to the frequency of interstate wars discussed in chapter 3, suggesting different potential causes. Civil wars appear to become more likely over time and are most likely during the 1990s, where scholars across perspectives tend to agree that the system is unipolar with the United States unchallenged. Periods of their relative absence are concentrated in the interwar period and during the Cold War. This departure from patterns of interstate conflict in chapter 3 is puzzling. Is the international hierarchy unrelated to domestic conflict? Does unipolarity allow the United States to intervene in the internal politics of others at will, creating greater conflict than otherwise would exist in bipolarity, as some neorealists suggest?[6]

As with international conflict in chapter 3, we must also remember that the probability of observing an intrastate conflict each year is dependent upon the number of states in the international system. More states means more opportunities to observe internal conflicts, and the number of states has increased from 23 in 1820 to 193 in 2007.[7] If we graph the number of intrastate conflicts by the number of states in the system, giving us an image that tells us the rough proportion of states experiencing intrastate wars rather than just the count, we get a picture that tells a very different empirical story.

There are some commonalities: the republican revolutions of 1848 remain a significant peak serving as the maximum in the per state graph. Relative jumps also seem to follow periods of instability, such as the collapse of the Soviet Union. However, the figure shows a decline in the rate of civil war onset given the number of states in the system, leading us to assume that despite the rapid proliferation of

Figure 5.1   Frequency of Intrastate War Onset, 1820–2007

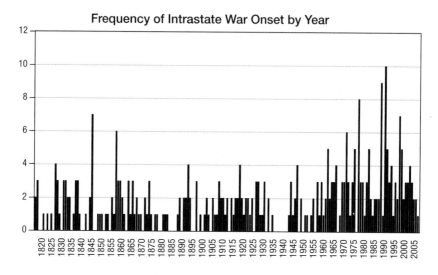

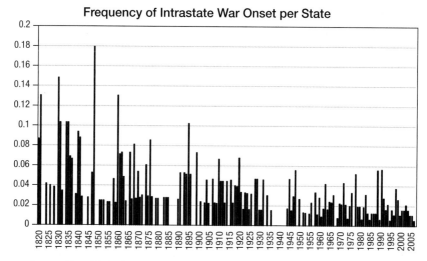

Source: Meredith Sarkees and Frank Wayman, *Resort to War: 1816–2007* (Washington, DC: CQ Press, 2010); Correlates of War Project, "State System Membership List, v 2016" (2017), last accessed August 17, 2019, http://correlatesofwar.org.

states in the international system, the proportion of states experiencing internal violence is falling.

The comparison of these two graphs demonstrates the importance of proper data specification, as failing to do so can lead to dramatically different conclusions about the outcome we are trying to explain. Furthermore, there is not necessarily a single right answer, but instead, the proper data specification depends on our question. As with the preceding discussion, if we want to understand how the system influences the internal hierarchies of states as observed in the presence or absence of internal conflict, controlling for the number of states in the international system that could experience such a conflict is a necessity. Regardless of whether we consider the system to be unipolar, bipolar, or multipolar, states cannot project power equally across geography. So we should ask ourselves in what locations are these conflicts most likely to occur?

Diffusion of Intrastate Conflict

Referring to the clustering of conflict in certain locations, remember that shatterbelts are geographic spaces that are "inherently more prone to conflict than other areas."[8] As such, we may expect that instability to extend beyond merely interstate conflicts but also include the politics within states, as well as interventions by competing powers in these shatterbelts. An outside power may help prop up an ailing civil war belligerent, increasing its capability and prolonging a conflict to the devastation of a nation. China, for example, provided dramatic support to the North Vietnamese in their civil war as the United States sought to prop up the South, with both sides support prolonging and intensifying the war.

Intrastate conflicts tend to cluster in geographic spaces in the international system, meaning that they tend to be nearby to one another rather than equally and randomly distributed across the globe. When one state experiences a civil war, the violence, destruction, and instability are rarely restricted solely to the territory of that state. As we have observed recently in the case of Syria, fighters, refugees, and weapons may cross into neighboring states, with the potential to spread political instability or even violent conflict. Interested major powers, as routinely occurred in the Cold War, may use these opportunities to attempt to export their interests, focusing on regime change or thwarting the interests of some opponent without engaging in direct conflict. This can lead to the active erosion of political authority not just in a single state but also by diffusion throughout an entire region.

Diffusive conflicts that might begin as a civil war can evolve, as actors join from the outside, into an international conflict. The Korean War, the Vietnam War, and even World War I all began as internal conflicts that rapidly escalated to include a much broader international audience. Major powers were on both sides of all three conflicts, attempting to expand their influence at the margins of their major power reach.

The decision on who to support in a conflict is often heavily driven by orientations toward the status quo. A rising challenger such as the Soviet Union may support actors only for their orientation against the system leader. Alternatively, alliances of convenience may materialize, as either dominant power or challenger seek to meddle in the internal politics of a state, perpetuating or promoting civil war. For example, the United States funded and supported the Mujahedeen in Afghanistan to inflict high costs on the Soviet Union. Without U.S. support, the rebels may have been easily overwhelmed, ending quickly what would instead subsequently become an internal conflict that lasted almost ten years and gave rise to the Al Qaeda terrorist organization. In contrast to the Soviet Union, China, which the United States looks to as the current challenger, is relatively satisfied, engaging in the fewest conflict interventions of any major power.[9]

BOX 5.1 | Syrian Civil War

Syria has been dominated by the authoritarian rule of the Assad family since 1970, with Bashar al-Assad taking control of the country following the death of his father in 2000. Alawite Shiites, the Assads maintain the backing of Iran, who view Syria as a key ally adjacent to both Lebanon and Israel. Syria has also allied with Russia, providing the Russians their last naval base outside of Europe or their own territory. Internal dynamics began to destabilize Syria starting with a severe famine that decimated the country, eroding support for the regime. Extremist Sunni Muslim groups, more moderate pro-democracy groups, and the excluded Kurdish populations in the country's north and east then challenged the government. These internal dynamics unique to Syria laid the groundwork for domestic conflict, but wrangling between regional and global actors outside Syria has helped transform the conflict into a uniquely violent civil war and the worst refugee crisis since World War II.

BOX 5.1 | **Continued**

Regionally, the erosion of support for the Iranian-backed Assad regime granted the Saudi government, who has been at odds with Iran for dominance in the Middle Eastern hierarchy, an opportunity to funnel support for Sunni militants. On the northern edge of Syria, the Turks have taken the opportunity to reassert their foreign policy engagement in the Middle East and exert pressure on proximate Kurdish populations. Indeed, the Turks have not only supported and harbored Syrian rebels but even purchased a suit for one of their commanders in preparation for a *New York Times* interview as well.[10] Meanwhile, the absence of a domestic hierarchy that could reach the northern portions of Iraq granted the opportunity for the extremist and apocalyptic development of the Islamic State of Iraq and the Levant (ISIL).

While the contested regional hierarchy in the Middle East exacerbates the conflict between internal groups in Syria, external pressures from outside major powers created further escalation. In 2015, as Assad's hold on Syria progressively eroded, Russia chose to enter the conflict directly in support of its ally. The United States offered support to anti-Assad militias or indirect support via Saudi Arabia. Russian forces attacked all opposing groups, whether Sunni, ISIL, or the American-backed Kurdish Peshmerga, keeping Assad's government afloat. Assad's forces, with Russian weapons and support, indiscriminately attacked areas of opposition, further deepening the humanitarian crisis with as many as 570,000 killed and almost 6 million refugees so far.[11] As of this writing, Assad appears to have the upper hand, with Kurdish opposition suppressed by the recent Turkish invasion of Kurdish territory near their border following the withdrawal of American forces. The Syrian case provides a clear example of how domestic political instability, driven by the erosion of the political capacity of a state internally, can then be exacerbated by the intervention of outside forces. Iran, Saudi Arabia, and Turkey have used Syria as a battleground through which to exert influence over the future of the Middle Eastern regional hierarchy. Meanwhile, the Russians have used Syria as a stop-gap to prevent further erosion of their influence in the region, demonstrating its dissatisfaction with the American system by protecting an ally that is clearly in opposition to the United States. External forces may not have initiated the conflict, but they certainly exacerbated the depth of its destructive force.

INTERNAL HIERARCHY AND INTRASTATE CONFLICT

Most intrastate conflict research focuses on internal causes. Although we focus primarily on geography and state capacity, other important variables are worth noting. In particular, poverty appears to be what we might call a "necessary condition" to observing civil war.[12] At or above US$5,000 GDP per capita, or the size of the economy per person, the chances of civil war in a country are below 1 percent and approach 0 percent as wealth continues to rise.[13] Among geographic spaces contested by major powers, as illustrated in chapter 6 on the Cold War, those comprised of poorer states experience the most internal disorder. Although both Western Europe and East Asia were within contested geographic spaces, the wealthy countries of Western Europe experienced little domestic conflict, while intrastate conflicts occurred throughout East Asia during the Cold War and often involved the intervention of one or both superpowers.

Political Capacity

Internally, an intrastate conflict is a challenge to the hierarchy of the existing state. In both civil wars over state control and attempts to secede from an existing state, the legitimacy and the authority of the state's government are challenged. All states face challenges to their defined role as the sole entity with a monopoly of coercive force over a territory, however small, including rogue actors and even interpersonal conflicts. But something as great as an organized war over control of its territory necessitates that the state lack sufficient hierarchical control within its borders in the form of state capacity to manage its internal affairs.[14] Compound this reality with the hostility of civil wars, in particular, where, in a competition over control of the state, stalemates are relatively rare as there can be only one victor. Thus, a rebel group would be hesitant to resort to violence unless the state itself is sufficiently weak as to grant the opposing side a chance of success. Something within the state itself must have changed, either in a reduction of political capacity of the state or in shifting population dynamics.[15] Indeed, one of the best indicators of who will win is the relative strength of the state, as strong states reduce a rebellion's chances at victory.[16] Within the Absolute Political Capacity Data, the capacity of states that experience an intrastate conflict is 33 percent lower than the average for all other states in the year leading up to the conflict.[17] Civil wars and secessionist conflicts are most likely when a state is so sufficiently weak in its political capacity that it can no longer exercise sufficient coercive force across its territory to prevent a movement from challenging its control.

Distance and Terrain

Geography, in combination with state capacity, plays, a crucial role in a civil war's onset and continuation. In most states, the nexus of power for the government typically resides in the capital. The farther from the capital, the easier it may be to challenge the existing government's legitimacy. Findings demonstrate the distance from the capital is strongly related to both the onset and the scope of civil conflict. As with Lemke's results on interstate conflict discussed in chapter 3, terrain plays an important role in civil wars as well. As you will recall, Lemke first sought to measure whether two states could *reach* one another and then determined their relative hierarchy as a condition for the onset of conflict in a region. Here we are most interested in those spaces where states *cannot* reach effectively throughout their territory, as civil conflicts are more likely and more extensive in their scope in remote areas where the state is less able to project power to take on an opposing military group.[18] Furthermore, terrain also matters in addition to distance, as dense jungle or mountains provide places where rebel actors can challenge the state's capabilities and operate relatively autonomously.

These challenging actors must have their own capabilities to challenge the state effectively. In Africa, these centers of power may reside around resources that the rebel group can extract to support its cause, such as diamonds or oil. The greater the relative capabilities of the rebel group, the closer it may be to the capital in challenging the state. Alternatively, intrastate conflicts may spread across borders, either as identity groups in neighboring states join a war or as refugee migrations and economic instability destabilize an adjacent state, causing neighbors of relatively lower political capacity to deteriorate into violence of their own. Inversely, states surrounded by stable states are less likely to experience conflicts, particularly stable democratic neighbors.[19]

In other words, "beyond the pale" of government control yet within its recognized territorial borders, rebels are better able to challenge the government, as well as one another. These actors with relative freedom of movement not only war with the government to create their own territorial space or overthrow the state but also engage in alliances and trade with one another as states might.[20] In very large states, such as the Democratic Republic of Congo (DRC), significant portions of territory may reside well beyond the government's control. Neighboring states, such as Uganda or Rwanda, may take matters into their own hands, crossing the border into the DRC to manage security threats from rebels as they are more proximate to the security threat than the DRC's forces based much further away in the capital of Kinshasa.

RESOLVING CIVIL WARS

The general rule for civil war resolution is either one side must be completely victorious over the other or the violent stalemate is so significant that both sides can no longer maintain the conflict. Because the actors often cannot compromise on who controls the state, options on the spectrum between stalemate and total capitulation are less likely. Conflicts that address political grievances or secession of territory may be easier to solve simply because a resolution that gives the rebels what they want does not necessarily threaten the existence of the state itself. This does not mean that these conflicts are less likely or severe, as a secessionist movement, such as the American Civil War,[21] can be extremely violent as well.

Just as the intervention of major powers can exacerbate the violence of intrastate conflict, so, too, can the intervention of a major power be an important contributing factor to the resolution of a conflict. Through intervention, either by the major power directly or by a group of major powers acting through an organization such as NATO or the United Nations, a major power may be able to (1) stop the fighting by inserting its own assets between the two sides to prevent them from doing harm to one another without also invoking the wrath of the major power and thus (2) get the two sides to sit down and talk with one another to reach some settlement. In this regard, major powers can act as conflict managers or referees, preventing further bloodshed using their own power projection and arbitrating the diplomatic discussion.

Biased Negotiators

All major powers are not equally effective in playing this managing role. First, a major power must possess sufficient capabilities to reach the conflictual space and possess the willingness to do so. Intrastate and extrastate conflicts between rebel groups and warlords in Central Africa's Great Lakes region are particularly challenging for any major power to reach, making an intervention to reduce conflict or support one side uniquely difficult. Second, they must have the willingness to intervene in a conflict and endure the potential costs of doing so. For example, the United States possessed the capability to intervene in the ongoing conflict in Somalia in the early 1990s. But after enduring the loss of eighteen of its soldiers, the United States quickly departed the conflict as it was unwilling to withstand further costs. The U.S. avoidance of African conflicts continued as it stayed out of future conflicts in Rwanda and Darfur despite tremendous violence. The willingness to engage is partially driven by the strategic interests the major power possesses in the conflict space as well as the potential for the conflict to create broader instability in the regional or international system, particularly for a dominant power that seeks to preserve the status quo.

However, if the major power can intervene in the conflict successfully, it helps to be viewed as unbiased.[22] This can create some tension with the need for the major power to possess a strategic interest in the space. If the major power's strategic interests align with one or the other side in the conflict, its ability to play referee to the two sides is unlikely to be successful. Take, for example, the prolonged conflict in Nicaragua during the Cold War. The two sides vying for control over the government were from different ideological views, one relatively pro-American in the government, and the subsequent Contra rebels, and the other, the communist Sandinistas. Neither the United States nor the Soviet Union could effectively play the role of unbiased referee, as ideological values that squarely aligned with each defined the conflict, and both superpowers provided material support to their respective sides.

This problem is one of perception rather than necessarily intent. If, hypothetically, the United States were to offer to moderate and assist in negotiations to resolve the conflict out of nothing but the purest motives, the Sandinistas still could not *trust* the United States would be reliable in doing so. Similarly, cultural cleavages can present clear roadblocks to trust in a third party by both sides to a conflict, as demonstrated in the ongoing difficulties of the United States in providing a path forward in the Israeli–Palestinian conflict. Indeed, for Nicaragua, ending the conflict with the Sandinistas required a peace plan from neighboring Central American governments that were viewed as unbiased but possessed a direct strategic interest in the resolution of the conflict given the political instability it created.

For this reason, the best global negotiators are often motivated but unengaged. Whether smaller states such as Costa Rica, perennial negotiators such as Switzerland or Norway, or unbiased major powers, these actors can be looked on as independent dispute negotiators working toward a reasonable resolution to the conflict. Thus, among the major powers, the most effective conflict negotiators tend to be those who are relatively satisfied and desire a resolution to the instability a conflict creates. China, France, and the United Kingdom, for example, have frequently used their assets to provide humanitarian aid and conflict mitigation under the auspices of UN guidance.

For example, China provides significant support for the UN mission in South Sudan, sending more security personnel than any non-neighboring state. In that distant geographic space, belligerents may view the Chinese as an unbiased actor with no historical or cultural ties to either side. Indeed, the Chinese are the most active among major powers in their personnel contributions to UN peacekeeping efforts, providing 2,497 persons to active missions as of this writing. France and Britain, likewise, provide 753 and 585, respectively. Compare those numbers to the United States (34) and Russia (74), both of whom are usually viewed as poor referees by civil war belligerents given their histories of intervention during the Cold War.[23] Indeed, although the United States is undoubtedly strategically interested in many conflicts throughout the globe, given its extensive reach it often finds itself on one side or other of a conflict, rendering it an ineffective future negotiator.

Hierarchy and the Provision of Domestic Order

Given their capabilities and interests, major powers often provide some of the greatest conflict mediation successes for civil wars. Not only are they able to engage, but they also possess the material ability to offer incentives to both sides. These incentives could be in the form of direct material aid payouts to one or both sides or an incentive more structural in nature, such as the promise of inclusion in international regimes. Either way, these incentives may overpower the political grievances of actors, making peace more attractive. Internal conflicts, like interstate conflicts, are complex with a myriad of potential causes. The hierarchy of the state over territory is an essential contributing factor to conflict's onset, while the capabilities and willingness of regional and major powers to intervene and resolve conflicts have clear consequences for their duration and outcome.

DISCUSSION QUESTIONS

1. In chapter 3, we talked extensively about balance of power. How could we apply balance of power logic to intrastate conflicts?
2. If neorealism is correct and all states are only concerned about power, can any state be trusted as an unbiased third party? Do states ever intervene or mediate conflicts for good reasons, such as ending genocide or the displacement of a people?
3. If a civil war is an observable challenge to a state's control over territory, are there types of political institutions or governments a state might implement that share political control between multiple groups to prevent conflict?
4. Under what conditions would a dominant state avoid intervening in a domestic conflict?

KEY TERMS

civil wars

diffusion

extrastate

intrastate

necessary condition

proxy war

secessionist conflict

FURTHER READING

Cederman, Lars Erik, Kristian Skrede Gleditsch, and Halvard Buhaug. 2013. *Inequality, Grievances, and Civil War.* Cambridge: Cambridge University Press.

Collier, Paul, Anke Hoeffler, and Mans Soderbom. 2004. "On the Duration of Civil War." *Journal of Peace Research* 41, no. 3:253–73.

Lemke, Douglas, and Jeff Carter. 2016. "Birth Legacies, State Making, and War." *The Journal of Politics* 78, no. 2:497–511.

6

The Cold War

THE CREATION OF AN AMERICAN ORDER

The Cold War is a period of regular tensions between the United States and the Soviet Union from 1945 to 1991. It is a "cold" war as the two primary belligerents, the United States and the Soviet Union, never engaged in a direct war with one another. However, despite the absence of global major power war, the period is filled with proxy conflicts involving both superpowers, alliance blocs pitted against one another, and numerous rivalries. The hierarchical arrangement between the two superpowers defined this more than four-decades-long period across all levels of analysis and thus provides an excellent example of how hierarchy and its absence influence both the conflict behaviors of the most powerful states and those throughout the international system. As a result, conflicts, rivalries, and domestic disputes related to this superpower relationship proliferated, with both sides forming a web of cooperative and conflictual interactions to bolster their relative position.

Immediately following the end of World War II, the United States began to impose a new form of order and normative values on the international system. This was not the first instance of the United States seeking to impose a new order on the system. It attempted to remake international politics with the League of Nations following World War I. However, at the negotiations that ended the war, the United States was unable to compel its allies to agree to strict and enforceable restrictions on issues such as peace and self-determination without first inflicting heavy punishments on Germany and Austria-Hungary. Those same punitive measures laid the foundation for German grievances that festered and eventually were exploited by Hitler's populist rise to power. Second, the U.S. government was unwilling to follow through on the imposition of order that Woodrow Wilson had intended. Despite the negotiations at Versailles and the agreement of the other major powers to join, the U.S. Senate refused to ratify the treaty, leaving the Americans out of the very institution its president had designed.

The United States approached the conclusion of World War II very differently. Although the United States repeated an attempt to impose a new set of rules, norms, and institutions on the international system, unlike in the Treaty of Versailles, it incentivized participation in that system and avoided unenforceable institutional provisions. Independent of their willingness to participate in American designs for a new international system, every major power in the international system had suffered severe losses of both population and infrastructure. Although the United States also experienced significant casualties, unlike its peers, it suffered no conflict on its territory outside the attack on Pearl Harbor. As an illustrative comparison, the United States suffered fewer than a half-million deaths from the war, while the Soviet Union, which emerged from the war as the second-most powerful state, suffered around twenty-five million deaths. In the years following the war's conclusion, the United States crafted a series of security and economic agreements designed both to create order and provide stability for the recovery of Europe. The critical pieces of this recovery were the North Atlantic Treaty Organization (NATO), the Marshall Plan, and the dollar reserve system of Bretton Woods. Part II on cooperation in the international system discusses the latter two in greater detail. Each of these institutions was designed to provide support for a recovering Europe while crafting a system the United States could manage.

Left out of all three, however, was the Soviet Union. The Soviets had a very different vision than the liberal capitalist designs of the United States and crafted a buffer of occupied territory of politically controlled puppet states around itself. Adherence to liberal capitalist goals, furthermore, was a pivotal requirement for participation in the Marshall Plan. The Soviet Union, alternatively, created the "Molotov" Plan, named for the Soviet foreign affairs minister at the time, which served primarily as a parallel to the Marshall Plan to promote the totalitarian communism of the Soviets. Within this sphere of immediate geographic influence, the Soviet Union crafted a space where it could impose its own rules, norms, and institutions. It frequently employed direct coercion rather than economic incentives like the United States. Thus, the battle lines of the Cold War were drawn, geographically, ideologically, and normatively, with the relative capabilities and resulting hierarchy between the two superpowers distributed across geography determining its course.

A BALANCE OF POWER OR A FAILED CHALLENGE?

There are two great empirical debates between balance of power and hierarchy camps in international politics. The first is the nature of unipolarity as either stable or uniquely violent, which both sides agree characterizes the distribution of power in the international system since 1991 and perhaps during the mid-nineteenth century. The second debate is on the nature of the Cold War as either a bipolar or unipolar distribution of power and therefore what conclusions we might reach about the behavior of states under the two types of power distribution. Neorealists use the Cold War as a prime example of bipolarity creating relative stability due to the absence of the global warfare that characterized the first half of the twentieth century.

On the contrary, hierarchical theorists operating in the power transition and hegemonic stability theories view portions of the Cold War as also unipolar, led by the United States, with a distant challenger in the Soviet Union. Hierarchical theorists concur with their balance of power counterparts that the Soviet Union was undoubtedly dissatisfied with the international system. However, the difference in opinion lies in whether their coequal power deterred both the Soviet Union and the United States or, instead, if the United States was globally dominant, with the Soviet Union possessing more limited control on its immediate geographic periphery and employing subversive tactics in spaces dominated by the United States. Hierarchical approaches would point out that while there was no direct war between the two superpowers, the Cold War was not always peaceful, as illustrated in figure 3.1. Analyzing patterns of behavior based on measures of power, as well as the incorporation of geography into our analysis, can provide us with answers to these competing outlooks. The competing theories provide us with two variables to discuss: first, the primary independent variable, or cause, that is the relative capabilities between the two powers, and, second, the dependent variable, or outcome that we are seeking to explain, the degree of peacefulness in the international system.

Comparing Power

Table 6.1 compares measures of power between the United States and the Soviet Union, and their constituent allies, in 1976 at the peak of Soviet capabilities in the Correlates of War Composite Indicator of National Capability (CINC) data.[1] At this point, the Soviet Union was at its peak in power relative to the United States, and many at the time believed the United States had fallen behind in the Cold War competition. Consistently, the CINC data show the United States as

Table 6.1   Capabilities Comparison of NATO and the Warsaw Pact

Country	CINC Score	GDP (billions)	Military Expenditures (millions)
United States	.142	5,899.81	91,013
Soviet Union	.176	4,143.01	138,000
NATO Members			
Belgium	.006	193.19	2,109.6
Canada	.012	545.57	3,640
Denmark	.001	106.31	939.6
France	.024	1,107.61	13,369.1
Iceland	.00001	4.72	0
Italy	.02	892.53	4,335.1
Luxembourg	.001	8.39	25.5
Netherlands	.007	306.09	2,898
Norway	.002	84.65	977.4
Portugal	.002	85.71	623.5
United Kingdom	.027	977.87	11,076.6
Greece	.003	105.86	1,559.9
Turkey	.01	312.08	2,534.8
West Germany	.033	1,226.04	15,278.2
Warsaw Pact			
Bulgaria	.004	94.71	2,100.3
Czechoslovakia	.009	215.49	4,017.1
East Germany	.009	334.38	4,881.1
Hungary	.004	84.98	1,657.4
Poland	.016	253.61	6,505.5
Romania	.009	115.77	3,180.9

(Continued)

Table 6.1   Continued

Country	CINC Score	GDP (billions)	Military Expenditures (millions)
Combined NATO	.466	11,856.43	150,380.3
Combined Warsaw Pact	.227	5241.95	160,342.3

Source: J. David Singer, Stuart Bremer, and John Stuckey. 1972. "Capability Distribution, Uncertainty, and Major Power War, 1820–1965," in Peace, War, and Numbers, ed. Bruce Russet (Beverly Hills, CA: Sage, 1972), 19–48; Jutta Bolt, Robert Inklaar, Herman de Jong, and Jan Luiten van Zanden, "Rebasing 'Maddison': New Income Comparisons and the Shape of Long-Run Economic Development," Maddison Project Working Paper 10, 2018, Groningen: University of Groningen.

Note: Gross domestic product (GDP) data from the Maddison data set lump Germany together as a single entity. Using the ratio of East German to West German capabilities from the Composite Indicator of National Capabilities (CINC) data, GDP is divided between East and West as an approximation. For military spending, we use the values listed in the CINC data. NATO = North Atlantic Treaty Organization.

19 percent behind the Soviet Union in national capabilities. However, available gross domestic product (GDP) data tell a very different story. In this comparison, the roles are reversed and more dramatically so. The Soviet Union is almost 30 percent behind the United States, which is a greater gap than the entire economy of France at the time and a degree of separation that very few would describe as two states of relatively equal power. By this measure of power, even in this best-case scenario for the Soviet Union of 1976 where they are at the peak of their capabilities, the world appears unipolar with the United States dramatically ahead. If we then aggregate the combined capabilities of their alliance blocs, the gap between the two sides only grows more severe, sharply calling into question balance of power logic. From a balance of power perspective, we should see states allying with the weaker side against the stronger. But if the Soviet Union was so weak, why did so few states ally with it, and almost none voluntarily, leaving nothing more than a collection of directly controlled satellite states? Indeed, the only significant instances of the Warsaw Pact engaging in conflict involved putting down uprisings against Soviet puppet regimes within their members: Hungary and Czechoslovakia. Rather than a balancing organization against the United States, the Warsaw Pact served as little more than an institutional mechanism for the Soviet Union to manage its European geographic periphery. Perhaps, spaces of both balanced projected capabilities and spaces of dominance existed simultaneously. In other words, whether

one state is dominant or two states are at a balance in power varies depending where we are in the world. Comparing these spaces may provide insights into both the conduct of the Cold War and the applicability of competing theories.

Compare the GDP figures to the CINC data at the peak of supposed Soviet capabilities.[2] You will immediately notice that the CINC score provides a much higher estimate of Soviet capabilities than the purely economic measure. Unlike GDP, which is an estimate of economic size based on types of activity,[3] the CINC scores are a measure of some indirect economic indicators, such as population, energy consumption, and iron and steel production, and some that are policy driven by the state, such as the size of military personnel and expenditures. Only in military expenditures did the Soviet Union seem to significantly outpace the United States,[4] and that data from the Cold War have been called into question. But, regardless of willingness, military spending is unsustainable without a strong economy to fund it. In GDP, economic productivity, and population, the United States was unmatched throughout the supposedly bipolar "order." Which of these indicators should we believe?

Unfortunately, reporting on military spending figures may also be politically motivated. The military expenditure and personnel data used by the Correlates of War is from the Arms Control and Disarmament Agency, a bureaucratic wing within the U.S. government. Developed as a price index by the Central Intelligence Agency (CIA), those same estimates were often used to justify increases in military spending to Congress. Of course, the incentive for the creators of the data to inflate those numbers is significant. The index the CIA used to calculate Soviet capabilities dramatically "overstates" Soviet military spending as well as the spending of its satellite states.[5] Therefore, the data that show near parity by the Soviet Union during portions of the Cold War is perhaps generous, highlighting the importance of not only using measures that most closely align with the concept of study but also ensuring that the data used are accurately and carefully coded. Unfortunately, reliable estimates of Soviet government expenditures, particularly for the military, remain difficult. Even with these likely inflated numbers, the combined military spending of the Warsaw Pact is, at best, at parity with NATO.

Evaluating Conflict

Consistent with the empirical story that the Soviet Union was a distant second to the dominant United States are the conflict behaviors of the two states throughout the almost-five-decade period. In each instance of a notable conflict between the two powers, the United States managed to force the capitulation of its distant challenger. Projecting power across geography provides important insights into where conflicts were more heated and where one side consistently reigned supreme. During the Cuban missile crisis, the Soviet Union attempted to challenge American hegemony within its hemisphere of clear dominance. Although the action was intended as a challenge to American dominance, the Soviet Union did not directly initiate conflict with the Americans. The United States, however, rapidly escalated the conflict to the point of potential violence, committing what is considered to be an act of war with the naval blockade. The escalatory situation was so tense that a nuclear exchange very nearly occurred. During the crisis, a Russian submarine crew was one vote short among its commanding officers of launching its nuclear weapons.[6]—a terrifying example of the dangers of potential nuclear war caused by mismanagement and error.

In another instance immediately following the end of World War II, the Soviet Union attempted to challenge the United States by closing access to West Berlin to remove the island of Western control from within Soviet-occupied territory. Like the Cuban Missile Crisis later, it was not a direct initiation of conflict against the United States but instead a targeting of a small occupied territory surrounded by Soviet control. The United States airlifted supplies in and out of West Berlin for nearly a year until the Soviet Union capitulated.

Conflicts such as these characterize the Cold War, where the Soviet Union attempts to poke at the margins of American hegemony and is quickly slapped down either by the United States or its allies. The Soviets provided military support to the Arab states, which were defeated swiftly by Israel in each occurrence. They supported internal conflicts, such as the Sandinistas in Nicaragua. In two cases, Soviet support may seem successful against the United States at least in terms of the relative outcome: the stalemate that ended the Korean War and the American loss in Vietnam. In both cases, however, Chinese support was far in excess of Soviet intervention, making it difficult to grant the Soviets credit. As the Soviet Union's capacity began to erode in the late 1980s, attempts to retain control over their geographic margins rapidly deteriorated.

Erosion of Soviet-Controlled Geographic Space

American support, albeit not direct intervention, helped to stretch thin Soviet capabilities in its last decade. First, the Soviet invasion of Afghanistan in response to the American-backed Mujahedeen rebels lasted almost a decade and ended in disastrous failure. Second, the margins of Soviet control in Europe slowly receded, with internal political movements pushing back Soviet control as the United States led a strong, nonviolent push to promote American liberal normative values. One of those values, freedom of movement, is what eventually led to the end of the Cold War. The expansion of liberal order, or, put another way, the attractiveness of the American status quo from blue jeans to McDonald's and all the other commercial artifacts of the American long cycle, became too much for the Soviet Union to combat. As a comparison that illustrates the erosion of Soviet strength, in 1956, in response to a liberal revolt in Hungary, the Soviet Union sent the tanks into Budapest and forced an immediate end to liberal reforms, but by 1989, it was unable to stem the tide of East Germans crossing into West Berlin, as borders between Hungary and Czechoslovakia with Austria had sporadically eroded. Rather than roll the tanks into Berlin and reinforce the crossing positions, as it had done in the past, the Soviet Union watched as the wall fell. Perhaps serving as the death knell of communism, on the final night of 1989, *Baywatch* star David Hasselhoff sang "Looking for Freedom" at the Brandenburg Gate wearing a leather jacket adorned with blinking lights.

BOX 6.1	Major Power, Global Power, Superpower

You may notice in reading international politics literature, as well as in the news or movies, that different names for the most powerful states—major, global, and superpowers—tend to be used almost interchangeably. However, these "clubs" have some significant differences. Major powers are uniquely powerful states, are much more active than other countries, and receive the status, or respect and legitimacy, as strong, active states from members of the international system.[7] Surpassing each of these thresholds creates a small club of uniquely powerful states that have large portfolios of responsibilities, such as possessing veto power in the United Nations or being expected to intervene in an ongoing conflict.

However, surpassing each of these thresholds does not inherently mean all major powers are also global powers. Describing a state as a global power is a statement about not only the actor's

(Continued)

BOX 6.1	Continued

capabilities, foreign policy engagement, and status but also its geographic reach. Can a state project power well beyond its borders to the opposite side of the globe? Is it global in its use of capabilities? Compare, for example, the United States and China today. Both are very powerful by most measurements of capabilities; however, the United States can effectively project power to most geographic spaces with the combined use of aircraft carriers, air and space capabilities, and logistical technology that facilitates troop movements. China, however, is more limited in its power projection, engaging in naval activity near its territory, and is far less able to project power, often using relatively dated Soviet equipment purchased from Russia. Thus, although both the United States and China may be labeled major powers, the United States is a global power.

Finally, superpowers are those that not only have capabilities well beyond other states but also possess the technological and logistical infrastructure to globally defend their interests as well as challenge any other state.[8] To reach this highest level of the powerful state club requires more than capabilities or desire, but the political capacity to translate resources into logistical material assets capable of effectively traversing global geographic space. In the present, these might include not only traditional military assets, such as submarines and aircraft carriers, but also include information technologies, including satellites and cyber capabilities, to both collect information and engage in the sabotage of enemy assets if necessary. Currently, there are six major powers: the United States, Russia, Japan, China, France, and the United Kingdom. For global powers, there is the United States and perhaps France, Russia, and the United Kingdom. The United States is the only state, however, that can be considered a superpower today.

RIVALRIES AND ALLIANCES SHAPED BY THE COLD WAR

When we think of rivalries in the Cold War, we think first of the relationship between the Soviet Union and the United States themselves. Although the two sides never engaged in a violent war, their repeated conflicts characterized the period, often dragging lesser states into their contests. Many other rivalries that proliferated during the period were driven, then, by the support of the two sides. As shown in figure 4.1, those rivalries terminated in coincidence with the end of the Cold War, as American dominance went unchallenged and Soviet material support for aligned states quickly diminished. For example, the long-standing rivalry between China and the Soviet Union ends, as disputed border areas became part of the new state of Kazakhstan. Similarly, many of the rivalries during the Cold War, and the corresponding conflicts that erupted, were at least escalated by the interference of the two superpowers. The rivalry ends between Thailand, often backed by the United States, and Vietnam, which was supported by the Soviet Union.[9]

Rivalries shaped by the Cold War also ebbed and flowed with the broader politics of the international system. The Arab–Israeli conflicts, specifically the Egypt–Israeli rivalry, began following the creation of Israel by a UN resolution and the support of the United States. As those conflictual interactions unfolded, the United States supported and funded Israel against the aggressor Arab states. Egypt took a balanced strategy, playing the Soviet Union and the United States off one another. They initially accepted support from the Soviet Union and then warmed to the United States after American refusal to support Britain's and France's attempt to retake the Suez Canal. Egyptian leader Abdul Nasser would oscillate back and forth between the powers in a policy that would be continued by Sadat. However, because economic conditions continued to deteriorate, Sadat used an American desire to see the end of that rivalry as a bargaining chip to receive economic aid. At great cost, as an extremist assassinated Sadat only a few years later, the rivalry ended with the Camp David Accords in 1978. Even in this heated, thirty-year rivalry, an engaged major power was able to secure a termination of the hostile relationship. Although Egypt could not trust that the United States was impartial, it could trust, given the global hierarchical competition, that the United States had a strategic interest in not permitting continued or expanded Soviet influence in the Middle East. Thus, both sides were able to negotiate a termination to the rivalry successfully.

INTERNAL CONFLICTS AND CIVIL WARS

Although there was an absence of major power war during the Cold War, secessionist, postcolonial, and civil wars were consistently present and at far higher rates than today (see figure 5.1). Both sides throughout the period sought to destabilize those allied with the opposing side, providing support for internal antigovernment forces. The United States, for example, helped overthrow the prime minister of Iran and installed the Shah, intervened in 62 foreign elections,[10] and even funded an invasion of Cuba in 1961.

Many prominent neorealists during the time held to George Kennan's domino theory.[11] Kennan suggested that communist movements throughout the globe, from Honduras to China, were in league. If the United States permitted a state to "fall" to communism, others would rapidly follow like dominoes. Interestingly, as he is often described as a neorealist, this theory explains behavior as caused by the spread of a competing ideology, more closely resembling constructivism. Although Kennan intended to advocate for a strategy of "balancing" against this threat, the emphasis on ideology rather than power suggests his perspective is rooted in a more constructivist concern with spreading norms. It could be construed as a hegemonic stability concern with a rising competing vision of international order, but the absence of meaningful capabilities behind this alternative, communist vision of the international system renders the threat less serious.

However, due to this pervasive fear of spreading communism, and the belief that the Soviet Union was surpassing the United States and sponsoring the advancement of these many internal domestic groups, the United States engaged in several interventionist conflicts. This apophenia, or seeing patterns where none exist, drove the United States into interfering in many other states' domestic politics, often with self-defeating outcomes. Fear of rising communist groups even led to the stifling of liberal democracy, such as support for coups in Chile and Iran, a normative value that the United States had actively promoted following the end of the Cold War.

Afghanistan

The Soviet invasion of Afghanistan previously mentioned provides an excellent example of how the internal politics of a space at the margins of the geographic reach of both superpowers can become a stage for confrontation. This confrontation then exacerbates the conflict's length and severity, increasing the costs to the internal population as well as one or both powers engaged in the conflict. Much as it had done in its European periphery, the Soviet Union crafted in Afghanistan a puppet state that shared its normative goals and whose foreign and domestic policies aligned mainly with those of Moscow. However, that government began to erode in the late 1970s as Wahhabist Islamic fighters from throughout the Middle East flooded to Afghanistan in an attempt to overthrow the communist state. Initially, this civil war was restricted to Afghanistan, as Islamist fighters and tribal leaders seeking to increase their political power fought violently against the state. However, seeing the power of the communist Afghan state begin to erode, the Soviet Union intervened directly. Similarly, observing an opportunity to undermine Soviet control on its immediate periphery, the United States began funding and providing material supports to insurgents. By 1989, the Soviets left, the government of Afghanistan was overthrown, and the Taliban and Mujahedeen, funded by the United States, were victorious.

This case from late in the Cold War illustrates the intersection of different levels of conflict discussed in this text alongside the impact of hierarchy and the importance of geographic space. Whether we are talking about the Soviet invasion, the current American engagement, or the Great Game struggle between Britain and Russia in the nineteenth century, Afghanistan has almost always resided in a peripheral geographic space where no one state is dominant. This absence of a clear hierarchy is then related to the frequent episodes of conflict which it has experienced. These conflicts involve internal political differences, such as those between the Taliban and the communist Afghan state. Seeing an opportunity to affect internal politics to its advantage, a major power then seeks to intervene in this geographic periphery but to mixed effect and increasing the severity of the conflict. The opposing power, seeing its opponent trying to exert influence in this contested geographic space, then reciprocates either directly or through proxies, whether the United States with the Mujahadeen or nineteenth-century Imperial Russia through Uzbek tribes. The conflict then increases further. In some cases, what was a civil war becomes an international war, as the civil war becomes a stage for major power competition in a contested geographic space absent a clear hierarchy.

Cold War Shatterbelts

In thinking about how these conflicts cluster geographically, imagine the intersection of the United States and the Soviet Union's power projection during the Cold War similar to how we have illustrated the current international system in figure 1.1. The spaces where the power projection of the two superpowers intersects forms a ring around the Soviet Union, beginning in Eastern Europe, intersecting the Middle East and Southeast Asia, and heading north through China and the Koreas.[12] Figure 6.1 illustrates this ring of parity and likewise shows

Figure 6.1   Interventions by the United States and the Soviet Union during the Cold War

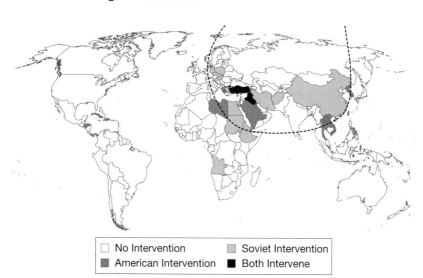

No Intervention   Soviet Intervention
American Intervention   Both Intervene

Source: Map made using historicalmapchart.net, governed by an attribution-sharealike 4.0 international license (CC BY-SA 4.0). Parity line added. Intervention data from Patricia L. Sullivan and Michael T. Koch, "Military Intervention by Powerful States (MIPS) Codebook, Version 2.0" (2008), last accessed June 23, 2019, http://plsullivan.web.unc.edu/files/2011/09/MIPS_codebook_Sullivan.pdf.

the spaces where the United States and the Soviet Union intervened during the Cold War from the Military Intervention by Powerful States data.[13] Evident are the usual suspects of Vietnam, Korea, and Afghanistan. More generally, the process of intervention follows a particular geographic pattern, mirroring the "shatterbelt" concept. A ring of intervention surrounding the Soviet Union geographically, as both the United States and the Soviet Union attempt to restructure both domestic and regional contexts to suit their security and economic interests. The dashed line illustrates approximately where the United States and the Soviet Union were at parity in the middle of the Cold War. Countries subject to intervention, not surprisingly, cluster around this peripheral line where the hierarchy between the two states, and therefore the imposed order, becomes muddled. Although there were many other domestic conflicts throughout the world during the Cold War, the intervention of the two superpowers prolonged these and made them more violent, including more than

5 million casualties across Korea, Vietnam, and Afghanistan. The legacy of instability created by these conflicts has long-lasting effects, as the United States continues to deal with instability in the Korean Peninsula, the Middle East, and Central Asia today.

SIMULATION: BALANCE OF POWER VERSUS THE TRAJECTORY OF CAPABILITIES

1. Separate into six groups, numbered 1 through 6. Each group represents a state that has the same amount of power. How do you balance one another? Go through the room and sequentially choose "side A" or "side B." Does the outcome reflect balance of power theory's expectations?

2. Now, reorganize the groups where the total number is five, but each group still has the same amount of power. Have each group once again choose either side A or side B, one at a time. What happens to the balance when the last group chooses a side? With equal power, both this and the previous round demonstrate multipolarity. Note how any one group, particularly when we have an odd number, can have a dramatic impact on the outcome.

3. Let's now change the power of each of your groups. Group 1 has ten units of power. Group 2 has nine units of power. This reflects bipolarity. Groups 3, 4, and 5 have one unit of power. Have groups 3 through 5 now choose to side with either group 1 or group 2. Can the last group to choose have the same impact they did in round 2? What would happen if we gave group 1 eighteen units of power and all other groups receive one unit each? Does it matter what decisions on any issue groups 2 through 5 make? Why or why not?

4. Now let us incorporate multiple turns into our game, reflecting the effect of time, growth, and the decline of a dominant power:

   a. Group 1 has eighteen units of power, and groups 2 through 5 start with two units. At the beginning of each turn, group 1 may choose to punish any or all of groups 2 through 5 by taking 1 unit of their power away. It may give that one unit of power to any other group it chooses. This could represent a dominant state attacking a smaller state or another type of punitive behavior such as an embargo.

   b. Now repeat the side-taking exercise from rounds 1 through 3 earlier. As with round 3, on turn 1, the behavior of groups 2 through 5 will not make a difference.

c. The turn is now complete. At the end of turn, group 1 loses one unit of power. Have someone flip a coin for each of the remaining groups. If it falls on "heads," that group receives +1 power. This represents that the source of power is internal to states and not dependent on the international system.

d. Now repeat the process. Because states usually recover from wars, after five turns, reimburse all the power points that group 1 took from groups 2 through 5 in any of the preceding turns.

e. As you continue this process, keep choosing sides at the end of every turn. How does the decision of group 1 to take power away from some but favor others affect the sides that members of groups 2 through 5 choose to join? How does the fact that you know we are going to keep taking turns affect your expectations about what decisions other groups will make?

f. No matter who group 1 favors, eventually it will be surpassed as it loses a unit of power each turn. When a group punished by group 1 has equal units of power, what do you think they might do to turn the international system governed by group 1 in its favor?

g. Throughout the exercise, we have been using hypothetical units of power. What if we increased the stakes? What if the winner of the game received money or points on a test? As the stakes go up, how would that alter your choices?

h. Finally, were there things that affected your choice of who to side with outside the rules of the game, such as having friends in another group? What might that represent in international politics?

DISCUSSION QUESTIONS

1. It is often repeated that no one expected the Soviet Union's collapse. What variables went ignored in the 1980s that could have provided American policymakers insights into the Soviet's eventual demise?

2. In the ring of parity that surrounded the Soviet Union during the Cold War, conflict is not equally violent in all spaces. What other variables might contribute to the recurring conflict in the Middle East or Southeast Asia that were not present in Europe?

3. The United States was more successful in creating order after World War II than World War I. Separate from capabilities, what if the United States withdrew from the world as it did in the 1920s? Alternatively, what if it overexpands like the Soviet Union in the 1980s?

KEY TERMS

alliance bloc

Great Game

Treaty of Versailles

FUTURE READING

Kennan, George F. [Mr. X]. 1947. "The Sources of Soviet Conduct." *Foreign Affairs* 25, no. 4 (July): 566–82.

Kugler, Jacek, and William Domke. 1986. "Comparing the Strength of Nations." *Comparative Political Studies* 19, no. 1:39–69.

Volgy, Thomas J. 1974. "Reducing Conflict in International Politics: The Impact of Structural Variables." *International Studies Quarterly* 18, no. 2:179–210.

PART II

Cooperation

HOW MIGHT STATES ACHIEVE THEIR GOALS outside violence? What policies might they enact and enforce? What role does the most powerful state play in achieving these goals, or does power not matter to such questions? Are development, free trade, and globalization not inevitable phenomena but merely the choice of the United States?

Stability, peace, and economic prosperity are all things most individuals seek, and as such so to do states. To achieve these ends, they create policies that form the basis of international institutions like the World Bank, the International Monetary Fund, the World Trade Organization, the North Atlantic Treaty Organization, the European Union, the North American Free Trade Association, and the United Nations. Together these institutions perform a wide array of functions, ranging from regulating conflict to promoting trade. But can these organizations exist without the support of the United States? Would they be as effective if they could?

This part of the text explores how the cooperative behaviors of states may also be rooted in hierarchy and what alternative perspectives may claim is their cause. Unlike our comparisons of power transition with balance of power, the hypotheses discussed in the next four chapters are not necessarily contradictions between theories, such as hegemonic stability and neoliberal institutionalism. Both may agree that institutions affect the behaviors of states, but their disagreement will lie in why these institutions exist and matter.

Analysis of cooperative behavior includes some of the most extensive data, with economic figures on growth, demography, development, and infrastructure. The challenge for the student seeking to engage international relations empirically will be parsing out what variables cause the outcomes you are trying to explain and which ones are spurious or causally unrelated.

7

Organizational Formation and Evolution

★ ★ ★

FORMAL AND INFORMAL NETWORKS

International organizations and agreements are relevant to almost all actions taken not only by countries but also by you, the individual reading this text. Everything from how or where nuclear technology can be used to the usability of a debit card is authorized and regulated by the accumulation of decades of agreements between states. The scale is so vast that it is difficult to think of a single component of modern society that does not have some form of global legality attached. Diplomacy is built not from the idea of fixing or finishing a single problem but that there exists a myriad of interconnected individual issues that continuously require management.

Two concepts are behind this process. The first is formal networks. These are the legislative, legal, and easily observable relationships among countries as well as, importantly, the process of how organizations make decisions. Organizational framework and management, hiring personnel, the location of the headquarters, and even the scale of their budget are all good examples. The second, informal networks, is as important even if these networks can be more complicated in measurement. These are the styles of international engagement, the expectations of law and arbitration, and the complexity of how trade can be arranged and in what area.

Trade relationships are one of the most common examples of international organizations (IOs) and may be laid out in broad agreements, such as the North American Free Trade Agreement

(NAFTA) or the Trans-Pacific Partnership, but they are continually adapted, tweaked, and negotiated. Similarly, nuclear technology will continuously be negotiated and regulated, given both its necessity to modern life and the potential for mass destruction. From water to disease, birds to whales, oil to wind, and the creation of new pharmaceuticals, a complex set of regulations are managed by specialized international organizations. The need to work beyond the borders of states is as constant as the need to work between and within them.

Defining Institutional Effectiveness

Within this discussion of empirics, there are two essential points. First, law is only relevant so long as it has an effect. This can be shaming of an actor who violates the law to the rarer occurrence of direct coercive punishment. Second, organizations need to have accomplishments and not merely be a series of press conferences or debates. The Warsaw Pact, for example, was not the equivalent of the North Atlantic Treaty Organization (NATO), and the African Union is not the European Union. Differentiating those that are merely forums for political posturing from those that facilitate organization among countries underlies attempts at measuring institutional strength.[1] Effective organizations can unlock vast levels of cooperation, as the successful international organizations rarely stay within their traditional boundaries but expand to other areas of potential cooperation between states. However, the very existence of them is not itself enough to be a cause of state behavior.

The practical importance of an institution is often driven by the hierarchy of the international system, as major powers are pivotal in their establishment and ability to succeed while their absence or antipathy can lead to stunning failure. As the states with the highest capabilities, they likewise hold the key to ultimate effectiveness. Law without enforcement is not effective, nor is an organization without power supporting its actions. Coercion, production, and costs are components of organizations and their effectiveness, and in their foundational moments will require major power support.

The list of organizations is long and well beyond the ability of this book to provide in detail. Table 7.1 is only a small list but illustrates the wide range of institutional functions: from human rights in a post–World War I era, such as the Red Cross, to controls over nuclear technology, such as the International Atomic Energy Agency (IAEA); from the results of Bretton Woods in the World Bank and the

Table 7.1   Select International Organizations

Name	Total Members	Start Date
African Union (AU)	55	2001
Agency for the Prohibition of Nuclear Weapons in Latin America and the Caribbean (OPANAL)	33	1967
Arctic Council	8	1996
Association of Southeast Asian Nations (ASEAN)	10	1967
Bank for International Settlements (BIS)	60	1930
BRICS	5	2011
British Commonwealth	55	1931
Commonwealth of Independent States (CIS)	12	1991
Council of Europe (CE)	47	1949
International Atomic Energy Agency (IAEA)	155	1957
International Bank for Reconstruction and Development (IBRD or World Bank)	189	1947
International Criminal Court (ICCT)	123	2002
International Criminal Police Organization (Interpol)	191	1923
International Federation of Red Cross and Red Crescent Societies (IFRCS)	190	1919
International Monetary Fund (IMF)	194	1945
International Olympic Committee (IOC)	202	1894
International Organization for Standardization (ISO)	121	1947
International Telecommunication Satellite Organization (ITSO)	149	1964
North Atlantic Treaty Organization (NATO)	29	1949
Organisation for Economic Cooperation and Development (OECD)	36	1961
Organization for the Prohibition of Chemical Weapons (OPCW)	192	1997
United Nations (UN)	193	1945
Warsaw Pact (WP)	14	1955
World Trade Organization (WTO)	164	1995

Source: The World Factbook 2019 (Washington, DC: Central Intelligence Agency), 2019, last accessed August 1, 2019, www.cia.gov/library/publications/the-world-factbook/.

International Monetary Fund (IMF) to defunct organizations such as the Warsaw Pact; and everything from crime to financial exchanges via central banks.

Nothing in the development of global policy is ever truly complete, and as the decades move, the complexity deepens. How this complexity limits or enhances the policy effectiveness of global and regional hegemons is of importance. Furthermore, are institutions important as actors or only as the visual examples of hegemonic power?

Role of Hegemony

Consistent with the logic of hegemonic stability theory, Ikenberry describes the dominant power as providing the international system with "system services," or types of public goods that keep the system as a whole stable and of which all states, satisfied or not, reap the benefits.[2] These institutions, by nature and treaty, rarely have enforcement powers of their own. Coercion requires capabilities, and at present, those capabilities remain the domain of states, with the dominant power being the most important. Keohane, in *After Hegemony*, suggested that the point of IOs is to address the problem of coordinating cooperative behaviors by states, known as collective action, by reducing the domestic influences of trade policy through binding international agreements.[3] States, including the hegemon, regularly have domestic stakeholders' pressuring political actors to reduce policies such as free trade. These barriers created through internal political dynamics, therefore, may undermine international cooperation and the ability of a hegemon to provide stability.[4] Pressure groups can be any industrial collective created not only to lobby the government but also through public displays of status, shaming, and diplomatic discourse.

What, then, does the dominant power gain from the provision of these costly "system services"? The most common argument is not the dramatic idea of total control over all lesser states but the more lasting goal of creating "rules of the game" or expectations. Through this rule making, dominant powers create a system based upon how they expect the world to operate. Expectations of states codified in organizations and agreements, both in their domestic and foreign conduct, are a vital foundation of the system's influence on state behavior, and, most important, created by the hegemon. As Susan Strange elaborated in the Cold War's final moments, the dominant power provides the security and economic backbone of the international order and thus creates the framework that "decides how things shall be done."[5] The benefits of providing this costly order are the ability to "to shape and determine the structure of the global political economy within which other states, their political institutions, their economic enterprises and (not least) their scientists and other professional people have to operate."[6]

Consider that after the fall of the Soviet Union, unlike after World War II, no parallel set of alternative institutions replaced those already in existence, nor is there any concerted attempt to develop them. We have the World Trade Organization (WTO) with no alternatives, the United Nations as well, and even NATO. Economic, diplomatic, and military, the three most essential components of international relations, are all governed through organizations composed of mostly similar democratic states with very few significant disagreements. As further evidence of the American foundation to all these organizations, the United Nations' headquarters are in New York, with the WTO, the World Bank, and the IMF all in Washington, DC, providing a direct territorial example of the influence of a dominating power in the physical location of its headquarters. In the case of the last three, they are explicitly headquartered in the capital city of the country with the largest total nominal gross domestic product (GDP). A change in location has not occurred since these institutions' founding, and the costs of moving to another country would be extreme. It remains to be seen if a move will occur should China surpass the United States in total GDP.

BOX 7.1 | **Theories and Measurements**

Just as we outlined the theory, hypothesis, and testing of power transition theory, we do the same here for long-cycle theory to illustrate how an idea can translate to a testable research question.

Long-cycle theory considers the organization of the world to be the physical representation of a hierarchical power whose strength originates in the advancement of a critical economic industry. International organizations are not independent actors, but the outcome of policy choices related to that economic dominance, such as the British creation of a free-trade regime. Because economic cycles are quite lengthy, the theory requires that studies

(Continued)

BOX 7.1	Continued

of international relations have far more years for evaluation than commonly undertaken in the conflict analysis literature, with historical research often going back to at least 1500 AD. Examining this century or longer processes, long-cycle theorists suggest that global leadership is a process of (1) global war, (2) world power, (3) legitimation, and, finally, (4) deconcentration.[7]

Hypothesis—As a dominant state's economic supremacy erodes, conflict will become more likely.

Measurements—Historical GDP, capabilities, military expenditures, naval assets, demography, and geographical controls, particularly sea lanes foundational to international economic activity.

Results—Large conflicts are most likely when social order deteriorates alongside a hegemon's decline and is restored when a new power emerges, typically coinciding with the global development of economic or technological sectors that establish new social order.

THE AMERICAN LIBERAL ORDER

The United States provides stability through the provision of certain public goods to the international system. As part of that provision of public goods, the United States established a wide array of economic and security architecture that also encapsulates American liberal norms and interests. Through these institutions, the United States has both encouraged and pressured other states to adopt policies amenable to American foreign policy interests. Initially, within the Soviet geographic sphere of influence, alternative Soviet institutions contested these organizations but, since the collapse of the Soviet Union, they have been unchallenged in their importance. We describe these cornerstone institutions in greater detail next.

The Economic Triad: The IMF, the World Bank, and the WTO
Bretton Woods is a resort town in northern New Hampshire, and it was here in 1944 that the forty-four members of the Allies from World War II convened to discuss the emerging financial system. It

became the foundation of the modern international order as well as shorthand for the establishment of international organizations in general, with the creation of two key institutions: the IMF and the World Bank. The purpose of both organizations is to facilitate and limit the damage of national financial collapse experienced globally during the Great Depression, which then led in part to the violence of World War II. When one country collapsed financially, that instability spread rapidly no matter what policy tools national governments implemented. This damage, in turn, can undermine previously stable countries leading to civil and even international conflicts. Indeed, the economic instability in Germany gave rise to the National Socialists. So, to ameliorate the potential severity of these economic collapses, the IMF was created to be the *lender of last resort*: the organization that countries rely upon when no other source of funds is available.

How the IMF operates is up for some debate. The formal rules of the organization are that it makes decisions based upon the voting of member states weighted to give larger, wealthier donors a proportionally higher amount of influence. The United States, as an example, is at 17 percent of the total votes. The research question would then be how independent is the IMF from national policies given this system of choice? Some suggest that the IMF operates only as the figurehead of U.S. economic policies, whereas others show that although the U.S. voice is far louder than its voting percentage would indicate, the IMF still retains institutional independence.[8] This combination of formal (number of votes) and informal (power of the country) influence is seen throughout discussions of international organizations in general.

The World Bank initially was tasked with helping to move the capital necessary to rebuild Europe after the war, generally originating as loans from the United States. Like the establishment of the IMF, lessons were learned from past attempts at managing conflict. Following World War I, the allies made the significant mistake of forcing their defeated foes to pay enormous sums, inhibiting reconstruction and causing massive unemployment for a generation to come, a generation that, in Germany, gave rise to Hitler and the Nazi Party. As populist and fascist political leaders rose across Central Europe, the idea of renegotiating these punitive agreements with force was a popular political platform. The newly victorious allies after World War II learned from this mistake, believing peace came from property rights and economic integration, which required the availability of capital to rebuild.

Building on the progress at Bretton Woods, three years later, a similar group of liberal states met to establish the General Agreement on Tariffs and Trade (GATT) to further trade liberalization in the same manner as the financial stability of the IMF and World Bank. Although initially not an organization but a series of agreements, the diplomatic framework evolved into a standalone organization that focused on the reduction of trade barriers.

With each successive treaty, the mechanics of trade and trade dispute resolution became more complex while the number of signatories, seeking to acquire the gains from trade enjoyed by GATT members, continued to grow. This led to the creation of the WTO: not only one of the most critical institutions in the world but also one of the more limited. The WTO's primary goal is a reduction of restrictions on international trade and operating as a judicial body when states have trade disputes. As a standalone institution, it both furthers the free-trade agenda promoted by the United States while also serving as a neutral third party that states can trust as disputes arise. Dispute resolution is standard in trade treaties allowing smaller, weaker states to have the ability to hold richer, more powerful ones to their contractual provisions. However, the WTO is limited in that enforcement of its rulings must be carried out by the member states.

The United Nations

As the premier diplomatic organization in the world, the United Nations serves as a prime case of managing international discourse and attempting to achieve a difficult to attain consensus. However, consensus restraining its ability to act may also serve as the United Nations' strength, solving many of the problems of its predecessor, the League of Nations. The League of Nations was founded immediately following World War I to encapsulate Woodrow Wilson's Fourteen Points, furthering a liberal order of peace, democracy, and human rights. However, the league was stringent, binding all nations to prevent aggressive acts by any rogue member but providing no means of enforcement capability. Given that restrictiveness, despite the strong support of Wilson, the U.S. Congress refused to ratify the treaty, and the world's most powerful state thus declined to join. Lacking the influence of the dominant power, the League was ultimately left unable to prevent the rising irredentism of Nazi Germany and to ameliorate the economic crises of the Great Depression and rising human rights violations throughout the globe.[9]

However, the allied victors founded the United Nations after World War II in support of four freedoms that mirror the League of Nations justification: of speech, of religion, from want, and from fear. Furthermore, reflecting on the horrors of the holocaust, the emphasis on human rights was expanded vastly with a thirty-article Universal Declaration of Human Rights signed by forty-eight of the fifty-eight members of the United Nations in 1948 and growing again with the Convention on the Prevention and Punishment of the Crime of Genocide in 1951. Both agreements were designed to limit state sovereignty and compel members of the international community to act when faced with human rights violations.

However, unlike the League, the United Nations was limited at the outset in its ability to act by acknowledging the importance of the most powerful states in its decision-making structure. This prevented it from being rendered ineffective when a particularly powerful state or states disagree with the majority opinion. The United Nations established that the five victors of World War II, which included the four remaining major powers (the United States, the United Kingdom, France, and the Soviet Union), received a veto over any issue brought before the security council. The fifth veto holder, the Republic of China, eventually lost its position in 1971 as the United Nations voted to recognize the People's Republic of China, with its greater capabilities, as the appropriate holder of the security council seat. Unlike the League of Nations, the United Nations managed the idealism of universal human rights against the reality of limited enforcement by the most powerful states.

This emphasis on the practical is essential to the survival of institutions. The United Nations has assumed increasing amounts of cross-national work that nations are either unwilling or unable to manage. Refugees, for example, are a UN-coded classification, with camps run and regulated according to the UN framework, managing their housing, support, security, and relocation as necessary. Cultural engagement is also supported by the organization, managing World Heritage sites, and the United Nations' Population Division collects some of the most important data to the study of international relations and political demography. The most resource-dependent activity, peacekeeping, is perhaps most controversial but also essential to its mission. This armed military force is given highly restricted tasks to support or protect populations within countries but is only allowed with unanimous security council support among the veto holders. These troops are only volunteered by member nations and are selectively allocated depending upon the location and context of the peacekeeping mission, as discussed in chapter 5. In addition to direct peacekeeping, the United Nations also oversees organizations that assume significant security functions, like the IAEA. This important group was given the responsibility to oversee treaties dealing with nuclear weapons, employing third party specialists to monitor and audit nuclear facilities. The United Nations independence and nonterritorial status allow for more considerable amounts of trust as a third party that, in turn, facilitates greater cooperation between states.

What then is the point of the United Nations? Above all else, it serves as an international coordination organization, especially on issues that individual nations are unable or unwilling to alleviate. Although there are many lofty, even utopian ideals that justify its founding, the United Nations' most practical function is as a discussion forum. Similarly, the United Nations serves as an institution through which the major powers, members of the Security Council, will always have an open means of communication even during times of extreme crisis. The United Nations serves as a focal point for the public airing of grievances, propaganda, and continuous diplomacy: all things that, in an era of nuclear weapons, are of practical importance. Issues change over time, but the need for a public forum to communicate is constant.

The classic criticism of the United Nations is that it is not designed to change and that it is ineffective. However, the United Nations was designed by the United States and its allies to provide stability for the status quo, not to allow dramatic change. The veto power of the major powers purposefully does not allow newly prosperous or nuclear-powered nations to also gain that institutional influence, thus succeeding in not incentivizing change-oriented behavior. Furthermore, although it provides an arena for the major powers to engage one another on issues between themselves or with lesser powers, it helps to prevent the violence, instability, and status quo–threatening outcomes of the world wars. As rising challengers, such as India or Brazil, continue to grow and surpass current veto holders, such as Russia, the ability of the United Nations, given its unchanging veto players, to preserve the status quo fostered originally by the United States will be tested.

NATO

Upon the conclusion of World War II, the United States and its allies crafted a separate collective security organization apart from the

United Nations to provide a stabilizing force against potential aggressors, specifically the Soviet Union, that might threaten the new American-dominated status quo. The United States worried that a rapidly approaching World War III may be on the horizon, necessitating the formation of an organization to coordinate the security policy of its members on everything from the quality of rations, the caliber of bullets, and the standardization of detailed measurements. Building on lessons learned in World War II, NATO initially focused on logistical concerns: Could American, Italian, Dutch, or British troops identify each other in a fight? What equipment would they have, how would it work, or would it be possible to share ammunition? The emphasis was on the practical side of the military, not the diplomatic. If war happens, what do the troops on the ground need to know about each other to fight it effectively?

These logistical questions then quickly evolved to cross force military exercises and games. These activities represent the continuous need to train and prepare for a conflict against a formidable foe albeit one that does not have a precise date of commencement. NATO engaged in constant preparation for a war no one wanted that could lead to nuclear Armageddon. By coordinating in war games, states' militaries worked with one another, facilitating further cooperation while also providing clear deterrent signals to the Soviet Union of their collective capabilities. This social or diplomatic aspect of the alliance is essential for its continued influence, particularly by its most powerful member, the United States. For both American and allied personnel, a NATO high command became part of a successful officer's career. Having a ship as part of a U.S. carrier group is a distinguished prize as is the increased connections within the defense industry as procurement becomes a cross-national policy. NATO is not a piece of paper but an evolving collective security organization with joint decisions under its umbrella directly influencing nearly every action taken by members of the combined militaries.

The most dramatic component of NATO is Article 5, which stipulates that an attack against any NATO member allows that member to request assistance from all NATO members against the attacker. Article 5 served to replace, in a more effective permutation, the collective defense stipulation of the League of Nations. Excising the security component of punishing aggressors from the United Nations charter was necessary to its effectiveness, so the key to preventing future aggression was built into the more tightly knit NATO where members shared both security concerns and more liberal norms. As discussed in chapter 4, NATO was initially targeting the Soviet Union as a defensive alliance. Article 5, however, has only been used once, on September 11, 2001. Having never been used against an opposing state does not indicate it has no value. Instead, this highlights NATO's effectiveness at deterring possible aggressors through the belief by potential opponents that all members would come to the defense of one. Contemporary Russia, for example, may chew away at the territory of its non-NATO neighbors, but it has refrained from committing similarly aggressive acts against contiguous NATO member states.

As an organization, the NATO alliance serves more than the role of security provider and deterrent. One condition of membership is to be a democracy with free and fair elections. Thus, the United States used the provision of security and inclusion within its nuclear umbrella as an incentive to also adopt other status quo values that were a part of the broader American order. In terms of American foreign policy, the United States was willing to tolerate strong-arm dictators in other parts of the world, but in Europe, where that architecture went beyond preserving security or thwarting Soviet activity, it was not. The effectiveness of the NATO alliance required a shared ideological commitment to democracy, individual liberty, and capitalist economics. That joint commitment to the suite of American liberal values strengthened the common interests of all alliance members, making the alliance more effective.

Following the end of the Cold War, NATO expanded eastward across Europe, alongside democracy and capitalism, despite the evaporation of the original security threat it was intended to guard against. However, its presence has continued to thwart attempts at alternative security organizations that would exclude the United States under the control of a major European power or the European Union. The French have long desired the creation of a separate "European Army," and although they may arguably possess the second-most advanced military in the world and nuclear weapons, they have been thwarted in this endeavor routinely since World War II by the United States. Given the unified security policy that NATO has developed among its members, despite shifting security concerns, the formation of alternatives has been viewed as unnecessary. However, as the European Union continues to develop as a robust supranational entity, it may begin to build its security apparatus. With the decline in U.S. power, increased belligerence from Russia, and instability of Brexit, an EU Army may become an attractive possibility. After all, the combined European Union has roughly the same GDP as the United States. Further political consolidation, therefore, could see the European Union challenge American dominance in security affairs.

THE EVOLUTION OF THE LIBERAL ORDER

Even in times of crisis, new organizations alternative to the American order may have interest but not sustainability. The alternative throughout the Cold War, the Warsaw Pact, was more of an excuse for the Soviet occupation of Eastern Europe than a group made of willing participants. Each system of institutions, the Warsaw Pact and NATO, are heavily based on the interests and preferred norms of their superpower patron. From a long-cycle theory perspective, we may expect organizational structures to survive beyond their creators to take on new versions of themselves in response to shifting social and economic order at the system level. However, the Warsaw Pact failed to outlast the Soviet Union. Could NATO survive outside an American dominated international system?

Institutions can last beyond the existence of their creators or original purpose, just as NATO survived and evolved beyond its initial purpose targeting the Soviet Union. They can be modified to suit new conditions and expand well beyond their original intent taking on additional responsibilities. Think, for example, of the Holy Roman Empire that spanned Europe as a supranational entity for a millennium. Through a repackaging of ancient Roman symbols and institutions, ambitious political rulers, from Charlemagne to Napoleon, would co-opt the institution and its trappings to grant themselves political legitimacy as inheritors of a relevant historical legacy and explicit territory, leaving the institution itself constantly evolving. Similarly, consider the innovation of free trade now embodied in the governing mechanism of the WTO. In its modern form, this antiprotectionist opening of barriers that is free trade was first applied to post-Napoleonic France by Britain to try to exert greater economic and political influence over a historical rival. After the British decline, the newly dominant United States retained and expanded this economic ordering principle, despite the attempted rise of competing alternatives, such as the Communist International (COMINTERN) system of the Soviet Union, or the currency-reserve balance-of-trade manipulations by the Third Reich or the Japanese Empire.[10]

Shared Hierarchy

When considering the political hierarchy of these institutional frameworks, and their respective areas of control, we have three levels of organizations and law aligning with the three levels of analysis in international relations. The first is *national laws* and state sovereignty. The classical idea of a state is defined both by independence and by a monopoly of violence within its borders. The second is *international law* created by agreements between states and later enhanced by international organizations depending on the issue area. The last and most dramatic is *supranational law*, which are organizations made up of states that have created a framework so vast that national law is no longer completely dominant, as we might observe today in the European Union.[11] This is the rarest as it is also the most controversial. Unlike organizing institutions that govern international law, supranational law supersedes and infringes upon the national hierarchical dominance of the sovereign state.

We can think about such arrangements as akin to early forms of federalism in the United States, where the individual states possessed *sovereignty* over some issue areas, but in other explicit domains, the federal government was dominant. Similarly, today, the constituent states of the European Union have sovereignty over most issue areas. But, in some, such as currency production, they surrender their sovereignty to a supranational institution. However, the rule of law is enforced by the actors with capabilities to do so, and those actors continue to be states. Think of the domestic level of the law, even at the most local. What matters more in practice, the law as written or the choice to enforce it? The effectiveness of institutions is determined by their ability to affect functional change. As sovereignty becomes shared across domestic and international levels, the functional effectiveness of institutions increases, as we see today in most of Europe.

The Role of War in Institutional Development

Most current significant organizations begin their creation and evolution after the industrialization of war in the nineteenth century, reaching its zenith in the conflicts of World War I and II and coinciding with the rise of the United States to the position of a global major power.[12] The scale of those conflicts and their carnage led to the belief that countries must reconsider how they interact with each other politically or the next great war will be a horror so great that extinction could be a possibility. However, this was not the first attempt at integration or fear of ever-escalating war, as at the conclusion of the Napoleonic Wars, Tsar Alexander of Russia suggested a European confederation that included the United States governed by major powers with a military ability to deter violence.[13] Yet conflict continued to become ever more destructive.

Military technological capacity evolved from small armies to mass conscription to fully mechanized warfare and the creation of chemical, biological, and nuclear weapons. At World War II's conclusion, World War III was not a mythological fear but a terror that could be the future of tomorrow. That technology had progressed to the point that conflict was no longer a simple extension of politics between states or a question of patriotism but an act that ushered vast destruction may have altered major power perceptions of war's utility. At this, point, the rise of the United States may have had a critical effect on the global concept of conflict, as its support of organizations built on the idea of decreasing conflict and promoting liberal human rights may have created the foundations of a world in which we observe a sharp decrease in international and civil conflicts, as illustrated in chapters 3 and 5.

Economies of Scale

Regionally, many contemporary international organizations started because of the economic advantage of economies of scale. In other words, being larger is cheaper, and in a world of gigantic competition, how do small countries compete? Absent the ability to acquire colonies or expand their territory, they grew not through conquest but treaty. One common approach is via a free-trade agreement, such as NAFTA, that focuses on reducing tariffs and expanding toward health, safety, and transportation concerns. The goal of these agreements is to create a process by which gains from trade can be expanded to benefit all parties to the agreement, resulting in the development of an institution to oversee those activities. The classic cliché argument for NAFTA was merely that a broader unified market could take advantage of a host of differing competitive advantages: cheaper labor from Mexico and natural resources from Canada, with technology and capital from the United States. This would allow production to increase as each category would be enhanced within a unified market, benefiting all three.

The more sophisticated version of these economic organizations is a customs union, such as Mercosur or the European Coal and Steel Community. In free-trade agreements, borders are still controlled by the nations themselves, but in customs unions, borders are functionally reduced as a barrier, governed by the same laws as stipulated by the terms of the union on either side. As a result, customs unions go beyond economic issues and incorporate security concerns, as the two or more nations in the union must coordinate security given their shared border. Furthermore, they must coordinate their trade policies outside the union with one another as well, as the trade policy of one state will then directly affect the other. This level of integration is purely political and an evident dilution of state sovereignty. The economic trade-off is that being bigger is more competitive, but on the security side, smaller is more controllable. Which would you rather be: a partner of a more prosperous group with less influence or a poorer one with more? Competition among these coalescing groups has the potential to continue to expand their size and scope, with some like the European Union clearly providing stabilizing public goods to their constituent members.

BOX 7.2	Establishing and Evolving the European Union

The most notable example of how the process of integration between states can unfold and the difficulty of a supranational legal system is the European Union: an organization with a parliament, courts, laws, and bureaucrats. All these aspects, in combination, begin to look less like an international organization and more like a state unto itself. The creation of this uniquely centralized organization and how it came into being is discussed throughout the text, but unequivocally, the European Union is the most remarkable attempt at integration in the modern era. It is also an example of how diplomacy works in practice over a decade-long series of political negotiations and wrangling. What we now call the European Union, with its current twenty-eight member states, started as the European Coal and Steel Community with six original members: Belgium, France, Italy, Luxembourg, the Netherlands, and West Germany. The intent of the organization was to moderate economic interests in the region, which had historically led to violent war. Signed in 1951, this was the seed from which the next sixty years of negotiation and integration would grow. Each progressive political movement integrated industries across increasingly more states at ever more complex levels, leading eventually to the establishment of the European Union (1993) and the eurozone common currency (2002).

FUTURE OF THE SYSTEM AND SHARED POLICY

Future study seems to be moving to the concept of networks, developing nuance through incorporating the informal or formal choices of states as they engage groups of IOs.[14] This emphasizes the depth of a state's integration into the global order rather than focusing on a single institution. Highly integrated countries are a part of many IOs, with each pulling countries together or dramatically increasing the costs of noncompliance.[15] Studying the European Union as an example without the IMF seems as if it would be a limited research endeavor as every member of the European Union is also a member of the IMF. States that are further engrained in this overlapping architecture are likely also more satisfied with the status quo and, consistent with the concept of authority discussed in the previous chapter, acknowledge the legitimacy of the United States as system leader.

Organizations reinforce the actions and shared policy of states. They can work as independent actors themselves, if permitted, but they require coercive power as support. Dominant states, be they international or regional, retain that coercive ability, and it is those whose policies are often advanced by institutions.

DISCUSSION QUESTIONS

1. Why did the League of Nations fail but the United Nations has not?
2. Although the purpose of international organizations is to mitigate some of the problems of cooperating under anarchy, if states make institutions too powerful, other states may not choose to join. Select an issue in international politics and design an institution to address that issue, making it powerful enough to be effective but not so punitive that it goes ignored by possible members.
3. Unlike the Soviet Union, China has not sought to develop meaningful institutional infrastructure separate from the United States. As the Chinese begin to implement policies such as "One Belt, One Road" that further regional economic integration, what institutional markers should we look to as signals that they are both challenging the American economic order and are dissatisfied?
4. A central stated purpose of the United Nations, according to its charter, is to protect against violations of human rights, but it has had mixed success in doing so. What do you think differentiates cases where the United Nations is successful in peacekeeping efforts versus where it fails?

5. If China becomes the dominant state, what institutions currently in existence do you think it will continue to support? How might those institutions change in both their structure and their conduct?

KEY TERMS

European Union
international law
irredentism
lender of last resort
liberalization

Mercosur
North American Free Trade
    Agreement (NAFTA)
supranational law
system services

FURTHER READING

Gilpin, Robert. 1987. *The Political Economy of International Relations*. Princeton, NJ: Princeton University Press.

Ikenberry, G. John. 2011. *Liberal Leviathan: The Origins, Crisis, and Transformation of the American World Order*. Princeton, NJ: Princeton University Press.

Keohane, Robert. O. 1984. *After Hegemony: Cooperation and Discord in the World Political Economy*. Princeton, NJ: Princeton University Press.

8

Regionalization and Trade

REGIONS IN SPACE AND POLITICS

Geography matters. Proximity influences all aspects of national and international politics. It contextualizes security concerns, determines your trading partners, and molds your national identity.[1] Geography is also history as populations flow to locations to access water, resources, and transportation. These locations are more valuable and provide the foundation for prosperity.[2] Geostrategic positions, likewise, are those that a state may seek to hold to protect those prosperous locations and the wealth they generate, such as straits, harbors, and mountain passes.

Conflicts have and will continue to be fought over essential geostrategic positions. The most important part of this geographic story, however, is that it is dynamic. The importance of a geographic location is not merely the space but also its connection to movement and trade. The ancient Silk Road of China is not the same as it once was, just as air travel renders mountains less effective as geopolitical barriers compared to the past. Likewise, as climate change continues, conflict over water politics is likely to rise.[3] The political and economic importance of space changes as nations rise and fall in their power and their interests likewise shift. What resources are valuable is malleable with products changing in value as tastes and technology change. Geography is relatively fixed, but its importance is not for humanity.

This chapter deals with three important interrelated concepts. The first is *regionalism*: the grouping of nations linked by political influence. We focus on the measurement of local political linkages moving beyond the traditional names of spaces, such as Europe/South America/South East Asia, instead exploring how states within those geographical spaces are bound politically and economically by hierarchy or its absence. What is the nature of politically relevant space? This concept highlights the importance of alliances, treaties, and even culture. The second is to consider the importance of trade in the context of regions. How is trade created and facilitated by geography, and what are its effects? Trade is the clearest example of an observable connection among people, and a traditionally useful method of illustrating cross-national linkages. Finally, the third is regional institutions. Groups such as the North American Free Trade Agreement (NAFTA), the European Union, or Mercosur are all geographically centric political organizations composed of sovereign states.

MEASUREMENTS OF REGIONS

Let us again consider the concept of power: the ability to coerce groups, people, or states. A significant part of that definition is the assumption that those you may wish to coerce are reachable. How does one force another on the top of a mountain or the other side of the world? What is the importance of stating policy goals if there is no physical ability to implement them? The trappings of power and the glitter of wealth are meaningless without the ability to transport. Hence, our understanding of regions is not geographic only but organizational as well. It is the locations in which states have the physical ability to engage. These overlapping spheres of influence between states are what evolve to become larger groups that we think of as regions today, such as the Middle East, South Asia, East Asia, or Europe. Countries in these spaces may not have the ability to influence globally but do have significant influence within their regions.

Within regions may exist a regional power or group of powers that have uniquely high capabilities compared to other region members and are active in organizing the politics of the space. Some may also be major powers, such as the United States in North America or China in East Asia, but these major powers consistently engage their regions above and beyond the rest of the world.[4] Others, however, may be strictly regional powers, such as India or Brazil. Finally, some other spaces may lack a regional power altogether, as no one state has the combination of capabilities, engagement, and status or authority to provide order to the space, such as the Middle East today. Such an absence of hierarchy may have important consequences for the politics of the region.

Table 8.1 shows how regions have evolved since the 1950s.[5] This measurement of regions entails a group of states that both reach one another as well as engage each other in their foreign policies uniquely apart from the rest of the international system. By defining regions analytically rather than arbitrarily or strictly geographically as we would by naming continents, we can observe how the politics within these spaces evolve. Thinking about regions as politically meaningful

Table 8.1   Regions, 1950–2010

1950s	1960s	1970s	1990s	2000s
North Central America	North America	Northern America	North America	North America
South Central America	Andes	South America	Andes	South America
Andes	South America	Europe	South America	Middle East
South America	West Africa	West Africa	West Africa	Europe
Europe	Gold Coast	Western Coast	Gold Coast	West Africa
Northern Europe	Central Savannah	Southern Africa	Central Savannah	Southern Africa
Middle East	Western Europe	Middle East	Central Africa	Central Africa
East Asia	Benelux	East Asia	Western Europe	East Asia
	Scandinavia	Northeast Asia	Scandinavia	South Asia
	Eastern Europe	Southeast Asia	Eastern Europe	
	Middle East		Benelux	
	East Asia		Middle East	
	Asia-Pacific		East Asia	
			Asia-Pacific	

Source: Data used to create the table are available at www.patrickrhamey.com/row. J. Patrick Rhamey Jr., "Regions of Opportunity and Willingness Data Codebook v3" (2019), last accessed June 30, 2019, www.patrickrhamey.com/row; Thomas J. Volgy, Paul Bezerra, Jacob Cramer, and J. Patrick Rhamey Jr., "The Case for Comparative Regional Analysis in International Politics," *International Studies Review* 19 (2017): 452–480. Note the 1980s remain absent due to the unavailability of events data.

spaces is essential to understanding their politics, as the composition of regions is not fixed.

Regional Evolution

We take for granted that there is a region called the Middle East that is central to American foreign policy. We might think of that space as unique given the dependence on oil resources, the dominance of Islam, or perhaps as a space particularly prone to conflict over the past few decades. However, the term *Middle East* was not widely used until the beginning of the twentieth century and has slowly evolved as decolonization, the establishment of Israel, and more recent American interventions continue to shape its politics. During the preceding period of British dominance in the international system, the term *Near East* was frequently used to refer to those spaces on the eastern littoral of the Mediterranean, overlapping with the territory of the Ottoman Empire but not including the Arabian Peninsula and the Persian Gulf. Now, because of changes in politics and economic engagement, the "Middle East" has supplanted the "Near East" of the past.

Table 8.1 shows how these regions develop and evolve during the Cold War period. Some regions come and go, such as Eastern Europe or Scandinavia, merging to form larger entities as the level of institutionalization and integration in Europe progresses. Others fragment, such as the division by the most recent period of Asia into East, with China and Japan, and South, with India. The politically relevant regional clusters that we observe often both integrate and fragment in coincidence with changes in regional hierarchy, either in the form of conflicts, which tend to fragment as Asia did during the Vietnam War period, or cooperation, such as trade and integration driving the consolidation of Europe into a single regional group.

The continent of Africa is an excellent example of the advantages of thinking about regions as evolving entities, with clusters shown in East Africa, Southern Africa, West Africa, and, last, Egypt in the Middle East. The linkages among nations created by the flows of trade, influence, and politics are not merely the coincidence of geography but also involve the conscious political decisions of states to turn their attention in one direction rather than another. This process can also be seen in South Asia with India as the central state but not in Southeast Asia. Indonesia, Malaysia, and Thailand are more closely associated with China and East Asia, despite some strong historical cleavages with the Indian subcontinent.

Effect of Hierarchy on Regions

In each region, the importance of regional powers becomes apparent. Some have a hierarchy led by a dominant power and, in some cases, challengers. Europe, for example, has a long regional history of repeated challenges among Britain, Germany, France, and Russia. Although the first three generally collaborate in providing order to Europe today, Russia remains a dissatisfied actor seeking to subvert those efforts. A region is not merely the cooperation of friendly states but also the conflicts that force the rest of the region to tie themselves to one or other challenging power. For example, in South Asia, much of regional politics coalesce around the sustained grievance between regional power India, and regional challenger, Pakistan. In the differing parts of Africa, it can be a wide range of countries, such as South Africa, Nigeria, or Ethiopia, each a critical authority within its region but not necessarily within the continent or the world.

The influence of regional powers grows and declines with their economy, both through trade and the capabilities available domestically to employ coercion. Table 8.1 illustrates how changes in the international affect the regional. The scale of a rising power such as China eclipses smaller regions nearby, pulling the nations within into its sphere of influence. Europe, likewise, was once split between East and West, divided between the United States and the Soviet Union until the Soviet Union's collapse. These borderlands between great powers are often the location of the most damaging wars in the twentieth century. A change in technology, however, can quickly alter where these spaces are, as the ease of projecting power continues to evolve just as it has throughout history. Only after technological advancements in sea power and navigation could European states craft global empires. The creation of roads, access to the sea, advancements in the construction of canals, and aircraft technology all changed the possibilities of where a nation can implement policy and at what cost.

EVOLUTION OF REGIONAL TRADE AND AGREEMENTS

From the invention of a professional military by the Romans with standardized training and national construction of infrastructure two thousand years ago to the mass production of modular container shipping technology only seventy years ago, the ability to transport and influence is continually changing. Our modern, interconnected world would be impossible without the shipping technology that is its veins. Perhaps in the second half of the twentieth century, the single greatest invention was not the Internet, the smartphone, or even the computer but the container ship which makes the ability to trade at current levels across great distance possible. As an example, for the United States from 2000 to 2017, the amount of "twenty-foot equivalent unit" traffic, a standard measurement of a container equal to the size of a sixteen-wheeler, has increased from 200 million to 700 million, more than tripling in volume. Add to this total the increase in air cargo capacity and the new normal for European consumers to expect fresh flowers in the middle of winter flown from Kenya or Rwanda. Such ease of transport and the degree of trade would seem beyond the imagination of science-fiction writers only a few decades ago.

What Does Trade Do?

With all this discussion of how linked the world has become, it is important to explain why. While there may be political reasons, such as the United States seeking influence in domestic societies, what are the economic justifications? To better understand the "Why?" think about the benefits of trade at an individual, personal level, as you might in an introductory microeconomics course. The scarcity of time makes trade beneficial. Individually, you possess skills, education, and an accumulation of experiences that make you better suited to certain occupations than others. You possess at your disposal certain qualities and resources, whether by talent, privilege, or luck. In combination, your abilities and context determine where in the market for labor you might be most effective. Given the scarcity of time, you are usually only able to pursue a single profession, at least at any one time. This means there are a variety of things you might wish to do, or things you might like to produce, that you are simply unable.

Because each of us is unique both in ability and environment, we each offer society a different set of strengths and abilities. The five-foot unathletic person cannot be a professional basketball player no matter how much they may desire it. Someone who cannot throw or hit a baseball cannot be a professional baseball player. These examples may sound silly, but they are the core of why trade exists. Should the world's greatest surgeon, capable of saving thousands of lives, instead spend their time mowing their yard, farming their food, or doing their home maintenance? The surgeon might be good at all of those things, enjoy them, and want to do them. However, the issue is *opportunity costs*. If this person is doing these things, they are not spending their time saving people's lives as a surgeon. And so this person's limited time as a resource is what makes trade attractive.

The surgeon engages in trade, hiring someone to do these other tasks. Farmers, lawyers, accountants, factory workers, teachers, carpenters, doctors, and filmmakers all specialize in one area and then exchange their skills with others so that they might all reap the benefits of their professions.

This process of exchange is trade at its core. You do not necessarily always trade what you are "good" at but instead trade what people in society will pay you to do. Trade is not just buying what you do not have or produce but also buying what you could produce but do not have the time as you are doing something that you are more effective at doing. This same principle applies to trade between states and is known as *comparative advantage*. States benefit from trade with one another as it allows a state to specialize in goods that it may create particularly well but still access products produced in other countries. Through trade, societies access greater amounts of labor, diverse talents, more resources, and the multitude of factors that go into the creation of an advanced economy.

The Limits of Geography

Who you trade with is a result of both comparative advantage and geography. If I produce wheat and you produce wine, we can trade with each other to have both. The comparative advantage is that my land and labor are better for the production of one crop or the other. If we choose not to trade and produce our own wheat and wine, we can enjoy relatively worse wine or flavorless wheat and both at higher costs because we produce less, resulting in greater scarcity. However, for trade to be preferable, we must be able to transport our wheat and wine across distances. Thus, trade is almost always higher among countries that are next to each other. States quite distant from one another still engage in trade, but the logistics of traveling great distances make it more difficult and thereby costly. For example, Mexico is smaller and produces less than China. However, China is thousands of miles away from the United States. As a result of the logistical issues surrounding distance, American trade with Mexico outpaces that of China.

Protectionism

The preceding discussion outlines the fundamental principle that guides free trade: I produce one thing, you produce another, and we trade so that everyone can enjoy these goods. However, the political reality is this complete freedom of exchange is rarely the case. Governments represent domestic producers, voters, and politicians that have a poor grasp of economics. Competing domestic constraints create policies of neo-mercantilism and protectionism. These policies aggressively seek to determine who within an economy wins or loses using government control, although they have different emphases. Neo-mercantilist trade policies, similar to neo-realist approaches to international politics, privilege the security of the state over any potential economic benefit. Therefore, even if a country is particularly bad at creating steel, cars, or airplanes, such industries must be protected in case the country goes to war and needs those industries to develop military hardware, even if consumers must suffer poorly made, expensive products in the meantime. Protectionism, likewise, often is rooted in reactionary politics, where workers demand protections even if the good being produced is inferior to alternatives and that worker's labor might be more productive doing something else. In both cases, the macroeconomic benefits of trade are not taken into account by the government but, instead, the priority is preservation of the status quo due to security needs or internal politics. The government dictates investment in cars, steel, satellites, or wheat because domestic groups demand it, not because the country will be good at it. This undermines the future by investing capital in unproductive ventures or losing access to foreign markets while the rest of the world, if trading with one another, is specializing and innovating, leaving the nontrading state to lag technologically.

From steel plants that produce no steel in Nigeria for almost forty years with thousands of employees to rice farms with an average worker age of sixty-five in Japan to Caribbean governments granting a single company a monopoly over all beer production, antitrade policies are popular. Institutionalizing trade, therefore, is an important step toward mitigating these policies and holding governments accountable. The point of signing onto organizations, such as the World Trade Organization, is to decrease the ability of future governments to change their minds on free trade and revert to protectionism. As much as trade may help an economy, the next election is always more important to politicians then what happens in twenty years. Short-run politics might make the termination of decades of trade liberalization attractive, as illustrated by the recent actions of the United States under the Trump administration. However, trade is subject to domestic politics and often implies sudden, and sometimes, dramatic change. No matter the macroeconomic benefits, individuals shy away from uncertainty, particularly if that uncertainty involves a new career, moving to a new location, or changing an existing way of life.

Protectionism is popular because it is a method by which people can push change further away from their lives and retain the status quo. The factory stays open even if it makes no profit, the farm is in operation even if it is not productive, and children go into the family business because they have no other choice. By signing onto a trade agreement, however, the rules of the organization can supersede domestic politics, making it much harder for a state to retreat on economic openness by making the costs of leaving the agreement more severe than those of continuing with liberalization, as the United Kingdom's attempts at Brexit illustrate.

EUROPEAN UNION VERSUS BREXIT

As of mid-2019, almost three years since Brexit began, we still do not know if planes will be able to land in Great Britain from Europe or if one of the world's top ten economies will have the ability to buy and sell on the global market. The largest car manufacturer, Nissan, does not know if it will be able to build or sell cars in the United Kingdom[6] all because of a nonbinding nationwide referendum on whether the United Kingdom should stay or leave the European Union and subsequently cancel almost every treaty related to trade with the continent for more than forty years. This expansive series of treaties since the end of World War II affect nearly all aspects of modern British life from the purchase of oil and pharmaceuticals to the manufacture of airplanes. The potential for economic disaster as a function of an uniformed vote by 52 percent of the British population has already begun to be felt and will likely become worse as the British government, now with Boris Johnson as prime minister, is struggling to find a path forward. So how could this happen to one of the founders of the modern international system of free trade?

The most straightforward answer is populism, rooted in political ignorance, scapegoating, and timing. The complexity of the European Union is beyond the scope of this book and, in detail, would fill volumes. But it is necessary to understand that it comes from a question of power. How could a region of small states, eclipsed by the size and might of the United States and the Soviet Union, continue to be relevant? Beginning in 1948, there was a slowly expanding framework of treaties, institutions, and organization among European states to create a single voice backed by the wealthiest combined population in the world.

So why would Britain leave? The problem is uninformed democracy, as is often the case when nationalist policies win over policies that materially improve the lives of citizens through further integration. In this instance, the European Union merged, not just linked, economies to such an extent that after three years how they might be disentangled is still unclear. However, political dissatisfaction with the decision-making structure of the European Union allowed populist political opportunists to suggest that because the international institution was not under voters' direct control, the policies of the European Union were not in their best interests. This message particularly resonated in parts of the United Kingdom where the economy continued to languish from the Great Recession or had not advanced technologically following the de-industrialization of World War II. Increased immigration from other parts of Europe was met with racism and group blame for personal struggles, while unionized factory workers faced an unknown future. Although London became an even greater center of international finance and a hub of services and wealth, other areas fell behind.

The use of the European Union as bogeyman became popular as the source of immigration, its lack of control by voters, and its headquarters on the other side of the English Channel. It was easy for politicians to convince people who did not quite understand what the European Union does that it was a villain: an elitist European sitting in Brussels not caring about true Englishmen. Furthermore, both major parties, Conservative and Labour, lacked a consistent, coherent message on the usefulness of the forty years of European integration policy. This process is a common problem in democracies transitioning toward a more globalized, liberal economy, as marketing and myth take the place of economic education and understanding. As a result, Brexit has cost the United Kingdom more than US$100 billion since the saga began.[7]

MERCOSUR

If the European Union is the example of a region attempting to have one voice, Mercosur, the African Union, and the Commonwealth of Independent States are all variations with differing degrees of success and clarity in achievable goals. All three are in regions either with a local hegemon with complex ideas of regional independence (Russia and Brazil) or one that has no overall power (Africa). Of these, Mercosur is likely the most effective organization outside the EU today. Mercosur is a customs union in South America, which is a group of nations without tariffs between them and negotiating as a bloc for trade. Much like the European Union, it was born from a region that worried about the possibilities of conflict, in this case, Chile, Argentina, and Brazil, with the latter two moving toward nuclear programs. Regional rivals and the importance of external influence in that region created the possibility of a devastating interstate conflict. These states also were governed by military juntas in the 1970s: juntas that could use these violent rivalries as a domestic means to shore up support. With the end of the Cold War, cooperation flourished, first with the Treaty of Mendoza among Chile, Argentina, and Brazil that eliminated chemical and biological weapons following the removal of their military governments. Furthermore, the Brazilian–Argentine Agency for Accounting and Control of Nuclear Materials, which publicized secret nuclear weapon programs by the rival juntas, oversaw the elimination of the programs and created an organization that would oversee both countries to verify that neither was once again attempting to create weapons of mass destruction. Resolving these violent relationships created the foundation of Mercosur's cooperative agreements, now with Brazil as the evident regional power. Mercosur than operated as a forum through which member states have reduced trade barriers, integrating societies and further reducing the propensity toward conflict internationally while bolstering liberal democracy at home.

From a regional standpoint, a shared policy is still evolving, and while the degree of instability in South America is less than it once was, a variety of international and domestic struggles remain, including political instability in Bolivia or Venezuela. Furthermore, while the regional power is Brazil with its historic rival Argentina now a part of its trade regime, Brazil suffers internally from a series of unstable governments leading to economic instability, undermining its willingness to further integrate the continent. However, the groundwork is there, for as of 2019, every other South American country is, in some way, a part of Mercosur.

South America's integration story is one that has not been given as much credit for alleviating regional tensions as it should. This region dealt with rival states moving toward a possible nuclear confrontation and instead moved to increased political and trade integration. Not coincidentally, this process coincided with the growth in Brazil's capabilities far surpassing Argentina's. Parity on the continent between the two rivals was no longer the norm. In the absence of balanced power between the two states, the probability of conflict is reduced as power transition theory suggests. As that chance of war decreases, the ability to cooperate between past belligerents rises. However, Mercosur demonstrates the difficulty of sustaining economic development, notwithstanding the movement from a seemingly inevitable series of wars to one of conflict only on the soccer pitch.

POINTS TO CONSIDER AND THE FUTURE

Regions evolve due to political influence and technological change. The waxing and waning of power, investment in transportation, or the products that are in demand move not only interest but also institutions. The Free Trade Association of the Americas is a concept that would have been the largest free trade area in the world with a NAFTA-like treaty of all the Americas: North, South, and Central. However, the agreement was lost, in part, due to the inability of the United States to deal with domestic pressure from agricultural industries, as well as the expansion of the global War on Terror, resulting in a combination of not being able to negotiate clearly while also being distracted by other issues internationally.

The Trans-Pacific Partnership is another lost opportunity, which was a far more elaborate free-trade pact between a number of Pacific Rim countries. This would have been the largest free-trade pact in the world and was the outcome of years of negotiation first under the Bush administration and later Obama. Trump withdrew from it. So what happens now? Underlying the idea behind the pact is the pacifying effect of shared governance, led by the United States. When the United States pulled out, the remaining members continued the agreement, meaning that now American exports to these states are all more expensive and, in the long run, less competitive than they would otherwise have been. The stated goal of this new administration is bilateral trade treaties and negotiations, rather than multilateral arrangements like the Trans-Pacific Partnership or NAFTA. This has yet to happen successfully in the third year of the administration, as execution of a trade treaty is a costly and time-intensive process.

DISCUSSION QUESTIONS

1. Free trade is a good way to generally acquire gains that make people better off, but what do you think should be the limits, if any? Are there certain sectors that should be protected?
2. If the state that created the current international trade regime withdraws from it, what do you think will be the consequences for everyone else? Will trade continue?
3. Would a reduction in trade help or hurt the security of the United States?
4. What is the relationship between trade and immigration?
5. How might satisfaction and status tie into who states decide to trade with and who they do not?

KEY TERMS

bilateral trade treaty
Brexit
comparative advantage
neo-mercantilism

opportunity costs
protectionism
regionalism

FURTHER READING

Easterly, William R. 2002. *The Elusive Quest for Growth: Economists' Adventures and Misadventures in the Tropics.* Cambridge, MA: MIT Press.

Krugman, Paul. 1991. "Increasing Returns and Economic Geography." *Journal of Political Economy*, 99, no. 3:483–99.

Volgy, Thomas J., Paul Bezerra, Jacob Cramer, and J. Patrick Rhamey Jr. 2017. "The Case for Comparative Regional Analysis in International Politics." *International Studies Review* 19, no. 3:452–80.

9

Development and Globalization

THE MEANING OF ECONOMIC PROGRESS

This chapter investigates one of the more challenging but vital topics to international relations: human and economic development as components of globalization. A harsh reality is that most of the economic growth of the twentieth century went to the same countries that enjoyed it in the nineteenth,[1] with the difference in growth outcomes creating *divergence*, or a widening of the gap between developing and developed world.

This divergence is often contrary to the expectations of adherents to free markets. The "why" has vexed generations of scholars from Marx to Keynes. How then do nations move from poverty to riches, and what are the consequences for major power politics? Looming over these questions are interrelated but differing concepts: growth, development, and globalization.

Economic Growth and Wealth

What is growth, and how can it be measured? Is it wealth? A composite measurement of life expectancy, literacy, and other aspects of human existence as attempted by the Human Development Index?[2] Why should we look at gross domestic product (GDP)? The underlying reason why so much of economics worries about GDP is not because it is a particularly useful measurement of an economy but that it is available. However, its components of consumption, investment, government expenditure, and net exports are all reasonably difficult to measure cross-nationally. The wide range of accounting quality, paperwork, taxes, and standardized measurements make quantification a difficult proposition, but GDP as a measure became popular during the Great Depression as the size of an "economy" moved from a theoretical concept to a direct concern of governments. It may seem shocking now, but previous governments worried about trade, tariffs, conflicts, and taxes, not the overall change of something as nebulous as an economy. GDP (and variations such as gross national income) is standard not due to quality of measurement but of ubiquity. We use it often earlier as a measure of capabilities for this same reason and the greater potential pitfalls of other widely used alternatives.

Figure 9.1 is a comparison of states' GDP divided by population, which has become a standard measure of relative wealth. The

Figure 9.1 Historical Growth by Nation

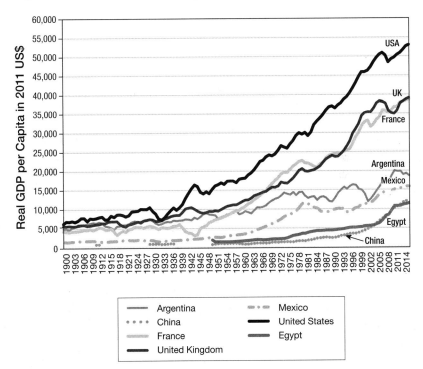

Source: Jutta Bolt, Robert Inklaar, Herman de Jong, and Jan Luiten van Zanden, "Rebasing 'Maddison': New Income Comparisons and the Shape of Long-Run Economic Development," Maddison Project Working Paper 10, 2018, Groningen: University of Groningen.

scale is significant, with 2016 having the United States near $55,000 and countries such as Argentina and China at $19,000 and $12,000, respectively. The European nations lie in between at almost $40,000. This is an excellent example of how countries that can be members of the Organisation for Economic Co-operation and Development, a club of developed large economy countries, can also be near a third to half of others who are in similar developmental categories. What does it mean for China to be a quarter per person as wealthy compared to the fully developed world and almost half as rich as the near developed world?

Per person, economics is a strange concept, but one that helps illustrate how income or growth is not the same as development. Would the average individual actually be wealthy in a country with extensive poverty and no education but, due to oil exports, a high GDP per capita? Why consider that to be equal to a country with the same GDP per capita, but high life expectancy, nearly no poverty, and universal education? Which is better?

The point is not a theoretical one but goes to the heart of current discussions of development. Growth is a part of it but not all. Wealth cannot simply be aggregated, but instead is dependent upon its effect on the population broadly. Always consider the importance of how things are measured when evaluating a ranking. In most cases, but not all, high economic size per capita means high levels of human development. But that does not necessarily mean the two are causally related.

Development

Most of the world today is very similar in life expectancy. Developed or developing nations are nearly the same, even with wide ranges of differing incomes. China is an example of a developing country that has a life expectancy of seventy-six years for those children lucky enough to be born within the last five years. Should this have been 1950, it would have been only forty-three. In other words, in indirect terms, what the Chinese have gained during the previous seventy years is thirty-three years of life. Think of all that can be accomplished in an almost double lifetime! In 1950, Argentina had a life expectancy of sixty-two, with the highest of the developed world at between sixty-seven and sixty-nine, in the cases of France, the United States, and the United Kingdom. Now in 2020, the United States is at seventy-eight, France at eighty-five, and the United Kingdom at eighty-one. Argentina, however, is at seventy-six. Convergence is getting closer for the most crucial variable of them all, life span. The differences between rich and poor are becoming minimized using this variable as our evaluator. Now all someone should gain by being an American versus Chinese is two years more of life whereas in the 1950s it would have been twenty years. That's a dramatic change, but what is equally important is that a country that is many times richer in GDP per capita creates only a handful of years more existence. Human development seems cheaper than economic growth.[3]

Globalization

So, what then is globalization? For some, it has a strongly negative connotation that implies the rampant use of natural resources or even the disregard of human rights. To others, it is the sum outcome of the post–World War II order that includes the enumeration of human rights and their codification in multinational treaties and the universality of liberties, including property rights. It is also the influence of global corporations or the aftereffects of proxy wars during the Cold War. Globalization is the interconnectedness of individuals and groups across borders facilitated by regional and global organizations, technology, trade patterns, and cross-border cooperative engagement, and it has important consequences for development. States must choose to be part of the system, against it, or a genuinely autarchic state cut off from the international community.

However, normative values can cloud attitudes, which can affect policies, certainly pertaining to perceptions of globalization. Even in a text devoted to the importance of empirical testing, the names of areas and issues affect the measurement of perception: first world, third world, developing, or developed. Although sometimes unjustified by specific measurements of income, life, and opportunity, these classifications lead to a belief in superiority and thus tensions as the world is more interconnected through globalization. The first world, for example, originally was not some measurement of development but a set of Western nations victorious after World War II: most democracies and reasonably wealthy. The second world was not necessarily less prosperous or developed but communist; hence, the first world includes Western democracies, the second world is communist, and the third world is everyone else. Over the years, this designation became synonymous with the degree of economic success even if it denotes political policy or the class hierarchy states themselves adhered too. Over time, alternative terminology was created by the World Bank dividing states between developed, developing, and less developed. Yet, these normative groupings remain and impact perceptions. Even under the new designations, some developing countries are mostly the same in human development as developed states, although not quite at the same level of GDP per capita. The terminology changes perceptions with common stereotypes of the third world versus first world based upon wording, not necessarily actual populations' differences.

THEORIES OF DEVELOPMENT AND MEASUREMENTS

Economics dominates the empirical social sciences, and in economics, growth theory is enjoying a resurgence in recent years. Macroeconomic approaches have come to dictate discussions of economic growth. The following are two classic examples.[4]

Marxism

Conceived as a unified theory of governance and economics, Marxism attempts to pull all aspects of human society into a measurable framework with the policy of material reallocation based upon empirical evaluations, principally concerned with social delineation of class. It assumes that labor is the only essential component of production. The policy recommendation is to redistribute wealth, measured by labor per unit, and then sustain that via continued redistribution.

Hypothesis—Reallocating labor will increase economic growth.

Measurement—Labor. Marxists assumed that labor is equal and typically measured it in hours to produce a good. They did not take into account skill gaps, organizational efficiency, or innovation. Hours to produce a good is often the primary measurement.

Test—Labor measured by hour was used in policies of redistribution and enforced equality. The assumption was that growth would be sustained as the workforce would have continued access to the fruits of their labor and hence the ability to maintain that production. The end was a failure. Innovation cannot be dictated, work per hour is a nearly useless measurement of total gain, and enforced equality undermines creativity as it does not allow for novelty.

The Solow Model

Considered the founding of classical growth theory and thereby most development policies in the second half of the twentieth century, the theory focuses on the creation of a unified series of policy prescriptions. It attempts to measure concepts, such as not only labor but also capital, which means that growth is the outcome of the interaction of those two variables.

Hypothesis—Economic growth is the outcome of change in labor (L) and/or capital (K). Either increasing in total amount or in productivity is sufficient for growth to occur.

Measurements—A wide range of variables from foreign direct investment, total investment, interest rate changes, female participation in the workforce, total participation in the workforce, rates of return of investment, the productivity of labor, and so on.

Test—The original testing of this theory generally reflected expectations given short-run time horizons. The limitation was that it did not have a means for measuring changes created by technological progress and the creation of new industries. The later neoclassical growth theory took the Solow foundation and added measurements of technology or innovation as a means to capture paradigm shifts, such as moving from an agriculturally focused economy to an industrial.[5] Short-term forecasts continue to be reasonable, and Solow remains a basis of that study.

The Importance of Politics

The greatest challenge to economic theories, as well as the reason behind their failure, is overlooking politics. Labor, capital, technology, and innovation are impacted by how a society is politically crafted, manipulated, and sustained. Integrating both economics and political reality is the key to unlocking development, and unfortunately absent in most twentieth-century development policies. Integrating the two leads to more nuanced, applicable, and complete conceptions of development theory:

- Economic development (measured by GDP) is often associated with human development (such as life expectancy, declines in mortality, or other associated benefits, such as education or clean water), but they are not necessarily parallel.

- Globalization is the connection between populations. It can be caused or enhanced by geographical access to trade routes, political linkages with global or regional hegemons, and, most important, the choices of the domestic regime to allow for international connections.

- All things are never equal, and although policy can be generalized, the specifics of the era (now vs. the nineteenth century or the Cold War) changes the outcomes of those policies. The details of the country itself are also critical. The age of the population, access to resources or transportation, and geography are all variables that need evaluation but may not be able to be changed.

- Markets are dynamic. What was once valuable may no longer be, and a constant need to change is a requirement for the sustainability of an economy, even without a clear understanding of what could be the future for the population.

DOES ECONOMIC GROWTH CREATE HUMAN DEVELOPMENT?

The classic argument in economics is that those with little can grow faster than those with much. It is simple math! If you have a single dollar and then double it, that is an incredible percentage growth of 100 percent: an extraordinary accomplishment mathematically. If you have a hundred dollars and earn a single additional dollar, that is only 1 percent growth, but in terms of actual earnings, it is equal. Scale that idea, generalize it, and move it to states. Poorer countries, given the same overall conditions, should grow faster as a percentage and hence should also attract more investor interest and then be able to converge, or move toward, the development of their more economically successful cousins. Their richer cousins, due to past successes, will thereby grow slower as a percentage due to scale and complexity. In a small number of cases in East Asia, this seemed to be the case. The rise of Japan, South Korea, Taiwan, and later China all have similar characteristics. However, throughout many parts of Africa, this claim does not seem to hold.

Dependency Theory

In earlier chapters, we looked at the effects of trade and how international institutions are created to perpetuate the policies of the more powerful states. Let us consider those intermingled when it comes to national development and globalization.[6] Classical development strategies span a range of industrialization policies from an emphasis on economic dependence to more neoliberal concepts, namely, *The Washington Consensus*.[7] From a dependency theory perspective, poor states may become trapped as underdeveloped as rich states exploit them for natural and agricultural resources. With no industry, development remains elusive, and agricultural or resource producers will always be "dependent" on the industrial world for modern technology. Therefore, the goal of an economy is not economic growth alone, but the types of goods produced. Specifically, states that produce industrial goods are more likely to be developed than those producing agricultural goods or natural resources. Interrelated with these industrialization concepts are essential questions about how independent countries should be from former colonial masters. Are you a genuinely independent country if you sell only to those that controlled you under colonialism and import all technologically advanced goods from the same? However, many states that used political coercion to try to escape this situation ended up in failed investments and financial collapse. The most extreme versions are communist countries suffering the consequences of planned industrialization and state ownership of production.

The Washington Consensus
The Washington Consensus is a prescription of ten policy recommendations that became standardized in the late 1980s and 1990s as what countries should do to economically innovate and transition away from communism.[8] Fiscal discipline, privatization, and property rights became part of how the United States sought to standardize how economies should grow. For this reason, many critics describe the consensus as a coercive policy of a hegemonic power. Smaller countries were strongly encouraged to accept these policies to be part of the American economic order. Democracy was assumed to also be necessary even without clear empirical evidence of effectiveness. Variations of this type of fiscal discipline are proscribed and used to this day by the International Monetary Fund and World Bank, such as the requirements given when taking a loan. Both are reinforcing an economic orthodoxy created by the United States.[9]

Both the consensus and dependency had and still have influence, but now, as economic growth moves from only a question of economics to that of politics, more complex issues of why these policies fail or see success need to be linked to the importance of the political. Does the political system, with all this nuance and intricacies, gain legitimacy and power if policy actors create economic success? Or do the people worry about other noneconomic issues? Perhaps the state is even weakened by economic growth and thereby seeks to avoid sudden changes in wealth. Policies cannot be universally generalized without an acceptance that the political system is more than just regime type (dictatorships or democracy) but the capacity of the state, the effectiveness of the policies' implementation, and the demands of the people.

A Holistic Approach Emphasizing Domestic and International Hierarchy

Economic growth, development, and globalization are a complex network of influences, choices, and outcomes. You cannot study one without understanding the others, but each is a concept that traditionally has been investigated singularly. To this end, more modern development practices and recommendations focus on markets more generally, advanced by governmental investments in infrastructure, social safety nets, stability, and legitimate legal systems. These recommendations are the following:

1. States must have access to international markets where they can sell goods, engage labor, or pursue opportunities for economic development, including access to foreign direct investment.
2. States must protect the property rights of individuals, defended by a legitimate and effective judicial system.
3. The political system is peaceful and stable, even if not directly democratic. The state must have the capacity to implement policies.

All three components of development that help to create growth are dependent on the mechanics of national competition, the degree of free trade, and political power.

First, access to a market is not guaranteed. Dominant powers usually are not only military but also economic. Control over the market is a crucial part of influence be it domestic or international. Tariffs (taxes on imports), regulations, and restrictions can all limit access to those with political ties and hence not distribute success to those who are better on price or quality. From the medieval era, requirements to pay to enter a market, such as salt taxes, road taxes, monopolies, corporate forced breakups, and trade wars, influence who can sell what and at what price. Political differences can reduce or even end opportunities.

During the Cold War, trade was not a given, but the outcome of the choices of domestic politics to be capitalist or communist and whether you resided in an irrelevant or useful geographic area. These conditions created the possibility of sanctions and restrictions on trade between competing blocs. These policies, if inflicted by the United States, undermined access to international markets and the global financial system, including both aid and foreign direct investment. This very first step into the worldwide market is a hurdle composed of difficult decisions and significant barriers to entry. Trade is a useful incentive, or even weapon, in the arsenal of a hegemon. The first choice of a developing nation is to accept the policy preferences of the international actor who has perpetuated open trade at the global level. Fairness, efficiency, and development are all secondary to that first choice.

Nations in a critical geographical location or with coveted resources can be far harsher in their domestic politics, as the United States will be more likely to ignore domestic illiberal transgressions, whereas those without such privileges need to be more consistent with international liberal norms. For example, if a state is trading a complicated item or service dependent on a highly educated population, the state is nearly required to be a free and fair democracy. But if the state is selling goods that use unskilled labor or are agricultural, it will need to have some limited protections and law but could be more oppressive than most liberal democracies. If the state is only selling natural resources, such as oil, it can pretty much do whatever it wants with no real pressures to change its domestic politics.[10] Think about the countries that were changed and those that were not during the Arab Spring. More developed advanced countries, such as Tunisia and Egypt, had movements that were lengthier and, in Tunisia's case, successful. Less sophisticated countries that were largely agrarian, such as Jordan, did not experience the same degree of dissent, although they grant their population a moderate degree of civil liberties. However, strong dictatorships, such as Saudi Arabia, that rely on oil exports both do not experience significant unrest and remain strongly oppressive. Free trade itself is fragile and is never entirely open. It is the accumulation of differing policies relative to the dominant actor in combination with economic context.

Second, property rights are the foundation of capital, and capital can be a powerful influencer. Depending on the physical size of the state in question, the importance of the domestic market can far outweigh the global. Economic freedom, at its core, is the concept that people can own, use, and rely upon the outcome of their work. How does one invest in the future without a reasonable expectation of gaining from that investment? Countries cannot create geography, natural resources, or in many cases, the politics of other nations, but they can control domestic institutions, legal systems, and structures.

As any quick look at twentieth-century history would illustrate, this concept of ownership leading to development was vehemently opposed by not just communists but decades of theoretical thought. Often, this debate over the degree to which governments should interfere in property rights is driven as a question of income inequality. Does the government cause impoverishment? Does it cause the concentration of wealth? Consider the modern investor in the United States. What is the most common attribute? Already being rich. What then is the policy recommendation to a newly developed country? Have rich people to invest? What causes this, and is it even an issue?

Income inequality is not the direct outcome of neoliberalism but often of government influence on risk to reward. Heavy investment requires the development of a capital structure, which takes time to accumulate resources to grow an economy. Furthermore, failure in investment is less critical when you still have other resources, particularly when developed countries will bail out the wealthiest investors. Concentration is also a generational effect and seen in nearly all societies with the exception of those who have undergone dramatic economic changes, such as violent war. It does have political effects that are still to be determined but are important to future research agendas.

Last is the stability of the political system. This is not a question of regime type but of consistency and capacity. Peaceful access to markets, even in situations of corruption or authoritarianism, such as Singapore, are more productive than those in which rapid changes in policy are the expectation. Business and growth are both dependent on long-run stability. Corruption is a cost but one that can be simply a part of the cost of doing business. Rapid, unexpected changes are not.

Problems associated with domestic politics are the current issue de jure of economics research with a host of development agencies and organizations fixated on trying to measure political variables:

something that political science has been doing for decades. A reason for the discrepancy is politics itself. The World Bank, with a multitude of measurements of corruption, was, by charter, not allowed to use the domestic politics of a country in its development strategies. If dictatorship, communism, or democracy were beneficial to development, it would be part of the plan, but that became politically loaded because of the Cold War ideological conflict. Although these are regime types, the restriction affected everything else. To talk about the effectiveness of the political system was a step too far. To remain in some degree of neutrality, the World Bank had to ignore the obvious: domestic politics matter. Hence, there developed an emphasis on "accountability" or "corruption" that are both rough attempts at measuring politics but ones that can, in turn, ignore the ideology of the political system. In so doing, international institutions could say that it was not necessarily an issue of regime type, just corruption of the current rules. Hence, the overwhelming amount of aid was allocated to physical capital infrastructure (buildings, bridges, electrical systems) and not to things such as education.

Suggesting that the whole of international aid is a failure, or highly problematic, is a common argument.[11] If it is an issue of GDP per capita growth, then it is a failure. For others, such as health or vaccinations, it is a success. Growth is elusive, but distributed medical advancements are not. Again, measurements matter to the question of success. Has post-1945 foreign aid been a failure if it has not been shown to create economic growth but has been shown to nearly eradicate a long list of diseases and increase human life?

Consistency and implementation are the two most essential parts of domestic politics and the lynchpin of development policy. How does one create a stable government? One that may have issues but is consistent that does not radically change its attitudes and thereby allows for the time needed for investments to grow. How do you create consistency in new countries that sometimes do not have some historical legitimacy but are instead created by chance? Many current borders in the developing world are little more than the outcome of forgotten negotiations decades ago by foreign empires. Increasingly aid is moving towards these goals by changing the older Cold War requirements of ignoring regime type and now taking the domestic political context and reliability of that regime into account when distributing the increasingly scarce resources of international aid.

The Consequences of Change and Globalization
Rapid change in technology and preferences can have a significant impact. Consider the problems of exporting. Perhaps you are exporting a product that is very valuable, but due to technological change or shifting preferences suddenly is no longer relevant. What next? Sugar, once the foundation of international commerce and central to the machinations of major power politics, now no more than an afterthought. Nutmeg, coffee, tea, and silks are goods that created the funds necessary to have international influence. These markets fueled the political expansion of, in these cases, European empires. This is the primary causal variable behind long-cycle theory: key economic activities that drive not just politics but also the dominance of a global power. What then does a former center of global trade do when its product loses its luster and alternative products become available?

Just think about the expansion of coffee production from East Africa to nearly all corners of the world. Supply increases far beyond the advance of demand and hence, due to the wonders of the market-reduced price profits diminish. This is why the island of Hispaniola, on which the nations of Haiti and the Dominican Republic inhabit, is no longer one of the most critical economic places on earth, whereas, if this were the sixteenth and seventeenth centuries, it would be the nexus of European empires in the New World. Trade leads to new production and, with it, new locations of importance or the birth of countries that can influence the world while others decline. However, within Hispaniola you see the consequences of different domestic political paths—Haiti has been plagued by ineffective governments, conflict, intervention by major powers, and state intervention in the economy. The Dominican Republic, on the same island with many of the same contextual conditions at its outset, has managed their domestic and international political circumstances differently, leading to superior economic circumstances.

POINTS TO CONSIDER AND THE FUTURE

Economic growth since the mid-nineteenth century was principally concentrated in the Western European powers. Then, it expanded to the United States, later Japan, and only recently China. Each is a story of domestic politics, including the capacity of the state, policy choice, technological development, markets, stability, and a little luck, usually in the form of geography. The United States, as we know it, does not exist without the sugar trade. A trade that it does not produce or sell but that fuels European colonial expansion. The independence of Haiti undermines the French Empire in North America by cutting off its financing, causing the Louisiana Purchase and the expansion of the American state.

Economic growth is only one policy politically, but it allows for the financing of others. Mistakes in choices of industrialization, production, and markets are all critical to future political concerns throughout a society with so much of domestic choice seemingly given to non-economic development-oriented ideas. It could be institutionalized racism, which undermines labor markets and excludes members from the labor force. It could be elitism, which concentrates wealth and undermines merit. Or it could be political tyranny by central authorities and loyalists using coercion to protect their resources. Regimes regularly take policy actions that have a negative economic impact decades into the future, even after decades of success. Economic growth and human development are affected by policies, both those made domestically and internationally.

DISCUSSION QUESTIONS

1. What policies would undercut current globalization trends? Would they need to be implemented by individual nations or a collective group? Could a regional or the international hegemon make a unitary decision?
2. Is GDP per capita growth more or less important than increases in life expectancy? Which would you rather support as a policy goal?
3. Marxism as an economic model failed, but its popularity lasted far beyond its effectiveness. Why? What brings people to consider it as an economic model after so many decades of failure?

KEY TERMS

autarchic

capital

dependency theory

globalization

Human Development Index

income inequality

privatization

Washington Consensus

FURTHER READING

Modelski, George, Tessaleno Devezas, and William R. Thompson, eds. 2008. *Globalization as Evolutionary Process: Modeling Global Change.* New York: Routledge

Romer, Paul M. 1990. "Endogenous Technological Change." *Journal of Political Economy* 98, no. 5:S71–S102.

Stiglitz, Josef E. 2003. *Globalization and Its Discontents.* New York: W. W. Norton.

10

Contemporary Regional Orders in the American Imperium

★ ★ ★

COMPARATIVE REGIONALISM

To examine variation in order and the consequences of hierarchy on stability and cooperation in international politics, in this chapter, we focus on comparing existing regional orders in the international system. In the examination of both international conflict and cooperation, we often focus our attention on the system at large. But, by focusing on regional spaces, we can accomplish two goals. First, we can zoom in on the interactions of states that are most important to one another: the politics of their immediate neighborhoods. Second, regions vary dramatically in their levels of stability, institutionalization, and economic development, as well as the extent to which they possess hierarchies and how they are engaged by the United States. Regions, then, operate as laboratories for different forms of order that we can examine comparatively.

We label this methodological approach to examining regions *comparative regionalism*.[1] This approach acknowledges that politics in regional spaces operate differently. Much of international relations theory extends from the European legal traditions in the nineteenth century and thus may be biased toward European conventions. By comparing regional spaces outside of Europe, we may further refine what causal relationships might be universal traits of states in regions versus what may be an artifact of only the European context.

From a policy standpoint, treating regions as laboratories means they offer cases where we can examine what policies are effective in managing issues and facilitating order, and what policies fail, similar to how states within the United States are treated in the federalism literature.[2] In federalism, states are laboratories for laws where the successful filter up to the national level. We can think of regions similarly, where the successful norms and practices in a region may filter up to the international level. What works in a region may provide effective policy strategies for the United States as a system leader.

American Foreign Policy and Regional Identification

Before we can examine how regions vary in their politics, given their hierarchical arrangements, we must first specify what a region is and what regions exist. We outline one way of measuring and identifying regions in chapter 8 by states' ability to reach and engage one another. In this chapter, we focus on how two highly institutionalized regions, Europe and sub-Saharan Africa, have evolved differently given their relative hierarchy. This variation in hierarchy has clear implications for institutional effectiveness, trading behaviors, and development. We can then juxtapose this comparison against a region such as South America, which has made some significant strides in integration and development, although not yet at European levels. But first, what are the policy implications of thinking about regions as analytically derived spaces constructed by the actions of states? By focusing on the relevant region, we can focus on the relevant hierarchy and then determine how variation in hierarchy across regions affects their politics. This analytical approach then can inform policymaking by guiding decisions on expectations of conflictual geographic spaces and threats to economic and security interests. By examining spaces contingent on the interaction and reach of their members, regions are capable of change and variation.

Thinking about how regions change allows for policy development that adjusts for shifting preferences among regional actors. From the perspective of the dominant power, this not only allows for the development of foreign policies specially adapted to the context of the states within a region but also allows them to anticipate future events that may alter the status quo.

Misleading definitions of regional space can likewise lead to inappropriate foreign policy choices. If we examine the U.S. Defense Department's command designations, some troubling incoherence becomes quickly manifest. North and South America are divided, with the division crossing between Mexico and the Central

American states. Recent events in the migratory crisis, which is a security issue for states throughout the Americas, spread across a geographic space divorced in the command areas of responsibility. On the other hand, all of Africa, except Egypt, is in its own command, making it the largest in territorial size. Although there are some shared security linkages between the Maghreb and the Middle East, there are few or none between southern Africa and the Sahara. Egypt, along with Central Asia, is included in the Middle East, which also includes Pakistan but not Turkey, who has recently reengaged the space in the wake of the Syrian Civil War. Finally, the remaining countries are grouped into Europe and East Asia. Although logistics and strategy drive the Defense Department's Areas of Responsibility, the bureaucratic division created can have important consequences for policymaking. If a "command area" is actually four or more unique regions, such as Africa, how might treating them as one massive entity result in policy mistakes? Likewise, does drawing a bureaucratic line between two spaces create a propensity to ignore how security issues might be interconnected between them?

Alternatively, we can look at the U.S. State Department's regional designations, which are very different and have their own questionable characteristics. Like the Defense Department, it is logistically derived according to diplomatic concerns and historical inertia. Once again, Africa, south of the Maghreb and Egypt, is treated as a single, monolithic region without nuance, making it also the largest in territorial size. However, the State Department treats the Middle East very differently. Unlike the Defense Department, it lumps Afghanistan and Pakistan with India. From a diplomatic perspective, this makes more sense, as the three countries are more heavily engaged with one another than they are with other neighbors, although often conflictual. Once again, however, Turkey is not included in the Middle East despite its recent strategic reengagement with the Arab south. Russia, along with Central Asia and the European states on its western border are lumped together, apart from Europe. Finally, the Western Hemisphere is one singular entity. How then do these divisions affect the way we think about the international system? More important, what are the implications of the differences between State and Defense Department definitions for how policy is created? Might it result in dissonance between the two departments in advising the president on appropriate actions to take when confronted with a crisis?

Regions Evolve

A significant problem facing both the State and Defense Department definitions, as well as others that are often referenced such as those used by the World Bank, the United Nations, and the Correlates of War Data, is that their regional designations are all fixed. We even see this problem in international relations scholarship. Regions do not change over time, either with pivotal events or responding to the shifting behavior of states. Failure to capture changing behaviors can result in oversights. We have, for example, mentioned Turkey twice now as a state whose recent behavior is increasingly less engaged with Europe and more with the Middle East in response to the cataclysmic events of the Syrian Civil War. The engagement of Turkey in the Middle East adds to the preexisting complex power relationships among Iran, Saudi Arabia, and Israel. The consequence of that added complexity is clearly observed in the unfolding of the Syrian Civil War and recent diplomatic crises involving Qatar.

To account for how regional politics vary, we must also account for how regions themselves may evolve. When does Europe go from divided between East and West to a single space? When is Southeast Asia a relevant space, and when is it not? Finally, how might the actions of dominant powers affect the composition of regions, including those in which they are not a part? As we discuss in this chapter, the United States has had a foundational role in the development of the European Union. However, it may have played a more destabilizing role in a region where attempts at institutionalization have also been frequent and extensive: Africa.

HOW DO REGIONAL POLITICS VARY?

Regional politics vary by geographic, security, and historical context. Existing findings demonstrate that the hierarchy within regions has important consequences for their stability. Regions with regional powers have less conflict than those who lack regional powers. Regions with major powers presiding over their politics are even more stable than those with less powerful regionally limited states as regional powers.[3] But how then does this hierarchy impact the diplomatic and cooperative architecture that characterizes regional spaces? For starters, we know from the section on conflictual behavior that regional spaces are significantly affected in their conflict behaviors by the extant hierarchy over their geographic space. First, regions with the most powerful regional actors at parity are more likely to experience conflict. Second, regions where projecting outside dominant powers are at parity are also more likely to experience conflict. Finally, these conflicts are not only interstate but also internal, such as civil wars and secessionist movements, that may be proxy policies of interfering external actors.

Regional Formal Intergovernmental Organizations

Given the confusion or absence of hierarchy is related to conflict, how might its presence relate to the cooperative architecture we have discussed in the preceding chapters? Figure 10.1 illustrates the number of FIGOs by region from the FIGO data as of 2004. Immediately you will notice that two regions stand out as uniquely populated by these formal institutions typical of those discussed in chapter 7, "Sub-Saharan Africa and Europe." However, as we know from data from the conflict section, as well as the discussion of trade in chapter 8, Europe

Figure 10.1 Number of Formal Intergovernmental Organizations by Region

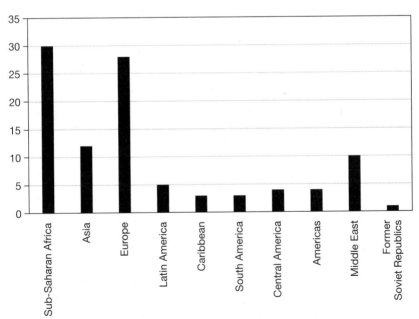

Source: Thomas J. Volgy, Elizabeth Fausett, Keith A Grant, and Stuart Rodgers, "Identifying Formal Intergovernmental Organizations," *Journal of Peace Research* 45, no. 6 (2008): 849–62, last accessed July 27, 2019. Data are available at www.u.arizona. edu/~volgy/data.html.

is much more stable and economically integrated than sub-Saharan Africa is. Despite similar levels of institutionalization, what accounts for this variation in cooperative and conflictual outcomes? Furthermore, there are less institutionalized regions, such as Latin America, that are remarkably stable as well. What accounts for this variation, and why might a relatively more institutionalized region such as the Middle East be such a hotbed of instability and conflict? Hegemonic stability theory would suggest that liberal variables, such as democracy, institutionalization, and trade, matter a great deal. However, they are only effective when supported by a dominant state that supports those values. Therefore, the treatment of the region by dominant major powers, as well as the presence and preferences of regional powers, may play an important role in explaining this variation. [4]

Why might hierarchy influence the effectiveness of cooperative architecture, like institutions and trade? The dominant power reinforces hierarchy in distant regions to preserve the stability of the status quo, and it may do so in different ways depending upon the region. The clearest example of this during the American period is engagement with Germany and Japan and their influence in their respective regions. Through these two states, the United States crafted security architecture, such as the North Atlantic Treaty Organization (NATO), as well as trading regimes that continue to act as conduits of American power. This, outside of previous colonial orders, is perhaps the first instance of a dominant power creating regional order among states beyond its own immediate geographic space.

American Engagement

In Europe, the United States crafted a complex order built around economic integration and collective security. To develop that order, it relied upon a West Germany that it had actively socialized and sought to craft in its image, with shared norms and values reinforced through the postwar denazification process. The United States relied upon this regional power to help provide further order to the region, even when states such as France or Italy would go through disruptive periods in their foreign policies. Asia and Europe are very different in their organization, owing to differences in American perception. Methodically outlining these distinctions, Peter Katzenstein suggests that Europe's institutionalization is derived from its high population of democracies, long history of organizational structure, and precedent of American security engagement during the war. [5] In Europe, the United States promoted a "Philadelphian" system of shared sovereignty between states that closely resembles its own founding. This system of over-lapping authority and institutions is in stark contrast to the "West-phalian" system, where the principle of state sovereignty underlies the behavior of states.[6] Institutions such as NATO and the European Union facilitate cooperation and information sharing among states, enabling high levels of effective cooperation. These overlapping institutions have grown and developed rapidly, as we outline in greater detail later, although not without their setbacks, such as Brexit.

In East Asia, however, this engagement has been more bilateral. Although there exists extensive economic integration, overarching institutions like those in Europe are relatively absent. Katzenstein identifies the roots of the variation in American engagement in the more direct, and less trusting, approach to Japanese reconstruction, wherein General Douglas MacArthur went so far as to take a direct role in drafting the Japanese constitution. Because divided Germany looked little like the Third Reich and politics on the continent were overshadowed by the Iron Curtain, Western European powers were able to overlook the evils of World War II in engaging multilater-ally with West Germany. The Japanese imperial legacy in East Asia, however, was more pervasive, creating greater wariness of Japanese leadership.

Further, in Europe the hierarchy was multipower in nature, shared across France, Britain, and Germany, also providing an impe-tus for the development of formal governing institutions with which regional powers would come to share sovereignty. However, only China would eventually confront Japanese power in East Asia. This alternative hierarchy led to the development of informal bilateral arrangements, usually economic, as the United States, too, would form bilateral security agreements throughout the region. These two cases provide some insights into how the United States exerts force and influence within regions and chooses to engage regional powers, but these regions are not unique. The United States has sought to develop similar regional orders in most places throughout the globe. Some, such as South America, have been steadily successful. Others, such as Africa, have been routinely ignored. And finally, in at least the case of the Middle East, American attempts at order creation and the reliance upon regional contenders, such as Israel and Saudi Arabia, have frequently destabilized the region. In the remainder of the chapter, we will examine the two extremes of American engage-ment and hierarchy to determine their relative impact: Europe and sub-Saharan Africa.

EXTENSIVE ORDER: THE EUROPEAN UNION

The development of European integration formally starts with the European Economic Community in 1958; however, the bedrock for this institutional experiment begins far earlier. Indeed, the idea was often broached following cataclysmic wars, such as the suggestion by Tsar Alexander after the Napoleonic Wars[7] and conflict between France and Prussia in the mid-nineteenth century.[8] However, it took the Marshall Plan by the United States to finally set in motion the integration process. The Marshall Plan, named after the World War II general and postwar secretary of state, was an ambitious aid package introduced in 1948 to Western European nations to both rebuild European economies as well as provide a bulwark against the attractiveness of communism. The distribution of these funds was carried out by the Organisation for European Economic Co-operation, which, as part of the funding package, worked to reduce economic barriers between participating states. The redevelopment funding by the United States provided the incentive for the European integration experiment to begin and set the trajectory for the development of the European Union.

As integration continued over the latter half of the twentieth century, additional European states joined the community. By the 1980s, signatories of the Schengen Agreement functionally dissolved the borders between them, which included all European community members except Ireland and the United Kingdom. As that process went into effect, the European Union was established immediately following the Cold War, which slowly expanded to include newly democratic states in Central and Eastern Europe. Rather than simply operating as a forum for information sharing and coordinating trade policy, the European Union established formal decision-making structures that were binding to members. Although it has undergone various revisions, the lawmaking structure begins with the European Commission, selected by the governments of member states, and the governments' leaders alongside the European Parliament, elected directly by citizens of the European Union, must approve all laws. The laws then passed by this body have, according to the terms of the treaty, the force of law in their member states, giving this unique supranational organization power most closely resembling that of a state of any international organization today.[9]

United States of Europe?

Given this legal and corresponding bureaucratic power, can we say that there is a United States of Europe? First, and foremost, the European Union lacks a security force. Because governments are territorial entities that have a monopoly of coercive force over their territory, the European Union cannot be considered a state. It relies upon the consent of member states to enforce its decisions. Recently, Hungarian prime minister Viktor Orbán has flaunted European prohibitions on restricting freedom of speech and the press within his country. Despite frequent warnings, he continues to operate outside EU rules. Instead of coercive punishment, the European Union more often relies on economic incentives (and potential economic punishments) to encourage the continued consent of its members, such as the use of aid packages and not-so-veiled economic threats to encourage budgetary and economic reform in Greece.

Although it lacks the direct means of coercion possessed by states, the tools at its disposal are uniquely powerful and well beyond those possessed by other international institutions. Perhaps most powerful is its monetary tool: the euro. Established in 1999, almost all European member states have adopted the currency, fully replacing their national currencies of the past. The economic consequences of going off the euro, replacing, reprinting, reminting, and transferring all accounts from euros back to a national currency, are enormous, no doubt outweighing any potential benefits. Beyond the currency itself, the standardized regulations that have progressively been instituted since the 1950s that ease the exchange of commerce between nations would also have to be reversed. These regulations are so extensive that even if a state is not on the euro, such as Britain, the logistics of leaving the European Union are daunting. As of the writing of this text, attempting to leave the European Union has been the undoing of two consecutive Conservative prime ministers in the United Kingdom.

European Security and Hierarchy

Not coincidentally, the United States controls the collective security arrangement that renders the development of a separate European Union security force unnecessary. Established before European integration, NATO provides security for the majority of EU member states, with those states who are not members, Austria, Ireland, and Sweden, essentially free-riding on NATO's security benefits. Although the United States was a strong driving force behind European economic integration, it has not been in areas of security integration, preferring to remain at the center of collective security decision-making.

Past rhetoric that suggested European integration, from Tsar Alexander to Winston Churchill,[10] failed to create powerful institutions that provide stability to the continent due to the absence of a dominating state able to encourage and promote the integration agenda. Beginning with the United States passage of the Marshall Plan, most states within Europe have increasingly integrated their economies, giving rise to a supranational institution with lawmaking power. The foundation of this effectiveness lies in American normative support dating back more than seventy years. The design of the institutions themselves, although essential to effective decision-making, cannot be solely given credit for the success of Europe.

What is interesting about Europe, however, is that although the United States has historically played a straightforward role in its politics, regionally it does not have a clearly defined hierarchy. Yes, as Katzenstein outlines, the United States did work through Germany extensively, particularly on economic issues. However, on security issues, it has always engaged more heavily with Britain and France. Of course, Russia is also present, and perhaps Europe's greatest challenges today are due to Russia not being integrated into its economic and security architecture in the 1990s as Margaret Thatcher recommended. But, even so, Europe appears somewhat *multipolar* between four potential competing powers. If we refer to chapter 3, it is this distribution of power that caused John Mearsheimer to expect a nuclear arms race to ensue on the continent following the Soviet Union's demise. However, at least three of those four powers have worked consistently to create order and stability, not compete over security. Is Europe an exception to the dangers of multipolarity? Indeed, in Lemke's analysis of regional hierarchies, he avoids analyzing Europe and North America because they contain global major powers with extra-regional reach. But, given the close proximate capabilities, why do the competing powers of Europe not engage in conflict as Lemke found to be the case in other regions?

The answer lies in the satisfaction with and engagement of the dominant major power that promotes the cooperative agenda in Europe. This agenda constrains leaders away from conflict into a "cooperative hegemony" that has pushed regional integration along,[11] and without the evolutionary process between the dominant power and satisfied regional actors, the prevalence of liberalism in Europe may not be the status quo we observe today. Challenges to that cooperative hegemony, however, are readily apparent as we look toward the future. First, the United States under the Trump administration has pursued a rhetoric of disinterest in European security. Second, Brexit threatens to remove one of the three cooperative powers from the integration arrangement. Third, Russia continues to be dissatisfied with the status quo and seeks to undermine its viability, pursing similar manipulation tactics in both national and European elections to those it used in the 2016 U.S. presidential election.

AFRICAN INSTITUTIONALIZATION

As many formal institutions populate Africa as Europe, and yet they are mostly unsuccessful at providing the same degree of integration and security as the European Union. Like Europe, many of the roughly thirty institutions in Africa are issue specific. For example, the African Intellectual Property Organization coordinates standards for patents and industrial-related logistical issues. Perhaps the closest organization to the geographic and issue area breadth of the European Union is the African Union. With membership including the entire continent, the African Union resembles in part the purpose of both the European Union and the United Nations. It seeks to both facilitate economic and political integration, like the European Union, and provide peacekeeping support to conflict-prone areas, like the United Nations.[12] The union has been successful in functioning as a discussion forum for African leaders, particularly in coordinating over security concerns. However, there has been little to no success in the type of economic integration that we observe in Europe, such as the reduction of trade barriers and economic development.[13]

Perhaps one reason for this failure is the incongruence between the African Union and the actual regions that exist within the African continent. If we review the evolution of regions in the Regions of Opportunity and Willingness Data, Europe is fragmented in the 1960s among three different spaces: a Western Europe, consistent with the developed Cold War architecture of NATO and the European Community; an Eastern Europe of Warsaw Pact states and Soviet allies; and a Scandinavia region. By the end of the Cold War, the only division remaining is between East and West, with a single European region stretching from Portugal to Russia by the 2000s.[14] This progression of regional expansion coincides with the development of the European Union itself, with the institution accurately representing the observed regional interests of constituent members and actively supported by most of the present regional powers. In Africa, however, there is never a singular African or sub-Saharan African region. With a diversity of economic and security interests, even excluding the northern littoral of the continent north of the Sahara, there are rarely fewer than three separate regions in the space. It is for this reason that the African Union has subdivided itself into eight different subunits in an attempt to develop smaller-scale integration.

American Disinterest

American foreign policy has not generated any attempt to promote greater integration in Africa as it had in Europe. The United States only created AFRICOM, the U.S. Command in Africa, as a separate strategic unit in the Defense Department in 2007. Unlike Europe, Africa has been, and perhaps continues to be, of relatively little strategic interest to the United States, labeled the "backwater of U.S. foreign policy."[15] The same support, including the material motivation of the Marshall Plan, never materialized for the African continent. Furthermore, also unlike Europe, the United States has been inconsistent in its engagement, pursuing sporadic interventionism without a clear foreign policy goal and destabilizing regional security and economies. The United States has concentrated a drone-based presence along the northern edge of the sub-Saharan space and engaged in occasional interventions that have frequently led to disaster, such as the Battle of Mogadishu in 1993 or the intervention in Libya following the overthrow of Moammar Gaddafi. In both cases, the United States withdrew, and these areas remain spaces of continued violent instability. Economic engagement by the United States through commercial integration and promotion of liberal norms that does not entail military intervention is relatively absent. As a result, in those spaces without a regional power, such as East Africa, politics looks like the chaos of the Middle East, which is also absent a dominant regional actor, with different parties vying for control rather than collaborating.

Internal and External Status Attribution

A key distinction between spaces such as East Africa and the Middle East compared to Europe is that the European powers are not only engaged by the United States cooperatively, but the European regional powers also receive the *status* of leadership from their constituent regional members.[16] As discussed in Part I, status is the attribution of leadership or authority from lesser states to regionally or globally dominant powers independent of capabilities, signifying acceptance of the status quo. In a region like the Middle East, there are many contenders with sufficient capabilities to be considered a regional power, but none possess status from the members of the region, leaving none able to create and enforce order. The closest thing to an order creator in the sub-Saharan context is South Africa, which has status in a small corner of the continent.[17] It has been successful in pursuing some economic integration, such as the creation of a customs and trade union, but only in a small part of the African continent. This again highlights the importance of the relevant region and its hierarchy. Regional economic order is relatively absent as you move farther north on the African continent, with attempts at regional integration, such as the West and Central African Franc, subject to dramatic corruption[18] and wrought with inflation as states were not also restricted by fiscal discipline requirements, as in the European Union.[19]

Looking ahead, as we observe attempts at order creation in Africa as the hierarchy and economic interests continue to evolve, it is worth noting that the Chinese have not neglected the continent. China has increased aid, acquired favorable trading relationships, and intensified its focus on resource extraction on the continent, and with that engagement comes a very different vision than the liberal order promoted by the United States.[20] As Africa continues to modernize and develop, it is likely to account for well over a majority of global population growth over the next century and therefore is expected to become a key area of influence for major powers. Whether that results in stability or conflict depends heavily on whether the United States pursues aggressive balancing and interventionist policies or instead builds the type of liberal order through free trade and collective security that characterized the development of Europe in the twentieth century.

ACTIVITY: DESIGNING REGIONAL RECIPES FOR PEACE

The purpose of this activity is to develop a recipe for a peaceful and stable region, defined in clear analytical terms, that abides by certain norms and rules operating through effective institutional structures. Keep in mind that "peace" does not necessarily mean the absence of conflict but instead includes the cooperative engagement discussed in chapters 7 through 9. This project can be done by breaking the classroom into groups for discussion and participation or as a multistep written project, allowing for the opportunity to work with and illustrate data of the student's choosing.

1. Begin with the region. Define regions according to observable and measurable criteria. When selecting those criteria, you must be sure that you are not defining regions by the very outcomes (trade, development, and institutions) that you seek to explain. The criteria should generally be applicable to all regions in the world while also variable across them.

   a. What are the rules about geography that restrict your regions? Do all states have to be contiguous? Can just water connect states to their region? How far?
   b. What are the merits of your regional designation?
   c. What are the potential pitfalls?
   d. If you have more than one criterion for determining a region, do they ever contradict one another? If so, how do you decide which is more important?
   e. Does it result in regional membership that is unexpected? Is that okay?
   f. How do regions vary over time according to your measure?

2. Of the regions created by your approach, select one to focus on for an analysis of regional order. Examine the level of hierarchy in the region, again, according to some measurable criteria. Next, carefully analyze the level of economic integration in the form of trade and investment as well as the institutional coverage in the region.

   a. We have discussed different ways a major or regional power may impact the behavior of other states. How is the behavior of states within your selected region affected by the regional power or powers, if there is one? If there is not one, how do potential contenders affect the behavior of fellow region members? What type of vision does the regional power or challenger have for the region?
   b. Do external major powers impact politics in the region? If so, who and how?
   c. Apply these hierarchical variables to the outcomes of economic integration and institutionalization in your region, developing a theory and hypotheses about their causal relationship. What are the independent variables? What are the dependent variables? If we were to test the relationship, how might we go about doing so?

3. Throughout the text, data are used as a means of illustrating possible causal relationships. Ideally, we would then statistically analyze those hypothesized causal relationships as is done in referenced

scholarly work, such as Lemke's *Regions of War and Peace* or Volgy et al.'s article "Conflict, Regions, and Regional Hierarchies."[21] For now, illustrate variables representing the causal relationship you discussed in point 2.c in a graph or table. The table or illustration should be simple yet compelling in depicting to the observer your proposed causal relationship. Now, compare that data for your selected region to another region you identified in step 1 where politics are quite a bit different. Interpret the relationship depicted by your graphical representation of the data, both within regions and across them.

DISCUSSION QUESTIONS

1. Can you imagine the development of a non-American order in regional spaces? How might it vary depending on who the next dominant power is?
2. What strategies can emerging African regional powers, such as Nigeria, Ethiopia, or South Africa, use to craft order and stability within their regional spaces?
3. The European order has historically been strongly supported by the United States. In the event of American decline or withdrawal, what strategies could the European Union and its constituent members pursue to maintain both extant economic and security architecture?

KEY TERMS

AFRICOM
comparative regionalism
contiguous
integration

Marshall Plan
Philadelphian system
Westphalian system

FURTHER READING

Hentz, James J. 2005. *South Africa and the Logic of Regional Cooperation.* Bloomington: Indiana University Press.
Katzenstein, Peter J. 2005. *A World of Regions: Asia and Europe in the American Imperium.* Ithaca, NY: Cornell University Press.
Lake, David A. 2006. "American Hegemony and the Future of East-West Relations." *International Studies Perspectives* 7, no. 1:23–30.

PART III

Key Issues Confronting the Twenty-First Century

★ ★ ★

IN THE FINAL SECTION OF THE BOOK, we examine the topics of deterrence and the democratic peace, how we might contextualize them in the current international hierarchy, and given that hierarchy is prone to change, what the future may hold. Deterrence and democratic peace represent the two theoretical ideas most akin to laws in international relations research. Two nuclear powers have never had a nuclear exchange. Two democracies have never gone to war.

In both cases, we are observing the absence of an event, not its occurrence, and although absence thus far is compelling, we must also recognize that the amount of time we have experienced to observe the effect of either nuclear weapons or democracy is limited to only a few decades. Hopefully their peaceful effects persist, but drawing on material from Parts I and II, we examine the international system in the present, and what lessons we may be able to learn from the last instance of a single state dominating the international system: the British Empire.

Drawing on each of these discussions, we conclude the text with a discussion of possible future trajectories for international politics, and how certain policies of the United States can promote, or hinder, the stability of the American order.

11

Deterrence and the Potential for Great-Power War

IN THE SHADOW OF THE MUSHROOM CLOUD

The core of deterrence theory is the development of policies expanding destructive military capabilities such that it reduces the likelihood of conflict. Nuclear weapons represent the zenith of that destructive force. Likewise, according to deterrence theory, a reliable nuclear arsenal should reduce the likelihood of conflict between similarly armed states to zero.

Traditionally, the primary concern was a conflict between the United States and the Soviet Union with their significant nuclear arsenals numbering in the thousands. However, the proliferation of these weapons has expanded to not only other major powers but also regional actors such as Pakistan, India, Israel, and North Korea. Some suggest that proliferation could bring about greater stability,[1] but how do we know?

Luckily, global wars between the most heavily armed states are infrequent, with none since the invention of nuclear weapons. Does this mean that nuclear weapons have made war irrelevant, or do nuclear weapons only exacerbate the dangers of a future major power war? We will evaluate deterrence through three theoretical lenses in this chapter: power transition, balance of power, and deterrence theories. Power transition theory surmises that wars are more likely at power parity; balance of power theory suggests the opposite, and deterrence theory considers how the use of threats by one party can prevent a challenge from another.

| BOX 11.1 | Hierarchy, Geography, and the Decision to Drop the Bomb |

One of the formative events that transitioned the United States and the Soviet Union from allies to rivals was the dropping of the atomic bombs on Hiroshima and Nagasaki in 1945. The conventional narrative justifying nuclear weapons' first and hitherto only use is that the only alternative would be a ground invasion of the Japanese home islands by the United States, which would cost the lives of hundreds of thousands of American servicemen.

Although likely true that a ground invasion would result in significant casualties, the political context unfolding around the Japanese islands between the United States and the Soviet Union sheds some additional light on the factors influencing the timing of Truman's decision and the Japanese surrender. Although the bomb certainly prevented the loss of American life in a hypothetical ground invasion, was it necessary to the outcome of the war? Why the rush to end the war in the summer of 1945? Why August 9? First, the United States was well positioned to continue the blockade and bombardment of Japan, making an invasion practically unnecessary. Before dropping the bomb on Hiroshima, the United States had engaged in extensive bombing of the Japanese home islands with conventional weapons that were far more devastating than either atomic explosion. Japan was ready to surrender but sought to preserve the emperor and other traditional institutions despite that devastation. What changed in early August? Notes from the Potsdam conference show that Stalin was amassing troops in Manchuria to attack Japan.[2] On August 9, the same day the bomb was dropped on Nagasaki, the Soviet Union declared war on the Japanese. Understanding the consequences of Soviet occupation, the Japanese surrendered.[3]

Given the importance of devastation to nuclear deterrence, was the bomb the sole or even primary reason for Japanese surrender? If not, was Truman misguided, or perhaps was he trying to send a message to the Soviet Union? First, the use of atomic weapons was billed as unnecessary to Japanese surrender by most top American military commanders. The U.S. Strategic Bombing Report conducted after the war stated that "in all probability prior to 1 November 1945, Japan would have surrendered even if the atomic bombs had not been dropped, even if Russia had not entered the war, and even if no invasion had been planned or contemplated."[4] What hastened both the Japanese decision to surrender and the American decision to use the bomb? The Soviets. By surrendering

BOX 11.1 | **Continued**

before the Soviet invasion, the Japanese left their fate in American rather than Soviet hands, leading to the development of one of the most important American bulwarks against Soviet expansion in East Asia in the crafting of a key American ally. The Americans may, in part, have sought to deter the Soviet Union through the use of a weapon it had and the Soviets did not. Although the complete reasons for the American use of the atomic bomb and Japan's surrender are likely a combination of many competing explanations, including tactical concerns over casualties, internal discontent in Japan, and the demonstration of nuclear capabilities, devastation, and deterrence are only part of the equation.

THEORIES AND MEASUREMENTS

In the following discussion, we outline the primary theoretical variations of deterrence with a summary of their causal process, a testable hypothesis, and variable measurements relevant to their analysis.

Classical Deterrence

War can be averted if the costs are so high as to render any benefit insufficient. The sheer destructiveness of war's costs maintains peace. This destructiveness itself thereby causes conflict to decrease.[5]

For classical deterrence, the primary hypothesis statement would be that as the costs of war increase, the probability of war decreases. Nuclear weapons, therefore, reach such a high point of cost that they are a *sufficient condition* to not observing war. Appropriate measures for this hypothesis would be the destructiveness of weapons produced and their ability or reliability in being delivered to their targets. To estimate the destructive costs of a possible war, measurements of potential population losses, industrial destruction, and even the elimination of infrastructure are critical parts of the investigation. The research question then is *how* much devastation is needed to have a viable threat, usually with the resolution being mutually assured destruction (MAD).

Perfect Deterrence

Game theory provides further insights into the classical deterrence model by building in perceptions, specifically of the credibility of the threat. The perception that a nuclear threat is not credible undermines stability because it adds the possibility that states may be mistaken in their perceptions, leading to disastrous choices. In other words, they do not *trust* the adversary to use the weapons they have available.[6]

For perfect deterrence, the relevant hypothesis is that the probability of conflict decreases if both a nuclear arsenal is sufficiently large *and* the threat of its retaliatory use is credible. In addition to the previous measures of weaponry and destructiveness, you would also need to measure trust, foreign policy consistency, or international reputation. Empirical studies of perfect deterrence focus on the probability of conflict and the absence of nuclear wars. Of course, it is challenging to study the probability of something that never happens, which is, in part, why many studies rely heavily on abstract game-theoretic models of deterrence logic as opposed to an empirical test that engages the hypothesis scientifically based upon observable events. This measurement limitation is controversial within the field with some suggesting that deterrence is not truly a theory but a strategy.[7]

Conditional Deterrence

Empirically moving from the fixation on nuclear weapons to conflict as a whole, conditional deterrence attempts to link evaluations of conflict suggested by power transition to the concept of peace via threat. The core of power transition is that a challenger state at or near parity that is also dissatisfied is the most common cause of significant conflicts. Added to this basic power transition logic is the total level of carnage capacity of nuclear weapons, and what level of grievance would be sufficient, if any, to cause a dissatisfied challenger or panicked declining dominant state to view the destructiveness of nuclear weapons as no longer outweighing the benefits of their use. Again, game theory is used to examine this question given the absence of empirical events, although empirics from past nonnuclear conflicts are also relevant.[8]

The main hypothesis of conditional deterrence is that as both parity and dissatisfaction of the challenger rise and information between actors declines, the probability of war increases.[9] Given this intersection of both system variables (parity), state preferences (dissatisfaction), and decision-making (information and credibility), this hypothesis is perhaps more complicated and thus challenging to demonstrate a causal connection.

In addition to previously mentioned measures relevant to other deterrence approaches, such as nuclear capacity and credibility, testing conditional deterrence requires broad measures of capabilities, regional alliances, and satisfaction. The conclusion of conditional deterrence from the power transition literature is that deterrence is unstable, or *imperfect*, even in situations with substantial potential losses. This does not necessarily mean that nuclear war is inevitable or even likely but merely that nuclear weapons are not a sufficient condition to observe peace between major powers. For states, capability losses contextually may erode credibility in times of crisis.

Within the last two hundred years, only sixteen conflicts are at a scale large enough to be classified as global.[10] Note that nearly all of them have been between belligerents with near-equal levels of power, and the consequence is hundreds of millions of casualties. Without nuclear weapons, these conflicts are already enormously destructive, supporting power transition theory's suggestion that most destructive conflicts are fought when countries are at or near parity. The insight, then, is that the dominant power has created a system for its benefit, which, in turn, creates reasons for dissatisfaction from the rising power and hence conflict. So why wait until parity to observe conflict? Because that is when a challenger thinks they can win. Think of a farcical but useful analogy. Would you want to fight a boxer that is the heavyweight champion of the world? It is unlikely that this would be a good idea, but what if you happened to be the second-best boxer in the world?

Maybe you can win, and if you do, you can change the system in your image. That is a pretty enormous benefit that might outweigh all kinds of possible devastating costs. The consequences of this type of choice, however, are millions of dead. When would a nation risk its cities, youth, and even future for the chance to change the international system? How much dissatisfaction is needed? Equally important, this assertion undermines the basic concept of balance of power, which suggests that if countries are equal, they will not fight because of the costs associated: that they would find peace due to the potential damage. The evaluation of wars historically suggests this is incorrect, although it retains its popularity with some scholars and policymakers, particularly in the context of deterrence, such as Kenneth Waltz suggesting the mass transfer of nuclear weapons to rival nations as a means to create peace.[11] However, just like the absence of nuclear wars presenting a challenge to deterrence approaches, conditional deterrence faces this same empirical problem, as well as the reality that cataclysmic wars forming the basis of the theory are rare and hence provide limited evidence.

EVALUATING THE DESTRUCTIVENESS
OF NUCLEAR WEAPONS

Weapons of mass destruction is something of a popular political catchphrase, playing a crucial role in the justification for the 2003 war in Iraq. The definition includes chemical, biological, and nuclear weapons, with the idea being that these are similar given their danger. However, chemical and biological weapons, although certainly destructive and horrific, do not have the casualty capacity needed to be in a higher classification along with the powerful nuclear weapons in existence. Both have significant limitations, including the direction of the wind or the process of infection. How exactly does one guarantee infecting hundreds of thousands of people or have them come in contact with a chemical? In both cases, why not drop an explosive device instead? These weapons are effective and reasonably cheap. Although both chemical and biological weapons have been used against civilian populations, including the use of chemical weapons in Ethiopia by the Italians or against the Kurds by Iraq, neither was more effective than a conventional bombing campaign in a contemporary interstate conflict.

The capacity for conventional warfare to enact extensive casualties is clear from the firebombing of Tokyo to the genocides in Rwanda. Chemical and biological weapons are rare because they are typically no more effective than conventional explosives, much less nuclear weapons that could destroy an entire city.

The higher casualty estimates for a great-power nuclear exchange are close to 80 percent of the total population.[12] Between the United States and the USSR or China, this would be more than every single person ever killed in conflict for more than two hundred years combined, all within less than a day: at the height of the Cold War, Secretary of Defense Robert McNamara estimated 60 percent of industrial capacity and 40 percent of the total population lost, assuming you could win the war.[13] Nuclear weapons offer carnage at a level unseen by humanity.

Geographic realities are equally crucial to evaluating a weapon's destructive force. Think, for example, about the nations that might be impacted by the development of an Iranian nuclear arsenal. States such as Egypt, Israel, and Saudi Arabia all have high levels of population density in a small series of urban areas. The Egyptian population is nearly entirely within a very short distance from the Nile. A river in which one of the largest dams in the world is situated. A dam that is easily targetable, which would, in turn, cause a wave of water resulting in an enormous death toll and long-term destructive consequences. Israel is small with dense, concentrated cities. Saudi Arabia not only is larger in geography but also has high levels of population density in individual cities. All of these would be different from Iran because it is far larger, as well as mountainous with lower population density, both of which would reduce losses and require a greater number of strikes. The number of weapons needed to devastate countries given geography and terrain is not equal.

THE LOGISTICS OF RETALIATION

Practically how do we prevent war? There are typically two suggested policy prescriptions: deterrence and disarmament. Deterrence is peace through fear. Nuclear weapons are an investment to counterstrike should an opponent attack. You destroy my population, and I will devastate yours. The alternative, disarmament, is the concept of ridding the world of these weapons, built upon the core principle of the classic 1980s' movie *WarGames*.[14] The best strategy is not to play the game. We will briefly discuss the latter toward the end of the chapter, but deterrence requires massive retaliation (MR), the mechanics of which are costly. How many weapons are necessary? At what point does a dispute become deterred from further escalation? Are there differences in types of nuclear powers? What happens when technology changes?

The individual costs of these decisions should not be ignored. Consider the United States. Now eighteen years into the longest war in American history, more than 5,000 American soldiers and others are dead. In no circumstance until the Trump administration has the possibility of using nuclear weapons been suggested. Whether Iraq, Afghanistan, Syria, or Iran, in each case erasing an entire society is the potential policy outcome of a decision of the president of the United States: a choice they alone can make without restriction. What level of civilian casualties, both foreign and domestic, do we accept in war? At what point does war become genocide?

Each step in a conflict involves the acceptance of potential nuclear exchange and the resulting deaths to civilians and soldiers on both sides, from Korea to the War on Terror. What is an acceptable ratio between enemy combatants eliminated to potential civilian casualties? What should the ratio be? Hundreds? Thousands? Even millions? Currently, most estimates are that with the expansion of conventional technology, such as night sights, drones, and other air forces, the expectations are in the hundreds of combined civilian and enemy deaths per American lost. The United States could have won the Vietnam War, saving thousands of American lives, but that would mean the death of as many civilians as people who were killed during the Holocaust. So, what is the acceptable price of victory?

Second Strike and the Nuclear Triad

Classical deterrence thought that, like balance of power theory, the creation of nuclear weapons would create a peacefully stagnant global system. The potential devastation would be so vast that the global powers would not engage in a battle against another so long as the nuclear-armed states understood the consequences of MR. The state understands that if a conventional war starts, escalates, and looks to produce significant losses, the other nuclear-armed state will end the war via the deployment of its arsenal through massive destruction and near-complete annihilation of the other country. In sum, to decrease, maybe even eliminate conflict, first limit the reasons for grievance but, more important, possess a massive nuclear retaliation. This was an exciting proposal first created by Brodie in 1946, a year in which World War III seemed almost inevitable.[15] His suggestion was that the scale of nuclear weapons would sustain the peace by undermining the advantages the USSR had in conventional forces. The state with the ability to massively retaliate at the time, the United States, would not need to use conventional war because of its vast capacity for carnage and could afford to be lenient and altruistic to its rivals. They would only be rivals in policy, not security.

The eventual consequence of this policy was MAD: production of weapons in enough numbers that both sides would suffer near-total devastation and the investment in just enough missiles to survive a first strike (or sneak attack) and still devastate the challenger. With the rise of the USSR as a nuclear state by the mid-1950s (with China soon after), MAD became the global norm with both Cold War rivals building and deploying nearly ten thousand warheads at the height of the conflict. The production seemed to take a life of its own and far outweigh the requirements for MAD. Neither country has tens of thousands of targets with the reality of a MAD war being mushroom clouds over already-irradiated wastelands: a comical yet terrifying concept of "I am safer than you because I can kill you dozens of times over" costing trillions of dollars. The idea suggests that it is the building of not just intercontinental missiles that is necessary but also weapons that can be deployed across multiple systems, such as submarines, silos, planes, and even artillery pieces. This threat from multiple avenues is known as the nuclear triad: weapons deployed by sea, land, and air. The danger is that as expectations of counter-strikes and first strikes increase, so, too, does the expansion in weapon production, design, and implementation. However, this also increases the likelihood of their use, even by accident.

When the expected use of nuclear weapons would be authorized continues to be of critical importance in the modern international system. Once MAD is reached, the assumption is that the scale causes a conventional war between nuclear adversaries to be unthinkable. Because of the lack of reliability in evaluating when weapons can be used, it acts as a means of sustaining peace between two rival great powers (the United States and the Soviet Union). Both engaged in proxy wars but never in an overt, violent confrontation between military forces.

Evolving Technology

Technological development can undermine these assumptions. Anti-ballistic missiles (ABMs) hold that possibility. A continuous worry is that investment in this capacity (in the trillions since the 1980s) would undermine MAD by limiting the ability of a rival state to trust that its deterrent was still functional. That, in turn, causes an arms race with the possibility of misunderstanding intentions or attempting preemption. New advancements in weapons with variable yield warheads are similar. Just think of how awful an idea that would be from a MAD perspective: building weapons that you can set to destroy small towns, medium cities, and large metropolitan areas, weapons that would look very similar to standard conventional warheads when in flight. What would be the point of that advancement but to increase the ability of it to be used in more situations when at its core nukes are supposedly defensive? That is a paradox. Increasing the technological variance means you are allowing future leaders to make a decision, most likely by using the smallest yield, which is something that rival states could not evaluate until detonation. Who would watch a warhead explode in a nuclear detonation and not strike back with an extraordinary counterstrike? Who would wait for the weapon to detonate in the first place? MAD suggests that all nuclear attacks are countered to the fullest without the need to wait for the evaluation of initial damage. Nuclear war is considered equivalent to an apocalypse, not merely small steps of escalation where you survive a first strike.

Alternatively, even a much smaller stock of weapons can create protection. Except for a series of skirmishes between India and Pakistan, no nuclear-armed nation has ever been significantly attacked by another state after the public deployment of these weapons. Publicity is essential. Adversaries need to know you have the ability, not just assume. Israel, in the 1973 war against Egypt, is a dangerous example: quietly nuclear-armed and waiting to see the outcome of a conventional war to determine if MR is the only remaining option.

NUCLEAR POWERS AND POTENTIAL

Many states could produce a nuclear weapon. Some would undoubtedly have an easier time than others. It could be the fruits of decades of investment or months, but the simple truth is nothing is secret about how to build the weapons themselves. The technology has existed since 1945. It cannot be kept secret. The greater challenge is the creation of effective delivery systems, but as we now know, these, too, are achievable by developing nations that are not major powers. More important, most nuclear technology has some level of dual usage, be it energy, medical, or research based. Nuclear technology helps cure cancer and find cavities, all the while keeping lights on throughout the world. What policies might keep the benefits open to humanity and limit the possibility of devastation?

Although the ability to produce a single weapon may be broad, the costs of producing large, deliverable nuclear arsenals are not. According to the latest publicly released information from the United States and Russia, each has around 1,400 nuclear weapons actively deployed through missile, aircraft, and submarine delivery systems.[16] However, both have thousands more in stockpile, with latest British estimates suggesting a total of around 17,000 warheads in the world today.[17] While sources suggest that other nuclear powers France, Israel, China, Britain, India, and Pakistan have but a few hundred each, such arsenals are more than sufficient to obliterate the urban areas of any potential opponent.[18] The reason for the disparity between the two Cold War powers and the others lies in both the costs and the traditional logic of deterrence: during the Cold War, the two sides believed a balance of such weapons was necessary to prevent an aggressive act by the other. In delivery, both powers, along with some others, can deliver weapons by air, land, and sea, ensuring a second-strike capability. In other words, if you can spread out the delivery of weapons, it would make them hard to liquidate in a first strike, though maintaining this diversity of these systems is expensive.

The arsenals for many of the non–Cold War rivals exhibit considerations of costs and the ability to inflict damage. For deterrence theories, it is an open question as to what level of nuclear capacity is necessary to, in fact, deter. Is it the destruction of everything, such as the United States and the Soviet Union, or is it the devastation of every major city? The ability to deploy weapons is an important point, as well. Are your security threats global or regional? If they are regional, then lower-ranged tactical missiles or planes are a more likely investment. If global, then large-scale missile production and probably submarine production would be necessary. In 2019, the era of the strategic bomber is over. To this end, France, the United Kingdom, the United States, Russia, and China all possess global deployment capacity with very long-range missiles. Pakistan, India, Israel, and North Korea have regional capacity because local politics are their more immediate security concerns.

Only nine countries are currently armed out of the hundred or so that have the capacity to build. Against the logic of deterrence, more states have given up their weapons in the past thirty years then have created them. The post-USSR nations of Ukraine, Kazakhstan, and Belarus, along with South Africa, had actual weapons. Furthermore, Argentina, Brazil, Iraq, Libya, South Korea, and Taiwan all had working programs for production that they eventually terminated.

These developments are seen as successes of the Nuclear Nonproliferation Treaty. In it, only the original nuclear-armed states, the United States, Russia, China, France, and Britain, are permitted to possess them, with each promising not to give them to others. The non-nuclear-armed signatories then have access to a plethora of technology investment in return. Those that do not, such as North Korea, Pakistan, and India, face restrictions in what they can buy internationally. These restrictions are so detailed that chips regularly used in consumer computers or cell phones may be considered illegal for export to those nations without an explicit waiver. Perhaps this key piece of architecture through access to the American commercial order is a pervasive tool in preventing further proliferation?

CONDITIONAL AND REGIONAL DETERRENCE

The core of deterrence is the attempt to create a policy that allows for stability. MR and mutually assured destruction may have been sensible in the global competition between the United States and the Soviet Union, but does the same logic suggest stability in the regional nuclear contests that have since developed? At the regional level, countries with small arsenals may be more likely to use them during what begins as a conventional war against a contiguous neighbor. Think of North Korea. Currently, it has, at best, a few warheads with low yield and may not even be able to reliably strike the mainland of the United States. Within its region, however, these few weapons could be incredibly destructive. Should it be attacked by a combined South Korean and American conventional force, it would undoubtedly lose that war. But it would also have the ability to destroy Seoul and the majority of the conventional forces arrayed against it. This is a local MR. It is not mutually assured destruction with the United States, but within the immediate area, nuclear weapons undermine the usefulness of a conventional attack. Similar situations exist with Pakistan, India, and Israel.

This conventional war to nuclear war is what worries scholars the most about the concepts of deterrence when applied to these regional, contiguous actors. Although deterrence is supposed to prevent conventional war, and perhaps has in the preceding cases, the line between the choice to lose a conventional war and a nuclear exchange is not clearly defined. It relies upon the discernment of what is acceptable during violent conflict. How great of a conventional threat makes a nuclear response likely? A battlefield loss or an invasion of an army?

What if only one side possesses nuclear weapons? A nuclear-armed nation facing a nonnuclear foe while losing a conventional war seems expected to use its arsenal. This means that classical deterrence may be unstable in theses regional contexts particularly given the complexities of territorial rivals in shatterbelts absent clear hierarchy, as discussed in chapter 4. Consider Israel, which is a nuclear-armed state in a region with at least two conventional nonnuclear contenders but has also repeatedly fought wars against its territorial neighbors. Why lose a war when you possess a certain tool of victory? Some evidence suggests that this scenario almost happened in 1973 during the war with Egypt. Nuclear weapons deployed, with possible use, during a conventional war was nearly a reality. Deterrence hopes for the creation of stability, but these more local, regional cases seem not to reflect the stability of the relied-upon Cold War case.

NONSTATE ACTORS AND THE REDUCTION OF NUCLEAR STOCKPILES

The genuinely terrifying possibility is of nonstate actors acquiring nuclear weapons, specifically terrorists. Mutually assured destruction assumes that modern states are in control of their arsenals, and an attack would be from a known adversary. Furthermore, both sides are considered sufficiently rational as to not intentionally take actions that would undoubtedly threaten their own survival. A suicide motivated terrorist would, however, be undeterrable.

Small groups hiding in a cave? Why would they care about counterstrike capacity? Does an attacked country then destroy the civilian population of another because a nonstate actor happens to be within their borders? How do you deter actors that have limited interest in the long-term ramifications of their actions?

Such a scenario, given the difficulty of not just acquiring but arming and detonating a nuclear weapon, is perhaps unlikely, but it is not impossible. One approach that could prevent this possibility is the reduction of nuclear weapons for anyone to use. However, classic deterrence theory suggests that reducing total nuclear arms will have the undesired effect of actually *increasing* their usage. The expectation for states is that as total weapons go down, so, too, does the threshold of acceptable losses. "Winning" a nuclear war becomes discussed. Our previous national examples are a useful illustration. Suppose you are an unknown regional adversary of the United Kingdom, which does not exist but let us use it as a supposition, and NATO is no longer in effect. The majority of UK deterrence is in four total submarines, with only one deployed at any one time, and all four stationed at a single naval base in Scotland. A paranoid, organized adversary could wait for an opportunity to hit both the deployed submarine and unprepared other submarines with a first strike, eliminating the whole of British deterrence. Now, of course, this ignores the existence of allies and who this adversary may be, but it is an illustration of the challenges created by moving arsenals toward zero. The first strike, winning, and acceptable losses all become more convincing to policy actors with conflict expected to increase.

So how then might we create nuclear disarmament? Trust is an important component of a global-zero policy: trust that Russia, the

United States, and others will not only reduce their arms but eliminate them. Note that this policy goal, although perhaps a noble end, ignores existing empirical evidence. It trusts, despite the proliferation that has already occurred, that no other nation would then violate that commitment, even rogue states such as North Korea. Furthermore, it assumes the credibility of the international system as a whole is high enough to support, sanction, and impose high costs on any who might break such a treaty. Do you believe that the international system is sufficiently credible? Credible to stop genocides? Credible to prevent the use of chemical weapons? Credible in the obligation to assist refugees? Who is credible and reliable is likely related to satisfaction, as satisfied states have little reason to proliferate.

This chapter presents some empirically motivated questions and concerns about deterrence as a theory that hopefully will not be tested by a future nuclear exchange. While the possibility of use under conditional deterrence is perhaps not the dominant view in international relations scholarship, the empirical challenges confronting deterrence theory and the potential destruction if deterrence fails make questions and challenges to the traditional deterrence logic worthy of consideration.

DISCUSSION QUESTIONS

1. What observable evidence would be necessary to confirm the superiority of perfect deterrence over conditional deterrence and vice versa?
2. What changes in technology could alter the effect of nuclear weapons on the decision of states to engage in conflict?
3. According to deterrence logic, if you possess nuclear weapons, are you better served by publicizing you have them or keeping it secret?
4. If deterrence prevents even conventional conflict between two nuclear-armed states, why not give all states nuclear weapons?
5. Was it necessary for the United States to drop the bombs on Hiroshima and Nagasaki?

KEY TERMS

credibility
massive retaliation
mutually assured destruction

nuclear triad
second strike
sufficient condition

FURTHER READINGS

Jervis, Robert. 1982–1983. "Deterrence and Perception." *International Security* 7, no. 3:3–30.

Kugler, Jacek, and Frank Zagare. 1990. "The Long-Term Stability of Deterrence." *International Interactions* 15, no. 3/4:255–78.

Quackenbush, Stephen. L. 2011. *Understanding General Deterrence: Theory and Application*. New York: Palgrave Macmillan.

12

Liberalism and the Democratic Peace

DEMOCRACY, HUMAN RIGHTS, AND POLICY

So far, we have discussed how the United States and its dominant power predecessors crafted a stable order through institutions, free trade, and collective security since the end of World War II. Furthermore, we have discussed how that stability can break down when hierarchy in the international system is challenged, not just internationally in wars between states but also destabilizing regimes internally leading to civil wars. In this chapter, we discuss how the United States has sought to create order globally through liberalism to not only create stability but also foster regimes that have shared values and preferences.

The Spread of Democracy

As figure 12.1 illustrates, the proportion of "free" liberal democracies in the international system has spread rapidly over time. However, that spread has seemingly peaked since the late 1990s in the mid-40 percent range.[1] What global variables may be responsible for its rise? Why has that spread seemed to stagnate over the last decade? What can we expect to happen in the future as the United States declines relative to China, India, or some other new dominant power? Although wealth, resolution of borders, education, and a number of other domestic variables are important causes of stable democracy, in this chapter, we focus on the systemic side of democracy's spread as we did in the chapter on intrastate conflict. In so doing, we will rely

Figure 12.1 Proportion of Free States

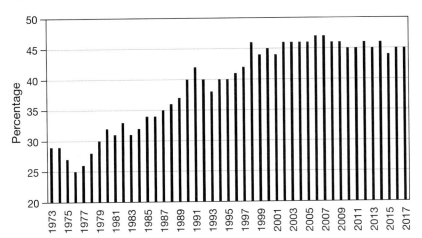

Source: Freedom House, "Freedom in the World Data and Resources" (2019), last accessed June 18, 2019, https://freedomhouse.org/content/freedom-world-data-and-resources.

on long-cycle and hegemonic stability theories to discuss the relationship between democracy and the current status quo in the international system and how that relationship may change.

The evolving location of liberal democracy also is concentrated in specific geographic areas, predominantly in Europe and North America. Not coincidentally, this same geographic space coincides with American collective security arrangements, primary trading partners, institutional development (particularly the European Union), and relative peace. Figure 12.2 shows the overlap between democratic institutions domestically and the presence of these economic and security related forms of American order.[2] The key takeaway from this diagram is that most of the almost fifty countries shown are members of more than one group, overlapping membership in institutions, trade centrality with the United States, and democracy. The outliers who are members of but one aspect of the liberal order, such as Turkey's membership in the North Atlantic Treaty Organization (NATO) or China's trading relationship with the United States, are quite rare. In other words, the liberal traits illustrated in figure 12.2 are not randomly distributed across the globe but concentrated among a core group of states under American influence that we might call, to borrow from Peter Katzenstein, the American Imperium.[3] Furthermore, that concentration is also heavily geographic, dominating Europe

Figure 12.2 The Liberal Order

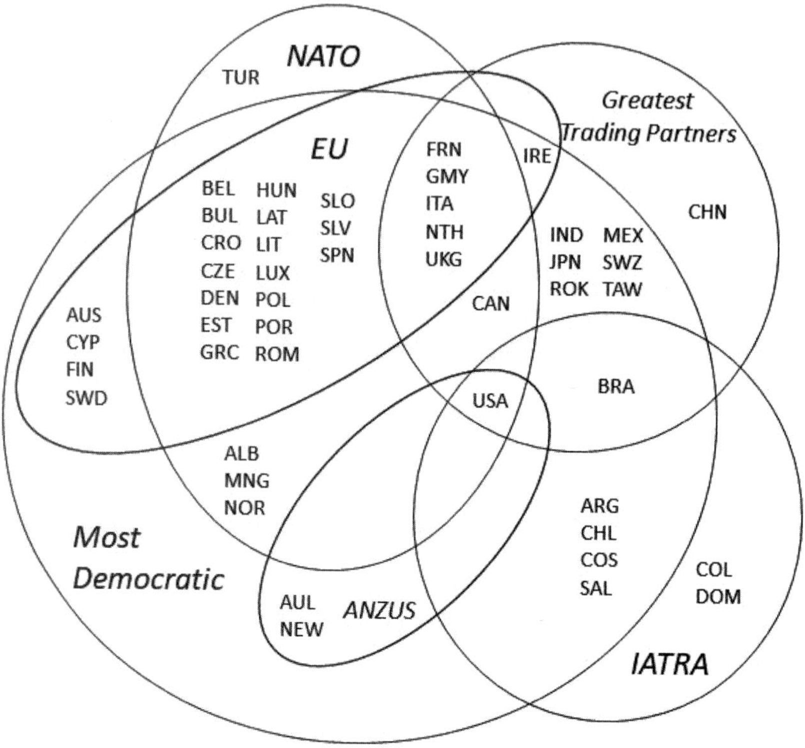

NATO

TUR

EU

Greatest
Trading Partners

BEL HUN SLO
BUL LAT SLV
CRO LIT SPN
CZE LUX
DEN POL
EST POR
GRC ROM

FRN
GMY
ITA
NTH
UKG

IRE

CHN

IND MEX
JPN SWZ
ROK TAW

CAN

AUS
CYP
FIN
SWD

USA

BRA

ALB
MNG
NOR

ARG
CHL
COS
SAL

COL
DOM

Most
Democratic

AUL ANZUS
NEW

IATRA

Note: Country abbreviations are those used by the Correlates of War Project (www.correlatesofwar.org). NATO: North Atlantic Treaty Organization. EU: European Union. ANZUS: Australia, New Zealand, United States Security Treaty. IATRA: Inter-American Treaty of Reciprocal Assistance.

with extensions in the Americas and Asia-Pacific. Completely absent are any states in the Middle East or Africa.

Taken together, these institutions, in their provision of security and promotion of trade, alongside the presence of democracy, represent what is called the "Kantian Tripod" of the *liberal* peace: institutions, commerce, and democracy. If we were to remove the United States from figure 12.2, the lynchpin that seems to hold the overlapping groups together, would the organization between institutions, commerce, and democracy hang together without the presence of such an uncontested dominant state? Does it depend on which state replaces the United States as the primarily dominant state in international politics? What, then, is the fate of democracy when America declines?

WHAT IS LIBERALISM?

Although we have focused extensively in this text on the differences between hierarchical approaches and neorealism, notably balance of power, liberal approaches that focus on the effect of domestic politics and preferences on external behaviors have offered some of the most conclusive findings in empirical international relations. Foremost among those findings is that democracies do not go to war with other democracies. Unlike neorealism, with its philosophical origins in a negative view of anarchy and human nature, liberalism has a relatively more positive perspective. Building on the philosophical tradition of John Locke, John Stuart Mill, and Immanuel Kant, liberalism in international relations proposes that anarchy does not cause actors to only fear for their survival. Instead, most of the time, actors are concerned with improving their position and thus can voluntarily engage in behaviors with others that benefit both parties. In other words, unless in a position of immediate security threat, actors are likely to be more concerned about absolute gains for themselves than acquiring relative gains over others.

Individual Liberty

The origin of these approaches lies in the assumption of individuals possessing "inalienable rights," as phrased by the Declaration of Independence and therefore not being subject in their beliefs, speech, or persons to any other person or government. Given that all individuals possess these rights, governments, as John Locke characterized them, exist only to protect individuals from one another and to peacefully resolve disputes as an unbiased third party. Beyond these two cases, individuals are fully capable of interacting without a "leviathan" state guiding or deterring their actions and choose to engage one another peacefully out of their self-interest. In the United States today, we might refer to this perspective as "libertarian" though it continues to be labeled "liberal" in most other modern political systems. Indeed, one of the earliest empirical examinations of the relationship between liberalism and peace referred to the finding as the libertarian peace, wherein states that valued individual liberty, both political and economic, were found to be peaceful in their interactions with one another.[4] Whether we refer to it as the democratic, the libertarian, the capitalist, or the liberal peace, all of these perspectives refer similarly to a type of political system that emphasizes the freedom of individuals. Each conceptualization of the cause of that peace tends to overlap with others. For example, most democracies value individual liberties and free commerce.

Incorporating Future Time Preferences

Liberal researchers, then, seek to identify what domestic conditions within and between countries make that ability to cooperate more likely. Speculating about what might lead states to refrain from conflict, Immanuel Kant suggested that three variables would so constrain states in their relations that war would become obsolete. The first is democracy, as the voting public would not endure the costs of war. The second is international law, which will facilitate cooperation between actors. And, last, states that engage in a high amount of economic interdependence will not wish to jeopardize the gains from trade by going to war.[5]

Some have suggested that this view is "idealistic"[6] and often in introductory course work, liberalism is portrayed, in contrast to realism, as viewing that human nature is good. This, however, is not necessarily the case. Liberalism requires only that human beings be self-interested and have preferences for their well-being that extend beyond the immediate present. For neorealism, you only worry about survival in the present because if you do not survive the present, the future is irrelevant. Liberalism suggests that because people all prefer to live better in the future, they benefit through cooperation with one another, making the use of physical force an ineffective long-term way of getting what they want.

Robert Axelrod shows that by incorporating time, actors begin to cooperate to get what they want, while those who fail to cooperate get left behind.[7] As with the simulation at the end of chapter 6, thinking about the long run versus only thinking about the short run has important consequences for the way actors behave. To win in the short run, exploiting others and violating their trust may be a more effective way to acquire gains. But if you repeat the activity over and over, actors will be less likely to cooperate with an untrustworthy person in the future and look elsewhere for cooperative partners. Furthermore, those actors cooperating will, through gains from trade and exchange, grow over time, while the untrustworthy actor will get left behind. In the real world, we might look to the example of North Korea or other states left out of the liberal free-trade regime managed by the United States. North Korea before the Korean War was far more populous and prosperous than the South. South Korea, however, was integrated into the liberal commercial order after the war, engaging in trade and cooperation with Japan, Taiwan, and the West. North Korea, however, became increasingly isolated. After a few decades of this isolation, South Korea has dramatically surpassed its North Korean neighbor in wealth and technological advancement.

Liberalism is a *progressive* theory of international politics. Advocates of liberal approaches suggest that over time, global politics will become progressively more liberal, as liberal values and institutions spread across the globe. This spread is considered inevitable as liberal practices such as democracy and capitalism are more effective at securing the liberty and well-being of individuals than the alternatives. The rapid spread of liberalism since the demise of the Axis powers seems to corroborate this perspective, particularly with liberalism's triumph after the collapse of the Soviet Union in the 1990s. However, liberalism's rapid rise coincides with the rise and dominance of the United States, a country founded on Lockean liberal principles that has routinely, albeit often imperfectly, sought to spread and support those principles in other parts of the globe. The spread of free trade and capitalism, the founding of liberal international organizations such as the European Union, and support for the stability and spread of democracy have all been central components to American foreign policy since the Marshall Plan enshrined their significance to the reconstruction of Europe. When the United States is no longer at the pinnacle of the international system, will these values that it has sought to spread and preserve continue their rise, or will the system the United States created decline along with it?

THE DEMOCRATIC PEACE

The democratic peace is what Jack Levy described as "as close as anything we have to an empirical law in international relations."[8] It is the empirical finding that democracies do not go to war. Although the statistical relationship is firm, the explanations for this empirical relationship are up for some debate. Some may argue that their shared norms of peacefully resolving domestic disputes grant democracies the ability to understand one another in resolving disputes internationally in a way that is not possible with their autocratic counterparts.[9] Others suggest that democratic institutions are open in their preferences, as leaders make statements to the public that bind their policies, forcing them to follow through on their promises. This makes it easier for democracies to know one another's intentions and preferences and avoid disagreements and misinformation erupting into war.[10] Finally, some suggest that democracies will only go to war if the potential benefits are significant enough to benefit the entire population.[11] The likelihood of two democracies both believing that they can win a conflict, and that the benefits of winning would be worthwhile to the people, is unlikely.

Not Unilaterally Peaceful

Researchers from across theoretical perspectives generally accept the existence of the empirical finding that democracies do not go to war. Initially, however, the democratic peace was not about the relationship between democracies going to war with one another, but instead that democracies would be overall more peaceful in general. In Kant's original discussion, democracies would not go to war, either against democracies or nondemocracies, simply because the public would not support it. In a democracy, the public calls the shots, and the public may not want to endure the costs of war. However, this original idea failed to generate empirical support, with countries such as the United States routinely engaging in conflicts throughout the globe, and conflict initiation often generates substantial increases in public support rather than declines.

Alternatives: Capitalism, Territory, or American Order

Not everyone agrees that democratic governance is the reason for the peace we observe between these states. Some suggest that democracy does not cause the empirical relationship between democratic institutions and peace but that something else related to democracy's presence does. In other words, democracy can be said to be *spurious* to the finding of peace between states. Some of these alternatives look toward other liberal variables, such as similar preferences guided by capitalism or ideology,[12] or something unrelated, such as territory. Perhaps democracies develop after a state has resolved its territorial borders. The resolution of territorial disputes, therefore, is the cause of peace, as states no longer have a reason for conflict with their neighbors, and separately the cause for the development of democracy.[13]

Like deterrence, the empirical democratic peace overlaps entirely with a period of American dominance, and whether the finding is likely to hold when the United States eventually declines remains to be seen.[14] Indeed, it would appear that the democratic peace seems to not only be limited to the American system but also is geographically concentrated in Europe and North America.[15]

FINDINGS OF THE DEMOCRATIC PEACE

Independent of the theoretical explanation, the empirical finding of the democratic peace literature is simply that democracies do not go to war. However, as discussed in chapter 2, our results can be heavily dependent on our measurements. How to accurately define and measure are both debatable and have important consequences for what our statistical outcomes tell us about this causal relationship.

Measuring Democracy

First, there are a variety of approaches to defining and measuring democracy. Historically, the most common approach is the Polity IV data set,[16] mentioned in chapter 2. This data set focuses its measurement on the degree to which democracies possess constrained executives: constrained by elections, legislatures, and other checks on unilateral decision-making. In his foundational article testing the democratic peace, Bill Dixon said that the greater the value of the lowest democracy score between two states, the less likely a dispute between the two states would become violent. When two states both had above a 6 on a scale of 10 to −10 of democracy in the Polity data (where a 10 is the most democratic), violent conflict did not occur. The two democracies, unlike dyads involving at least one nondemocratic state, were able to prevent their disagreement from escalating to war.

Usually, democracy implies the state is also *liberal*, meaning the government, whatever its form, protects the rights of its citizens from abuse, both from other individuals and itself. The presence of elections in a state may be related to liberal governance but not definite: a majoritarian democracy, for example, may vote to oppress the physical or political rights of a minority no matter the extent of executive constraints. One example that is often used by those critical of the democratic peace is the War of 1812 between the United States and Great Britain. However, in the United States, while there was an executive balanced by a legislature and independent judiciary, a large portion of the population was enslaved, and women were unable to vote. In Britain, likewise, suffrage was also restricted to men, and although Parliament constrained the power of the monarch, representation was often bound to landed titles, with seats representing financial interests rather than a representative election of a constituency. Given these evident, antiliberal qualities, although the form of government may be relatively restrained rather than a personalistic dictatorship, such as contemporary France, we still would not characterize either state as a liberal democracy.

There are, however, alternative measures of democracy that seek to more fully capture the importance of liberalism. The Freedom in the World index from Freedom House attempts to evaluate the degree of freedom experienced by the average individual within a state, both personal and political. Generally, the two data sets align fairly closely, given the clustering of states identified as democratic by Polity and "free" by Freedom House. However, there are some outliers between the two approaches, and those differences may be significant enough to result in different statistical findings in explaining outcomes. We could also explore the "V-Dem" data, which focuses neither just on executive constraints nor just on individual liberties but on a more comprehensive series of indicators that include both.[17] Once again, as we discussed in chapter 2, different measures of the same concept, such as democracy, can have significant consequences for whether our hypotheses are proved correct or false.[18]

It matters how we define both democracy and war.[19] Most analyses restrict the measurement of democracy very narrowly. At minimum, they use a shared value of "6" or greater on the Polity IV scale. However, others define it as higher, some restricting the pool of tested states to just a "10" on the polity scale. The higher we place the threshold, the more states, and therefore more conflicts we exclude. Are the United States and Britain democracies in 1812? What about Israel and Lebanon in their recent conflicts?

Measuring War

Second, we must define what qualifies as a war, and precisely who is at war with whom. The definition of war is usually a conflict with more than 1,000 battle deaths between two states. However, once we identify a war, how do we determine who is involved? For example, World War II includes many belligerents, some of which are considered democracies. Finland, a democracy, was supported by Nazi Germany in opposition to its territorial neighbor and historical aggressor, the Soviet Union. Thus, Finland, a democracy, was technically at war with the democracies of the United Kingdom and the United States. Furthermore, in one instance, the United Kingdom and Finland did engage in violent combat, with an assault on Finnish naval forces during the war. However, the number of casualties were limited to the double digits.[20] Although technically at war and having engaged in a violent exchange, the absence of greater levels of hostility between

Finland and the democratic members of the Allies often lead to the exemption of the observation.

Restrictions on what constitutes "war" between two states are important for determining what types of conflict are excluded as well. Most scholars use the traditional threshold of 1,000 battlefield deaths, as discussed in chapter 3, but many conflicts involve violent uses of force below that threshold. For example, a series of disputes over fishing rights in the North Atlantic between Iceland and the United Kingdom took place between 1958 and 1976, involving shots fired and a couple of casualties, including one death. However, given the traditional democratic peace hypothesis that democratic disputes merely do not *escalate* to war, the observation does not disprove the theory. These examples demonstrate that, regardless of theoretical veracity, careful operationalization choices have important consequences for proving or disproving our theories.

THE HIERARCHICAL ALTERNATIVE

From a long-cycle perspective, the international system's norms and regimes are part of the current American leadership wave, with its dominance maintained by a cycle of economic superiority in critical economic sectors.[21] In the twenty-first century, we might consider this to be the development of technology, such as the Internet. Democracy and liberalism, then, are part of that American economic cycle, as liberal political principles are integrated into capitalist economics by definition. As economic complexity continues to develop and new sectors in other countries take a more primary role in global politics, long-cycle theory suggests that this economic change may coincide with a point at which a war of global leadership is likely. If America ceases to be the global leader, the liberal norms at the foundation of the American order may cease as well, with clear consequences for the democratic peace.[22] Alternatively, perhaps democracy as an institution may prevent the next conflict over global order?[23]

The American Order Is Liberal

Rather than think of democracy as a variable that magically appeared without explanation within states and expanded rapidly over the past few decades, it might be prudent to consider instead the coincidental timing and location of democracy's spread.[24] The last transition in global order occurs in 1945 with the total defeat of the Axis powers at the hands of the Allies and the subsequent rapid creation of political order through agreements and institutions by the United States, much to the opposition of the Soviet Union. As illustrated in figure 12.2, the United States set about crafting a web of overlapping liberal order: an order that reflects its domestic politics and therefore, its foreign policy preferences. In designing this order, the United States sought (1) to alter the status quo in its favor and (2) to recraft the operation of the international system away from the realpolitik, Westphalian world of the nineteenth-century European system into one that is remarkably more *American*.

As the sole, relatively unscathed victor at the end of World War II, the United States could remake the world in its image using both carrots and sticks.[25] Unlike the conclusion of World War I, when the American government was opposed to foreign engagement and the devastation from the war was more geographically limited, the United States sought to avoid a third round of devastation after World War II by remaking the world in its image. In defeated Germany and Japan, it sought to restructure societies, both politically and socially, as satellite versions of American liberalism. In Japan's case, the restructuring was so direct that General MacArthur and his staff wrote the constitution, still in effect today. Within this liberal order, or the American Imperium, politics between states are not quite so anarchic after all. In the exercise of order creation, the United States extrapolates outward from itself its values and institutional methods of dealing with the logistics of day-to-day politics. Foundational to the American system is the idea of constrained governments as opposed to the Hobbesian ideal of an all-powerful sovereign state. Therefore, the idea of sovereignty, where a leviathan state is supreme over the entirety of its territory with no external constraints, is anathema. From a Lockean perspective, governments are the object that requires restrictions, not individuals. Therefore, the idea of states sharing sovereignty with international institutions or restricted in their ability to infringe upon the commercial or social activities of individuals is wholly consistent with American order.

Benefits of Democracy to American Foreign Policy

Within all democracies, disagreements are resolved through normalized processes. As such, in the creation of global order, American democracy promotes institutionalized means of resolving political issues peacefully. This goal is manifest in the creation of new democracies, such as Germany and Japan, as well as the structure of international institutions that mirror democratic processes, evident in the design of the United Nations, the World Trade Organization and the European Union. Indeed, that democracies resolve disputes peacefully internally and thereby do so externally with one another is the core of the empirical examination of the democratic peace done by Bill Dixon twenty-five years ago. But, rather than that being the cause of the democratic peace unto itself, focusing on hierarchy and hegemony in world politics suggests that the proliferation of democracy since the 1970s, and its effectiveness in preventing disagreements from erupting into war, is caused originally by the establishment of a global order by the United States. Casting aside the realpolitik values of the eighteenth and nineteen centuries, the United States expects its constituent members to conduct themselves according to democratic, institutional, and liberal norms.

THE LIBERAL FUTURE OF THE INTERNATIONAL SYSTEM

The international system has been described as Westphalian, referring to the treaty that ended the Thirty Years' War in 1648. That treaty established that sovereignty, or each ruler determining the politics of their state, would govern international politics, while the international system would operate absent one dominating interstate force, such as the papacy. However, some have argued that the American liberal order is changing, or at least amending, this system of global sovereignty, creating a network of overlapping responsibilities shared between states and different types of organizations.[26] Beginning with Wilson's Fourteen Points following the conclusion of World War I, the United States has sought to impose certain liberal principles on the international system. After World War II, the Marshall Plan, the Dollar Reserve System, and the creation of international institutions, such as the United Nations and the World Bank, institutionalized this process.

A Philadelphian System

The Westphalian order became slowly transformed into a Philadelphian system,[27] where the liberal principles that governed the United States were extended into the international system, promoting values where sovereignty was no longer exclusive to a territorial state. There are limitations on what a state can do internally, whether in harming its people or governing its commercial affairs. These limitations are not always imposed, with the United States frequently turning a blind eye to brutal dictators that promote American economic or security interests. But, by and large, the supremacy of sovereignty as an ordering principle has slowly eroded. Think, for a moment, about the European Union. Before World War II, Europe was a collection of powerful sovereign states. Germany's internal affairs, no matter how barbaric, were its own. It took an aggressive foreign policy of territorial conquest, violating the sovereignty of others, before the other major powers would take action. Only by violating the sovereignty of Poland did Germany finally cross an unforgivable line. Perhaps learning lessons not only from the past but also from pressure by the United States to cooperate, the European Cold and Steel community was formed to promote economic ties between France and West Germany. That cooperative arrangement slowly evolved into one where states would surrender to an international organization one of the most powerful tools of economic sovereignty, their national currency.

Creating Satisfaction

The question then remains, what do we expect to happen to this international system? The decline of the last dominant power may hold some lessons; lessons that are important not to repeat, given that violent transition. As liberal and global leadership theories suggest, the most powerful state may transform the rules that govern the international system. The Westphalian system was not, itself, primordial and true of every nation from ancient Greece to Nazi Germany. It was created following a lengthy, violent conflict, by the victors. Likewise, the United States worked to develop its own order following the defeat of the Axis powers, who had a very different vision for the future of the international system. Similarly, thinking back to our discussion of satisfaction in chapter 3, the United States may seek to promote values, including liberalism and democracy, in rising powers, so that when a rising power does eventually surpass the United States in its capabilities, it shares its values and retains much of the liberal order that the Americans created. Indeed, one of the best indicators of whether a state is satisfied with the American status quo lies in whether it is also a democracy.[28] Therefore, employing elements of soft power that emphasize American values should bring rising challengers, such as India and China, further into the fold. This should result in satisfaction in these rising challengers, making the coming transition acceptable to a declining American hegemon and peaceful for the international system.

From our discussion of liberal leadership, we may expect that with the rise of a new power, some aspects of the American system may be retained while others will fall by the wayside, rendered obsolete to the new dominant power. Who that new power is, and what norms and values they view as important to international politics, is pivotal to what survives. Whether that be China, India, Europe, or someone else will have essential consequences for the survival of that order and is the topic of chapter 14.

DISCUSSION QUESTIONS

1. Identify and discuss some specific foreign policy strategies the United States might employ to foster liberalism in rising challengers, particularly China.
2. If liberalism is fundamentally about individual freedom from coercion, then can a state use violence to spread liberalism? Why does this appear to work in Germany and Japan but fail in Iraq and Afghanistan?
3. If China were to become the next system leader today, what parts of the American order do you think it would retain, and which would it not?
4. According to long-cycle theory, the cycle of dominance is based upon key commercial sectors. Today, perhaps that key sector is the Internet and global communications. Speculate about what might be the key sector in the next long cycle. What consequences might that have for liberalism?
5. How might the United States promote the spread of democracy without using coercive force? Does it matter what type of democracy?

KEY WORDS

liberal

realpolitik

majoritarian

FURTHER READING

Ikenberry, G. John. 2001. *After Victory: Institutions, Strategic Restraint, and the Rebuilding of Order after Major Wars. Princeton*, NJ: Princeton University Press.

Rasler, Karen, and William R. Thompson. 2005. *Puzzles of the Democratic Peace: Theory, Geopolitics and the Transformation of World Politics.* London: Palgrave Macmillan.

Ray, James Lee. 1995. *Democracy and International Conflict: An Evaluation of the Democratic Peace Proposition.* Columbia: University of South Carolina Press.

13

Lessons for the American Imperium from the Decline of the British Empire

Who rules East Europe commands the Heartland;
who rules the Heartland commands the World-Island;
who rules the World-Island commands the world.
—Sir Halford J. Mackinder[1]

THE DECLINE OF THE BRITISH EMPIRE

As the strength of the British Empire progressively waned in 1904, the director of the London School of Economics, Sir Halford Mackinder, addressed the Royal Geographical Society on the emerging competition for global dominance. Drawing parallels between the rise and fall of great nations over four centuries and the geostrategic realities that helped or hampered their ability to shape history, Mackinder outlined Britain's key strategic goals in confronting growing powers on the European continent.[2] He characterized the threat confronting Britain as a sprawling resource-abundant land power that seeks to achieve global dominance controlling the "pivot," or the interior, of the vast Eurasian landmass which he called the World-Island. If any power is able to control the immense resources of the Eurasian heartland and develop military reach through naval strength, they could easily subjugate the entire globe. Thus, Britain's grand strategy should be to use its global empire and unparalleled naval strength to restrain potential challengers, working to prevent any single Eurasian state from dominating the others while working to thwart any alliance between such states. The timing of Mackinder's fears was not coincidental. In 1902,

Britain and Japan had signed the Anglo-Japanese alliance, targeting any naval expansion of Russia in the Pacific. In 1904, the same year as Mackinder's address, Russia went to war with Japan over access to Port Arthur and the surrounding territory. Britain believed that if Russia were successful, it could set in motion the geostrategic fear of a state with both resources and power projection capable of overthrowing British global dominance.

This British fear, however, was not to come to pass. Japanese forces successfully defeated Russia as internal discontent and the difficulty of transporting military assets across Asia plagued Russian efforts. However, Mackinder's concerns were realized a short time later in the rise of Germany. Britain was in a steady decline, which accelerated with the enormous costs of World War I and the steady erosion of its global empire. At the start of that war, its capabilities lagged both Russia and Germany, although it retained naval supremacy. Although internal politics would remove Russia from the short-term competition as the Bolshevik revolution overthrew the tsar, Germany, despite its defeat, would come to nearly destroy Britain twenty years later. Just a few decades prior to the two World Wars, Britain was unchallenged in its dominance with 50 to 90 percent more capabilities than its closest competitor, depending on the measure. Although this historical example is more than a century old, the British case is the most recent instance of decline by a previously dominant state. This chapter explores the process of British decline beginning in roughly 1880, its relationship to global hierarchy, geographic reach, and political capacity and what these lessons might mean for the United States in the twenty-first century.

The decline of the British Empire provides essential examples of how international hierarchy may interact with domestic context to bring about the demise of a once unchallenged global power. British perceptions of threat were as global as their empire. One example is the Great Game: a mostly artificial Russian threat to British interests in India. As Britain nearly controlled the entirety of the Indian subcontinent at the turn of the nineteenth century, it viewed Russia's relatively proximate territorial presence as a potential threat to what was perhaps their most essential colonial holding. However, to threaten India, Russia would need to traverse some challenging terrain including passing through the Emirate of Afghanistan: a space that, as the American military has discovered, is extremely difficult to project power across, blanketed with mountainous and inhospitable terrain.

First in 1839 and again in 1878, the British sought to control Afghanistan as a means of defending their interests in India and balancing Russian capabilities in the region. The first military excursion ended in disaster, and the British retreated in disgrace.[3] Their second Afghan war was successful but at the cost of thousands of military casualties. However, the Russians never seriously considered a military expansion to their south, and the entire threat was imagined by the British.[4] Although the Russians did engage in internally destabilizing tactics, similar to those discussed in chapter 5, by arming Uzbek tribes in response to British engagement, the idea of a Russian threat that could extend south to the Indian Ocean was a fabrication. In 1839, British capabilities on every dimension were dramatically outpacing those of a Russian state that was still grappling with its internal Asian frontier. Although British capabilities began to decline by the 1870s, the completion of the Suez Canal in Egypt meant dramatic gains to British naval power projection, further ensuring Britain's control of the Indian subcontinent. So why in these cases, as well as other conflicts, do the British persistently imagine threats to their dominance and feel compelled to attempt to balance opponents in distant geographic spaces?

The Thermopylae Myth

Pervasive throughout the British discussion of why they must balance Russia in Central Asia was the Thermopylae myth, a frequent feature of domestic political justifications of external foreign intervention.[5] Thermopylae, of course, is the battle from ancient Greek history where King Leonidas defended a narrow mountain pass with but a few thousand soldiers, including 300 Spartans, from the advancing Persian Army. As the story goes, although nearly all the Greeks perished, the Spartan stand so depleted the Persian Army that it allowed the remaining Greek city-states to repel the invaders. Unfortunately for Leonidas, the Persians managed to overrun much of Greece anyway. But the underlying idea behind Thermopylae was that the Greeks had to confront the enemy "there" or they would soon be fighting them in their towns and homes. This maxim is reminiscent of the "we must fight them there, so we do not have to fight them at home" logic that is often used in defense of American foreign interventions and was a frequent feature of British foreign policy rhetoric of the nineteenth century. Once domestic policymakers begin using this justification and receive public buy-in, they then may become "trapped by their own myths," perpetuating ineffective and failed foreign policies for their political preservation.[6]

In the Great Game example, the prevailing argument at the time was that Britain had to confront Russia there, in the remote parts of Afghanistan, lest they are forced to confront them first in India, then Europe, and finally at home in the British Isles. The rhetoric was a frequent component of other excursions,[7] including the Crimean War designed to restrict Russian expansion where Britain deployed more than 100,000 men with almost half becoming casualties.[8] Yet, in this dispute, the war was started not by Russian expansion but by a French desire to exert more control over the Near East and designs by Lord Palmerston of Britain to dismantle the Russian Empire. This internal pathology in Britain of whether to commit her forces to continued expansion and intervention as opposed to nonintervention and free trade defined the British decline.

Liberals versus Conservatives

In particular, this internal political struggle over how Britain should use and maintain its resources can be observed in the oscillations in government control between the Conservative and Liberal parties in the second half of the nineteenth century and the debates between Conservative Benjamin Disraeli, and later his ally Robert Gascoyne-Cecil, against liberal leader William Gladstone, who entered and left the office of prime minister on four separate occasions. The Conservative governments consistently favored continued imperial expansion, including the wars in Crimea, Afghanistan, and sub-Saharan African, with a constant insistence on maintaining large deployed naval forces. At one juncture, the Conservative government under Gascoyne-Cecil risked conflict with the United States over British possessions in the Western Hemisphere and again with Russia by allying itself with the Japanese. The Liberal Party led by Gladstone, as it oscillated into power, would then roll back these expansionist tendencies, ending conflicts in Central Asia and Africa and espousing home rule in some colonies. However, it would still use military force to maintain some British interests, particularly maintaining the openness of the sea lanes to commerce as in the case of occupying Egypt to secure the Suez Canal.[9]

Despite less expansion, liberal governments also sought to isolate and punish first Russia and then Germany both economically and diplomatically, with Britain's last Liberal prime minister presiding over Germany's punishment for World War I at Versailles. However, given the pressure of domestic policy interests, foreign policies of liberal governments were also often fitful and inconsistent, intervening in some places while avoiding others.

| BOX 13.1 | Domestic Politics, Overexpansion, and Van Dieman's Land Company |

Costly expansion in an attempt to preserve imperial glory and stifle potential competitors continued even after British power was clearly in decline in the 1890s. While often nominally victorious, the British victories in a nightmarish twenty-year conflict with the Mahdi army in Sudan, continued struggles against the Zulu and Dutch colonists in southern Africa, and interventions in Asia continued to "overstretch" British military forces even as their relative capabilities declined, particularly following German unification and industrialization. Much of this somewhat incoherent British foreign policy, as costly as it was, was not part of some broader grand strategy for the preservation of the empire but instead a result of "logrolling" domestic economic and political forces seeking to commit British resources to endeavors that benefited the interested domestic groups without clear strategic necessity.[10] As but one example in the mid-nineteenth century, the Van Dieman's Land Company lobbied the British Crown for control and support of establishing an agricultural industry in what is now Tasmania. In a profound display of expansionary hubris and despite enormous effort and expenditure, the company refused to acknowledge that the seasons were reversed in the Southern Hemisphere[11] bringing about years of agricultural failure in addition to the destruction of the native population and extinction of animal species.

Overlooking the Rise of Germany

By the time we reach Mackinder's address on the geostrategic realities confronting Britain, the British decline has already passed a critical tipping point, reaching parity with both Germany and Russia. Although the Russians, given their low levels of urbanization and industrialization, lacked global competitiveness with the British Empire, the Germans did not, as the initiation and conduct of World War I would demonstrate but a decade later. British attention was seemingly focused on the wrong competitor. We know from British foreign policy, as evident in the Mackinder speech, that concerns over Germany and Russia, and their control over key geostrategic points in eastern Europe, were paramount to British strategy. Britain's plan seemed to be one of force and punishment, hoping that they might, through continued colonial expansion and resource extraction while stifling their competitors, stave off the inevitable.

However, working against their efforts were not only independence and self-governance movements as distant as Australia and as nearby as Ireland but also their own relative decline in population. Germany grew rapidly, both through the initial consolidation of formally independent German states with Prussia as well as industrialization, urbanization, and technological development. Although at a disadvantage in capabilities at the foundation of the German Empire in 1871, its population immediately outpaced that of Britain,[12] providing an opportunity for more rapid growth and allowing them to make up the capabilities gap.

As Britain reaches the tipping point of control in the international system around 1905, its emphasis remains heavily fixated on Russian growth. However, although Britain understood the importance of geopolitics and the dangers of Russia's enormous population and resource wealth, it failed to capture the degree to which Russian political capacity internally inhibited the effective deployment of resources to achieve foreign policy goals. Although Russia's population was over four times that of the United Kingdom, its urbanized population was almost half, in stark contrast to Germany. With such a disparate, rural population heavily dependent on subsistence agriculture, extracting resources was far more challenging for the Russians. This became quickly evident by the end of 1905 as Russia conceded defeat to the Japanese Empire in the Russo-Japanese War. For the next decade, the Liberal Party, with its more ambivalent foreign policy, would retain control of the British government. Rather than acknowledge the inevitable decline of British power and take steps to ease that decline, the Liberal Party implemented policies that would attempt to hamper the military and economic growth of competitors, believing that if they were sufficiently constrained, they would not overthrow the British system. These punishments, whether military, diplomatic, or economic, did little to stop the rising capabilities of these competitors and instead would only serve to increase their dissatisfaction and exacerbate the likelihood of violent conflict between major powers.

The Origins of Offshore Balancing

Although the Conservatives were much more hawkish, the Liberals were by no means doves. Instead, they set about crafting a naval centric balancing policy that closely resembles what neorealist policy practitioners today call "offshore balancing." Through offshore balancing, the dominant power maintains the expenses of power projection through naval expenditures but avoids costly direct territorial intervention unless necessary.[13] Instead, proxy regional powers supported by the dominant state will provide stability to their regional spaces, balancing possible regional antagonists and thus preventing those undesirable states from expanding their power unchecked. Unlike the policies of British Conservatives that were heavily expansionist and interventionist, offshore balancing emphasized greater restraint; however, it is still a heavily interventionist form of foreign policy, requiring significant military engagement and the selection of regional partners to create regional balance. As we will see, this grand strategy failed because it ignored that parity between regional actors increases, not decreases, the odds of conflict, as discussed in chapter 3,[14] leaving Britain to be sucked into conflicts unprepared and culminating in two world wars. The late foreign policy of the British Empire is explicitly the basis of the offshore balancing grand strategy prevalent in American foreign policy circles today[15] and also responsible for the violence surrounding the British Empire's decline.

Contradictions in Liberal Grand Strategy

Liberal governments sought to constrain further expansion of military development by Britain's competitors, prompting the Hague conference of 1907. It was mostly unsuccessful in achieving its aims, aside from upsetting rising powers, notably Germany. Throughout the decade between the Russo-Japanese War and World War I, Britain consistently sought to thwart German expansion while favoring allies, notably the French as they rapidly took control of western Africa.[16] They employed an early form of offshore balancing strategy as exemplified by Liberal prime minister William Gladstone's slow dissolution of the British Empire's centralized authority through increasing autonomy of localized actors. Once independent, it was thought that they would provide for their own defense costs while still promoting British strategic interests. However, from Ireland to India, the policy faltered as local populations sought full independence for their nations, leaving British forces overstretched in attempts to provide internal political stability to Britain's own holdings.

The Liberal governments of the late British Empire were successful in avoiding many of the quagmires of past Conservative government's interventions, but they failed to recognize the importance of constructively engaging rising challengers. The combination of reluctance to engage with a desire to punish possible competitors diplomatically or economically continued through World War I, which even unto Britain's entrance, the Liberal government sought to avoid.

Unfortunately, its own policies made the entrance inevitable. Despite its preference for peace, Britain's rising opposition to German expansion and favoritism for France are what forced its hand into the conflict. Building on the inevitable consequences of French bias and a dissatisfied Germany, domestic anti-German sentiment in Britain pressured the government into issuing Germany an ultimatum about Belgian neutrality, fed by popular Conservative figures, such as Rudyard Kipling, who once quipped that "there are two divisions in the world: human beings and Germans."[17] However, Germany offered to compensate Belgium for damage in return for safe passage to France and continuing neutrality: a similar agreement to what it offered Luxembourg. But the Belgians refused.[18] Although the government of Britain entered a unified national system between the parties, Liberal composition rapidly declined, with Lloyd George serving as its final prime minister. Incorporating the Conservatives into a national government created further incoherence in British foreign policy, mixing the caution and economic favoritism of the Liberal Party with the hawkish expansionism of the Conservatives.

Further Conservative Interventionism

Expansionist designs from Conservatives during World War I led to a series of events that have conflictual consequences lasting through the present day. The Sykes–Picot agreement would divide the Arab territories of the Ottoman Empire between Britain and France, creating the current borders in Syria, Lebanon, Iraq, and Jordan that are central zones of conflict today. The Balfour Declaration, in an attempt to garner support from Jewish populations in allies and opponents alike, promised a "national home for the Jewish people" in Palestine. However, the British government had already promised the territory to the Sharif of Mecca in return for support against the Ottoman Empire. These contradicting promises infuriated Britain's Arab allies. Conflicts over control of these former Ottoman territories began with British promises and evolved into some of the most violent and frequent of the past century.

Though a Conservative before 1904 and after 1924, Churchill was a Liberal party member for economic reasons in the interim. However, his pro-imperial foreign policy stance remained staunchly Conservative. Serving as First Lord of the Admiralty during the war, Churchill sought to engineer the expansion of the conflict through the entrance of the United States. President Wilson had a strong repulsion to submarine warfare, although Germany was required to employ the new technology to have any hope of competing with Britain's superior surface navy and breaking blockades on German ports. Exploiting this tactic, Churchill would disguise naval vessels to appear as civilian vessels to confuse German submarine captains. This tactic would then lead Germany to fire indiscriminately at vessels coupled with announcements of war zones to warn away civilian shipping from non-belligerents.[19] Knowing this would place the civilians of neutral nations in danger, Churchill wrote at the same time as Germany's pronouncement of submarine warfare that "it is most important to attract neutral shipping to our shores in the hope especially of embroiling the USA with Germany . . . for our part, we want the traffic—the more the better and if some of it gets into trouble, better still."[20] Three months later a German submarine would sink the *Lusitania*, and the United States would enter the war. Arguably, this was not the intent of the Liberal politicians in the national government who decidedly preferred the United States not be involved in dictating the terms of the war's conclusion.[21] However, it does illustrate another example of Conservative politicians working through the national government to advance more expansionist strategies. This trend would continue, as they would then use Woodrow Wilson to advance punitive measures against the Central Powers at Versailles in return for tepid support of his liberally oriented Fourteen Points.

Consequences of World War I

A combination of disengaged hesitation due to a failure of imperial offshore balancing polices merged with offensive expansionist designs by increasingly powerful Conservative party voices characterizes the end of Liberal governments in Britain. By the end of Lloyd George's tenure as prime minister, the combination of conservative expansionist designs with liberal values in the national government began to resemble neoconservatism in the United States today. The end of World War I saw both the demise of the Liberal Party and its international laissez-faire policies that were a more successful aspect of British foreign policy at the time. But the attempt to corral and punish rising challengers remained, contradicting that past laissez-faire orientation. This resulted not in preventing new challenges to British hegemony following World War I, but instead creating challengers even more dissatisfied with the international system than those they just defeated.

First, although Lloyd George supported an agreement at Versailles that relied on some liberal principles, such as the importance of democratic institutions and international organizations in resolving disputes, he heavily punished Britain's competitors. Germany would be crippled while Britain dismantled the Austro-Hungarian and Ottoman Empires.

Second, Britain managed to garner the support of the United States for these punitive measures by making promises toward cooperative liberal policies. The punishment of Germany included saddling them with the war debts of both sides, which resulted in German economic disaster. Furthermore, it removed German populations from within the newly drafted German borders. Opposition to both these measures would eventually become the foundation of the Nazi political platform and rhetorical justification for their hostile expansionist foreign policy.

This British commitment to punishing the Central Powers at Versailles was effective at provoking Germany and underscored a series of mistakes. First, by failing to recognize the source of capabilities in population, Britain overlooked the inevitability of German recovery. As mentioned previously, the phoenix factor suggests that, given an intact population, a country can recover from the economic and infrastructure destruction of war within a couple of decades, which, as we know, Germany did. Second, going along with Woodrow Wilson's Fourteen Points and establishing the League of Nations made sense from a liberal institutionalist perspective, but there were no military capabilities to support the League's strict conditions, particularly after the United States failed to join. This left the League ineffective. Finally, the Liberal Party's demise brought about the end of the classical liberal opposition to conservative expansionist policies. It was replaced by the progressive populist Labour Party, which was more insular and isolationist, espousing protectionist economic policies. A successful combination of both military restraint and economic openness no longer possessed a foothold in British politics.

Further German Dissatisfaction and the Rise of Nazi Germany

The succeeding Conservative governments sought to maintain British hegemony through controlling, punitive policies. In addition to the Treaty of Versailles severely limiting any attempts at German rearmament, the Washington Naval Treaty of 1922 limited the total tonnage of naval vessels states could possess. Considered the pinnacle of war fighting technology at the time, battleships were particularly limited, resulting in only Britain deploying a new vessel until 1935. The treaty gave the United States and Great Britain much higher thresholds for maximum naval force sizes, leading signatories Japan and Italy to renounce the treaty's terms alongside Germany's renunciation of Versailles and subsequent naval rearmament.

The punitive measures of Versailles and the realpolitik policies of succeeding Conservative prime ministers not only failed to prevent future challenges to British order but instead birthed a dissatisfied challenger of unparalleled proportions in Nazi Germany. To underscore the relationship between global hierarchy and the domestic level of analysis, the rise of Nazi Germany is a direct consequence of the reshuffling of international hierarchy that took place in 1919. Hitler's grievance-based message accusing foreign actors for the economic ills of the 1930s resonated precisely because of the British foreign policy of the early 1920s.

British foreign policy created substantial dissatisfaction among the German population and laid the foundation that allowed the radical nationalist and populist National Socialist party to come to power. That political movement would both eradicate liberal governance within the German state and present the greatest challenge to the British international order. The Nazis sought to transform the system into one that was uniquely illiberal, starting at home with the Holocaust and spreading through their European conquest. The last prime minister before the war, Neville Chamberlain, thought he could appease Hitler with territorial concessions of historical German possessions while maintaining offshore balancing. Indeed, Chamberlain sought to use Hitler as part of Britain's offshore balancing strategy. By bolstering Hitler, British conservatives thought they might balance Nazi Germany against the Soviet Union and prevent conflict.[22] They were mistaken.

THE DECLINE OF THE UNITED STATES

Figure 13.1 compares the decline of the British Empire from 1890 to the outbreak of World War I against the trajectory of American capabilities over the past thirty-five years as a percentage of their nearest competitor. First, the United States is still a long way from reaching the period of parity experienced by the British beginning in the last decade of the nineteenth century. The United States is, at this point, approaching the point in their decline where the British were around 1880. The mistakes made by the British during their final few decades of dominance can offer crucial lessons for the United States, demonstrating the types of policies that may benefit or harm American interests as well as prevent the onset of the next global war.

Figure 13.1 American and British Decline, 1889–1914 and 1991–2016

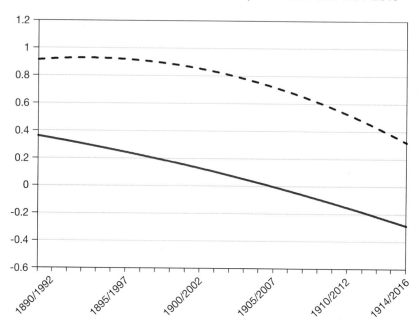

Source: Solid line represents the proportional difference between Britain and its closest competitor in the Correlates of War National Material Capabilities (v5.0). See J. David Singer, Stuart Bremer, and John Stuckey, "Capability Distribution, Uncertainty, and Major Power War, 1820–1965," in *Peace, War, and Numbers*, edited by Bruce Russett, 19–48 (Beverly Hills, CA: Sage, 1972). The dashed line represents the proportional difference between American and Chinese capabilities in gross domestic product from the World Bank: "World Bank Open Data" (2019), last accessed July 17, 2019, https://data.worldbank.org. Both capabilities measures are smoothed using a polynomial function for ease of comparison.

In carefully outlining the period of steady British decline, there is one immediate concern relevant to our current time: How do we, in the coming decades, keep from reflecting the errors of the British fall? It is worth noting that although the conclusion of the British Empire was easily the most violent transition in world history, it is not alone. The Napoleonic Wars, during which France attempted to supplant Britain at the head of the system, restructured Europe. The Thirty Years' War, during which Sweden, France, and the Dutch contended against the Holy Roman Empire and Spain, was the most violent war in Western history until World War I. Are there lessons to be learned from British mistakes that can reduce the chances of the United States committing equivalently dangerous blunders that result in equally or more violent events whereby millions may perish? To engage this question, we must first make a series of assumptions, none of which should be controversial. First, the United States is in decline. Second, a dissatisfied challenger is more likely to go to war with the United States than a satisfied one. Third, the United States has an interest in avoiding global conflict, particularly involving nuclear weapons.

If we apply these three assumptions to the same circumstances surrounding the decline of the British Empire, a bleak evaluation of its foreign policy choices remains. First, the British foreign policy community, as evidenced by their attempts at agreements restricting military assets, increasing naval spending, and a geostrategic policy resembling offshore balancing designed to set land-based European powers against one another, refused to acknowledge its inevitable decline. Their failure to understand the sources of power in population and capacity, which no foreign or colonial policy can ameliorate, drove their oversight. Second, despite some small disputes in the Western Hemisphere, the British sought to improve relations with the United States. They reasonably preferred the United States as a rising power over the German or Russian Empires but again missed the importance of population to capabilities, not realizing that their simple favoritism could not sufficiently augment the distribution of challenging state capabilities. Finally, the British Empire assumed, as illustrated in Rudyard Kipling's war propaganda, that the German (or Russian) Empire was incapable of acknowledging the *goodness* of British norms and values. Therefore, French, American, or sometimes Japanese interests should be privileged over those of these potential adversaries. Although restricting the potential relative power gains of adversaries may be sensible from a realpolitik or neorealist perspective, these attempts failed to recognize the demographic inevitability of Germany's challenge rooted in their domestic demography, which could not be constrained by punitive or institutional limitations.

We can also learn some positive lessons from the British experience that are directly applicable to the United States:

1. Geography matters.
2. Domestic political and economic conditions are the source of state power.
3. Challenger states are neither inherently satisfied nor dissatisfied, and the actions of the dominant state may augment their level of satisfaction.

Geography

First, Mackinder was undoubtedly right to identify the essential recipe of geographic space, power projection, and resource control in determining the challenges that would come to confront Britain in the twentieth century. Furthermore, naval assets, as an essential tool of power projection, are pivotal to the ability of a dominant power to maintain order globally; hence, the dominant power has been naval in orientation since the dawn of global politics.[23] Today, we see apparent attempts by the Chinese to expand their sphere of influence across the Asian continent, even unto Mackinder's "Heartland" of Eastern Europe. China's current "Belt and Road Initiative" seeks to create a trading network that reaches throughout Asia, crossing into both North Africa and Central Europe. Although economic in orientation, this rising level of influence in a crucial geostrategic space would give Mackinder pause.

Unlike Russia or Germany, China is primarily a geographically maritime state with most of its population residing on the coast, access to shipping lanes, and the ability to develop a year-round blue-water navy. So expecting China to remain a land-centric power into the future is implausible. Close analysis of geography and power projection allows the United States to identify places of likely conflict, such as issues between India and China over both territory and vital shipping lanes. However, this logic does not necessarily lead to an offshore balancing policy that would see the United States promote one of the two states' interests over another as Britain did with France over Germany. Doing so would only serve to create a relationship of parity between the two states that is more, not less, prone to conflict. The intervention of the declining dominant power will only cause greater dissatisfaction in the unsupported challenger. In other words, if the United States supported India over China, resulting in the appearance of parity between the two states, it would both increase China's dissatisfaction and the probability of a regional conflict between the two powers, thereby increasing American chances of being sucked into a war between the two.

When evaluating the possible threats posed by rising challengers, the dominant power should not overlook geography. Britain made this mistake by overestimating Russia's power projection throughout the nineteenth century. However, as they would discover in late 1905, Russia had difficulty reaching the remote portions of its own territory against a fledgling Japanese Empire. Similarly, the Chinese military may be quite large in terms of personnel, but it lacks the technological sophistication to project meaningful power. Indeed, the running joke in the American policy community was that if China were to attempt to invade Taiwan, it would be the "million-man swim."[24] The sheer distances required to occupy and hold American territory by China are so dramatic as to make the likelihood of a realistic Chinese territorial threat still quite distant. Compound the problems of American distance with the more proximate geographic concerns that China would have to resolve before considering a projection of power to the Western Hemisphere.

Internally, China must address its domestic political problems and contestations to its hierarchy, whether in the western parts of China, including Tibet, or Hong Kong. Second, it has two declining major powers (Russia and Japan) and one rising regional power (India) on its immediate borders, and China has had border disputes with all three that largely remain unresolved. When all these issues are taken together, the geographic landscape for China both near and far is prohibitive to demonstrating any significant threat to American interests that would not harm Chinese interests more extensively by orders of magnitude. As Chinese power grows, it will be ringed geographically by a dominance vacuum where hierarchy is contested. This doughnut of contested geographic space will be riddled with interstate conflicts, civil wars, and political instability that will present more pressing threats to their security interests than a declining United States. The United States would do well not to overestimate the Chinese security threat, lest they commit similar exaggerated foreign policy blunders of the late British Empire. Committing resources unnecessarily toward quagmire conflicts that result in, at best, pyrrhic victories will lead only to overburdening American capabilities and hastening its decline.

Domestic Capacity in the Challenging State

Second, the origins of the next dominant power's strength will lie in a productive, large population and the ability of the state's government to extract resources from that population. For these reasons, the United States must not presume that the challenger will inevitably be China, just as the British committed the error of assuming the Russians were the most likely candidates to challenge their order. Although China's population is the largest in the world, India is close behind and on track to surpass it within the next few years. China, unlike India, suffers from the "middle-income trap." Due to its aging population, and the necessary resources required to care for them in combination with the declining working-age population, further economic development will become increasingly difficult. In recent decades, China has rolled back policies that facilitate this population imbalance, such as the one-child policy, but related problems abound. For example, due to a preference for male children, the gender imbalance in the working-age population is 1.18:1, and the labor force is shrinking in raw numbers.[25] If we take a decades-long view, not only is India likely to be the most populous country in the world but even Nigeria is expected to approach a population equal to China after the turn of the next century.

Population alone does not predetermine capabilities. The state must have resources and the political capacity to extract those resources, and both contenders currently have significant political challenges. Regional factions and ethnic/religious divisions severely limit the coordination of national policy in India, as well as an ongoing unresolved border dispute with Pakistan. China has steadily modernized its nominally communist system but remains unquestionably authoritarian. As the population grows and acquires greater wealth with the development of a middle class, the endurance of such authoritarian institutions may erode. Alternatively, the next challenger may not even yet exist, as Germany did not exist in the early nineteenth century for Britain. A hypothetical United States of Europe, for example, would have both a large population and the political capacity to extract resources. The United States should recognize China's rising power and the eventual possibility of it surpassing American power globally, but it should not presume such nor focus on China exclusively.

Satisfaction

Finally, a rising challenger does not create the potential for violent conflict on its own. As Britain declined, the Americans and the French were both relatively satisfied powers, unlike Germany, and to a lesser extent, Russia. Furthermore, Germany's satisfaction, as represented by policy preferences, was not fixed. Under Bismarck, Germany's conduct was relatively satisfied. Only after Germany began to seek external colonies in earnest was it routinely thwarted by Britain. Both Conservative and Liberal governments in the late nineteenth century then continuously restricted Germany, fostering the growth of dissatisfaction and distrust. In the area of satisfaction, the British case shows that policies of the dominant power can amend the evaluations of the status quo by rising powers. In the short run, a declining dominant power such as Britain in the nineteenth century or the United States today is less concerned with the future contest and may cooperate quite nicely with the rising challenger.[26] However, as the reality of their being eclipsed by a competitor becomes more proximate, panic may set in as leaders look at the decline of their current capabilities and assume not only that they are being surpassed but also that their decline will continue unto their destruction in the absence of some dramatic action. This panic, then, creates ineffective attempts at restraining the challenger.

An example of a more effective policy by a declining dominant power, also from the British case, is the attempt to create satisfaction in potential challengers as Britain did with the French and Americans. Following Napoleon's permanent ouster, the English both promoted their style of institutions but incorporated the French into the first free-trade regime. Britain unilaterally reduced trade barriers and was effective in reciprocal reductions in France and the United States. This exchange of goods, as with trade today, increases contact between nations, generates shared interests through mutual gain, and reduces the probability of conflict.[27] To initiate trade liberalization policy at the time required the dominant state to open its markets and employ material capabilities to provide stability to shipping lanes. Although the United States may be the current "liberal leviathan," many aspects of our current order were established by the British Empire for both expanding its economic interests and creating stability.[28]

Industrialization and free trade are, from a long-cycle perspective, the innovations that Britain provided to the system and continued as the United States took on the costs of providing stability. However, the United States did not preserve all aspects of the British order, particularly colonialism that was steadily rolled back in favor of self-determination. But more of the British order was preserved by the United States than otherwise would have if the new dominant state had been a dissatisfied Germany or Russia.

Where the first part of the book examines how parity can create conflictual processes, the second part provides guidelines on how, given inevitable parity, conflict may be avoided. Preemptive warfare as a means of crushing challengers is both costly and often unsuccessful. Ameliorating dissatisfaction through diplomatic and economic engagement provides a greater chance of success. The former characterizes British treatment of Germany and Russia, while the latter represents their engagement of the United States and France. All four rose in capabilities regardless of British policy, but the latter two remained satisfied. The United States may replicate this process of nurturing satisfaction by being inclusive of rising challengers in both institutional and economic activity, avoiding trade wars and exclusionary policies.

Preserving the American Status Quo

The American status quo is a liberal order, and for the past seventy years, that liberal order has continued to expand and dominate international politics. The triumph of liberalism, through the expansion of trade and globalization, the formation and effectiveness of institutions, and the extension of that order to regional space exists as it is promoted by the United States. Thus, fostering those liberal qualities elsewhere will assist in it preserving the status quo.

However, the United States must be wary of promoting liberalism through force. British attempts at coercing its will, even when successful, were also successful in generating dissatisfaction against the British order. Economic and collective security has been an effective means of incorporating states into the existing order without intervention and conflict. Take, for example, Germany and the former Warsaw Pact states. Most all were included in both NATO and the European Union and are reasonably satisfied. Russia, however, was excluded, and its conduct over the past years demonstrates its apparent dissatisfaction. Interestingly, beginning with the Soviet Union's collapse, the idea of Russia's inclusion in Western institutions has been a recurring question. Mikhail Gorbachev even suggested that Russia be included in NATO when Germany reunified in 1990, a policy Margaret Thatcher supported.[29] Unfortunately for Russia's integration in the American order, that did not materialize. Russia today is limited in its domestic demography and unlikely to present the same level of challenge to the American order that it did when it was the Soviet Union. Dissatisfied challengers on the horizon, with their burgeoning populations, are not as restricted in their likely future capabilities. How much more dangerous would a power at parity with the United States be if it was similarly excluded from America's liberal institutions or confronted with persistent offshore balancing threats directed at its interests?

As America approaches the same period of decline that began for Britain in the late nineteenth century, it would do well to emphasize the aspects of American order, commercially and diplomatically, that generate satisfaction globally as a means of managing rising challengers and providing stability to unstable geographic spaces. The decline of the British Empire demonstrates that conflict as a means of order creation is both costly and ultimately unsuccessful. Its policies of sporadic intervention and offshore balancing not only hastened its decline but also destabilized the international system, contributing to the onset of both World Wars and the rise of Nazi Germany. If the United States relies on inclusive cooperative architecture and economic integration in its decline as opposed to intervention and conflict, then when it hands the mantle of power to the next dominant power, it will more likely be one that shares American liberal values.

DISCUSSION QUESTIONS

1. Give examples of specific policies that the United States could implement with China, India, or others to promote satisfaction. What types of policies should it avoid?
2. Thinking about British behavior in the early twentieth century, if conflicts do erupt between rising challengers, what course of action should the United States take?
3. How can the United States engage in free trade and collective security without alienating potential challengers?
4. How should the United States and satisfied European allies react to destabilizing liberal elements within China and corresponding Chinese suppression?
5. What variables should the United States focus on in the present to identify the likely major powers of the future?

KEY TERMS

grand strategy
geostrategic
interventionism
logrolling

middle-income trap
neoconservatism
offshore balancing

FURTHER READING

Mackinder, H. J. 1904. "The Geographical Pivot of History." *The Geographical Journal* 23, no. 4:421–37.
Modelski, George, and William R. Thompson. 1988. *Seapower in Global Politics, 1494–1993.* Seattle: University of Washington Press.
Snyder, Jack. 1991. *Myths of Empire: Domestic Politics and International Ambition.* Ithaca, NY: Cornell University Press.

14

American Decline, Chinese Rise, and the Unexpected Future

★ ★ ★

WHAT'S NEXT?

The culmination of this text is what to expect from the future given an empirical examination of the past. Is it the resurrection of great power politics and undermining of classical deterrence? Is it the inevitable process of one hegemon being eclipsed by another with all the resulting turbulence and trauma? International relations, as an empirical field, is rife with measurement debates. Trying to precisely predict the future using imprecise measurements is challenging, given the complexity of state decisions and likelihood of unanticipated events. Actual policies of states are the outcomes of more than just simple theories: they are the combination of domestic politics and international influences. Decline, growth, development, and government capacity are all variables that affect global order. Rather than predict the future, we outline four possible outcomes and what the lessons from the text suggest for American foreign policy.

The purpose of this chapter is for you to consider possible future outcomes and reflect on what policies may lead to relative stability. Consider the following scenarios:

1. China rises, but due to its policy choices relating to demography and economic growth, its capabilities do not significantly grow beyond those of the United States. This failure to develop before aging results in the *middle-income trap*. Therefore, all the most

fruitful strategies for China are exhausted, but growth was never high enough for such a large population to escape poverty. This could be a worst-case scenario from the perspective of power transition theory as it may lead to two rival states that may be relatively equal in power for an extended period.

2. The European Union organizes, unifies, and takes its place as the largest economy in the world and possibly the most powerful state. Wealth does not mean power alone, but it can finance it. The choice for member states to work as a group and to no longer think of themselves as individually sovereign states creates a new actor on the international stage more powerful than the United States. By merging resources, they become more powerful than the existing dominant state almost overnight.

3. Technological upheaval upsets the American order. Technology has the potential to create radical changes that we currently cannot predict, from artificial intelligence to the consequences of global warming. Imagine thinking about the world today from the view of a person in 1900: landing on the moon, weapons so large they can destroy whole cities, air flight so common it is boring, and nearly all diseases eradicated. These events would be considered science fiction, and each was written about at the time as a possible future and signal of a golden era. But they did happen and are no longer fiction. So what then happens in our future? Massive wars due to environmentally forced migrations? Is it collapsing ecosystems? Conflict moving from physical to cyber? Alternatively, does the continued automation of jobs create questions of humanity's purpose in a new era of artificial intelligence?

4. The United States withdraws from its own order. For the last seventy years, the United States has defined the international system: free trade, democracy, and the rule of law. Prior major powers created empires of direct control, which were dismantled by the American shift in norms after World War II. Globalization and commercial integration meant the development of shared norms, laws, institutional structure, and the creation of stable alliances. To be clear, every foreign policy decision during the Cold War may not have lived up to all these ideals, but the fact remains that liberalism as a core principle of government was supported and incentivized by the United States. If this is no longer the interest of the United States, what happens next? A rise in dictatorships? Additional conflict among increasingly militarized states? Does this even matter

to the United States, which, surrounded by vast oceans, has the benefit of geography? If the United States abstains from the world, what are the consequences?

THE RISE OF CHINA?

What is necessary for sustainable economic growth? The rule of law, access to markets, property rights, and stable governance, all of which, in 2019, are under threat in the Chinese system. The following are issues that may challenge or affect China in its quest to become the next dominant power:

1. The state is increasingly controlled by a corrupt elite, using kidnappings and internment of thousands for political purposes.
2. Products are increasingly controlled by large, politically well-connected conglomerates who rely on government support for continued market success. This, in turn, causes wealth to flee the country.
3. Comparative advantages in labor are in decline as an aging population demands social services and expanding industries, such as steel, require increased protectionism.
4. Domestic political power is more concentrated than at any time since Mao. The state values loyalty over efficiency or productivity.
5. Conflict is rising with the trade war against the United States alongside more troubling territorial issues with nearly every single contiguous state in the region: the South China Sea, borders with India, islands disputed with South Korea and Japan, and, of course, Taiwan. All potential issues of possible violence and undermining China's rise as a peaceful hegemon, resulting in significant increases in military expenditures.
6. The stability of the international system supported by the United States benefits China greatly, potentially creating a rising challenger satisfied with the status quo. Access to markets, technological development, investments, and safe shipping are artifacts of the current post–World War II order. All are expensive, fragile, and dependent on the dominant state's engagement and patronage, something it may no longer be willing or able to do.[1] Does a satisfied China continue to support what is in its economic benefit, or does it undermine the system that helped it rise to a position of dominance?

Will China's growth lead to global dominance? Development seems to be nearly inevitable, given the largest labor force in the world being pulled from inefficient agricultural regions into low-skilled and then increasingly complex industry. Furthermore, it is either the first or the second-highest recipient of foreign direct investment and transitioning from a top-down communist state to one that is more market-based and competitive. As the middle class grows, people will demand the freedom to speak, learn, move, and create. However, authoritarianism does not seem to be receding.

Yet, the middle-income trap remains the most significant challenge to China's rise as the population continues to age. The trap part suggests that the highest levels of growth have ended, and with it, the potential for future Chinese power. Figure 14.1 illustrates the change in the Chinese population over the next hundred years using two overlaid population pyramids.[2] The darker pyramid is from the 1950s. It shows the total amount of women and men in the nation by age cohort. Notice that the vast majority of the population is young

Figure 14.1 Demography and the Rise of China

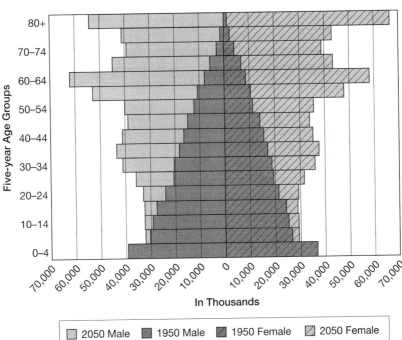

Legend: 2050 Male ■ 1950 Male ▨ 1950 Female ▨ 2050 Female

Source: United Nations, Department of Economic and Social Affairs, Population Division, *World Population Prospects: The 2015 Revision*, DVD edition (New York: Department of Economic and Social Affairs, United Nations, 2015).

and hence can be moved to industry, cities, and productivity. This was the fuel of China's rise: a large, youthful population. Consider the expectations by 2050 in gray. The largest generation is the oldest, a substantially smaller labor force, and growing resource costs associated with higher levels of education needed for the young and the maintenance of an elderly retired population. This is no longer the demographic foundation of a fast-growing economy but of a society that has the same cohort characteristics of the highly developed world.[3] A developed world of which even after two full generations of incredible economic success they are still not members. So what does China do with hundreds of millions of elderly and retired people? No longer a young society, China has now aged with a labor force diverted from growth industries to sustaining a retired generation.[4] The greatest challenge will not necessarily be liberalization and democracy but instead social services. This could lead to a *geriatric peace*[5] in which China's population is too old to be aggressive, but it also could lead to demographically driven dissatisfaction and aggressive foreign policy.

THE RISE OF THE EUROPEAN UNION?

There are many challenges to potential European integration. Foremost among them is integrating national identities, convincing the French to defend the borders of the Poles. But what if European states could overcome these national divisions and the European Union evolves from an international institution into a centralized state: a United States of Europe?

What is gained? At the international level, it elevates declining powers into a position of dominance. The European Union is born from economic integration, which, to be fully competitive, needs labor mobility and therefore the erosion of national borders. But to achieve such integration requires not only a change in border policy but also the laws that govern economic exchange, security, and migration. This integration potential then is faced with a series of challenges. Shifting elderly populations will strain welfare state finances and managing the security challenges of an integrated economy would necessitate the formation of a European security force with the ability to project power.

As with China, most of the European Union is stagnant in population growth and, in many cases, is rapidly aging. The expectation is that, within a decade, substantial labor shortages and aging populations will be the domestic reality of most of the continent. Initially, rich Western states hoped to remedy this inevitable demographic challenge by pulling youth from Central and Eastern Europe to fuel their labor needs. However, that process has been exhausted as postcommunist states reach high levels of development and similar domestic economic demands. To survive, wealthy Europeans must accept more migrants from Africa, the Middle East, and Central Asia.

A unified European military is a policy that was first suggested more than fifty years ago but never got beyond dramatic statements. Why create overlap with the North Atlantic Treaty Organization (NATO) while also surrendering national military policy both within Europe and abroad? Would a new foreign minister of the European Union or president have the ability to send troops overseas? The current security arrangement beyond NATO is disorganized with significant amounts of defense spending wasted in attempts to support national industrial programs. Radars, missiles, planes, tanks, and a host of other small arms are created to demonstrate the status of having a defense industry but not for practical defense purposes. Going from some inefficiency to a coordinated supranational defense policy seems, at present, unlikely. To be unified, the European Union would need to increase the power of the existing institutional structures, particularly the elected parliament. Democratic legitimacy would be critical to its expansion.

THE UNEXPECTED

Technology leads not just to an increase in productivity but has the potential for the radical reorganization of what humanity can accomplish. DARPAnet, created by computer scientists at Caltech and the University of Chicago with funding from the U.S. government, was initially designed to be a system of communication highly resistant to nuclear war. This program evolved into email and database transfers. Unexpectedly, it led to the rise of personal computers. The intersection of U.S. research spending and consumer products led to the innovation of modern personal computing that reshaped the world. You carry in your pocket a computer that you call a phone, which is more powerful than the system that took Americans to the moon: an excellent example of a transformative technology.

Thinking about technological advances, what will be the effects of artificial intelligence (AI)? As governments develop plans for using AI techniques for everything from bombing strategies to employee scheduling,[6] what is the effect of removing human judgment from the decision that kills people? Cheap drone swarms controlled by AI, supersonic independent drone wingmen flying with next-generation fighters, and even wholly controlled armored tanks and submarines may fight the next war. This is not science fiction; it is actual, contemporary research agendas. As this technology develops, it becomes cheaper or even ubiquitous. Given all this, the political systems of the world are not prepared for such dramatic change in the tools of coercion. Once a major technology is developed with a high-demand market, it will explode, and we may be unprepared for policies enforced by computers instead of people. This is not the first time sudden technological advancement has created instability. The invention of machine guns and mustard gas did not alter perceptions about the status quo in Europe before World War I, but they did change strategic and tactical decisions that likely made the war more violent.[7]

Climate change presents serious security challenges as well. In 2019, Europe experienced its hottest summer in roughly five hundred years. The national hurricane service is discussing the possibility of increasing the measurement categories by adding another category to tropical storms. Wide variation in weather is highly disruptive to agriculture, industry, and economies, which means it affects state capabilities and hierarchy. Countries that are still in the process of developing and have a labor force highly dependent on the agricultural industry are more directly affected than those that are industrialized. Therefore, the poorest countries, regions, and populations in the world will be the most directly impacted, with severe implications for the development of future conflicts. Both AI and climate change do not challenge hierarchy but create unexpected shocks to the system that can destabilize the current order.

TWENTY YEARS OF FAILURE: U.S. FOREIGN POLICY IN THE TWENTY-FIRST CENTURY

Over the past twenty years, trust in American institutions has eroded. Coinciding with that distrust and the increase of political influence by the baby boomer generation is the deterioration of expectations regarding America's role in the world. Today, advocacy for withdrawal from the world is likely higher than its been at any point since the 1930s. This does not mean an aversion only to intervening in the politics of foreign countries but any foreign engagement. Not only does it oppose neoconservative interventionism and adventurism, but also offshore balancing, and, as recent Trump administration tariffs demonstrate, international commerce and free trade.

As America seems prepared to withdraw from the world, it continues to meddle in a series of conflicts that are still unfolding in Iraq, Yemen, Libya, Somalia, Mali, Nigeria, Syria, and the waters off the coast of Iran. Like Britain at the end of the nineteenth century, America seems to contradict itself by both wanting to withdraw from the world while continuing costly interventions without clear objectives. Troops are on the ground, in combat, without accessible media evaluation or congressional voting while a disinterested American public ignores the ongoing wars. This apathy extends to accepting continued costs of global conflict with no clear guidelines on objectives, adversaries, or tactics. What is the end goal of the policy, or is the policy of perpetual war the goal? Whom are we fighting and how do we win are simple questions currently without answers.

The focus of this text is examining empirical approaches to international relations through the lens of hierarchical theories. As the current dominant state, the United States sits atop that hierarchy, having established an elaborate cooperative architecture of trade, investment, institutions, and collective security. As America inevitably declines, what policies originating within the domestic political context will preserve American power or prevent global conflict? Can policy lessons of the future be learned from the empirical lessons of the past?

When we examine international politics puzzles empirically, we might also hope to extend those scientific lessons about peace to engineering. Engineering in international relations means applying our empirical knowledge to create foreign policies that achieve stability, just as physics knowledge allows a civil engineer to achieve stability when building a bridge. What we propose from the intersection of empirics and theory is that the most effective approach for America in the twenty-first century is neither the overextension of military assets across the globe that resulted in the collapse of past empires nor the retrenchment of the British Empire's violent latter decades.

Peace, Commerce, and Honest Friendship

Perhaps the best advice for America to look to as it confronts the twenty-first century is the advice of its founders: "peace, commerce and honest friendship with all nations; entangling alliances with none." When Jefferson wrote these words, he was thinking of the realpolitik policies of contemporary European monarchs, using bilateral and often secret offensive and defensive pacts to balance one another on the continent. America's foreign policy should not try to dictate the capabilities of others but instead influence their satisfaction. This is not isolationism but instead open engagement with the world through free trade, a liberal immigration policy, and engagement in international organizations, avoiding entangling bilateral agreements consistent with Jefferson's idea of alliances but maintaining our collective security architecture. If the American imperium is a liberal leviathan as Ikenberry suggests,[8] then the United States must preserve the status quo by embracing the liberal order rather than withdrawing from the very system that it created.

Engaging the world does not mean engaging in conflict. Perhaps the greatest flaw of the past two decades of American foreign policy is the idea that liberalism, an ideology rooted in an aversion to coercion, can be coercively forced on other states. After relative success in Germany and Japan, American attempts at democratic evangelism have been met everywhere with resistance and failure. However, the population of democracies has skyrocketed. Where democracy has spread, from South Korea to Eastern Europe, it has coincided with domestically driven demands for liberal political and economic systems that correspond with international engagement in American-led international institutions and security agreements. The strength of the American status quo lies not in military force but in the stability of economic and diplomatic engagement. Military force, ineffective in promoting the liberal order, is a last resort in protecting the United States from external security threats. Today, those threats are pirates and terrorists with remarkably limited capabilities, not a rising China.

Promoting Satisfaction

If China reaches a position of parity with the United States despite its challenges in development and an aging population, it is not necessarily true that it will also be dissatisfied. Current Chinese foreign economic policy involves the provision of funds for infrastructure creation to facilitate global trade in Asia, Africa, and Europe. Promoting the exchange of goods and services across borders is not contradictory to the values of the American status quo. So long as China believes the American values that govern the international system benefit its interests, it will not be dissatisfied. If America, however, attempts to isolate China and exclude it from the liberal economic order, Chinese dissatisfaction could cause the next global war.

Just as Britain was wrong to assume their next challenger would be the Russian Empire, so we should not assume that China will be the next challenger to the United States. Like Russia in the nineteenth century, China faces a litany of domestic political and economic challenges with no clear solution in sight. If it fails to confront those challenges, it might be rendered as irrelevant to the next transition in power as was the Russian Empire. For this reason, the United States should not overlook India. Despite its lower levels of development and currently dysfunctional political institutions, India has a growing population projected to surpass China as the largest country in the world. Thinking about the trajectory of power in the long run, the United States should seek to incorporate both India and China into the current order as satisfied rising powers, not only to bolster support for the American status quo, but also to prevent potential conflict between the two.

These prescriptions are often contradictory to those of offshore balancing advocates from the neorealist school of international relations, though the goal of reducing American interventionism may be shared. Offshore balancing would suggest that the United States should balance a rising China by supporting regional competitors. Furthermore, they also often advocate reducing free trade, particularly with potential competitors, resulting in both excluding competitors from the liberal economic order as well as impinging on the economic liberty of American citizens. However, empirical evidence demonstrates that parity creates conflict among states, not stability, meaning that the United States would only be promoting conflict in other parts of the world by pursuing offshore balancing strategies. As with World Wars I and II, these regional conflicts born of a balance in capabilities can quickly spread to include not just other regional actors but also the entire world. Indeed, the late British Empire's policy of offshore balancing, instigating regional conflicts from the Anglo-Afghan Wars to the division of the Arab world, not only aided in its undoing but also began conflicts confronting the United States today. Rather than promote a noninterventionist strategy as intended, offshore balancing would unintentionally lead to America's engagement in more conflicts created as a result of its policies. The best way to avoid future military intervention is to incorporate rising global and regional powers into the American order of institutions, trade, and liberalism instead of relying on military power to balance regional opponents.

While the focus of this text is on the wide variety of empirical topics prevalent in international relations and how hierarchical theories explain them, theories of international relations lend themselves to grand strategic orientations, hopefully with clear implications for American foreign policy. This is perhaps uniquely true for hierarchical approaches, wherein the United States as a dominant power plays a paramount role in the system's future. From a hegemonic stability theory perspective, the United States should provide stability through cooperative order, not destabilizing violence. From a power transition perspective, it should be wary of both global and regional parity and even more wary of dissatisfaction. From a long-cycle theory perspective, its resources are better focused on economic and political regimes which reinforce its leadership rather than punitive measures against future opponents.

DISCUSSION QUESTIONS

1. Dominant powers often overlook their future replacements. Outside of India, China, and a consolidated European Union are there other states, or configurations of current states or societies, that might challenge the United States in the future? Explain why.
2. How might the United States observe the behavior of a regional power to determine how a rising challenger may behave as a future dominant power?
3. What great future technology do you speculate might shape the next long cycle?
4. Imagine the distant future where space capabilities are as common as commercial flights or boats. How would this technology impact the effects of geography and distance discussed in this text?
5. As discussed, there are many operationalizations of power. What currently ignored indicators may be relevant to measuring power in the near future?

KEY TERMS

artificial intelligence
cyber warfare
DARPAnet

isolationism
population pyramid

FURTHER READING

Horowitz, Michael C. 2018. "Artificial Intelligence, International Competition, and the Balance of Power." *Texas National Security Review* 1, no. 3 (May): 37–57.

Ikenberry, G. John. 2012. *Liberal Leviathan: The Origins, Crisis, and Transformation of the American World Order*. Princeton, NJ: Princeton University Press.

Larson, Deborah, T. V. Paul, and William C. Wohlforth. 2014. *Status in World Politics*. Cambridge: Cambridge University Press.

Glossary

AFRICOM—the U.S. military joint command overseeing the African continent.

alliance bloc—group of nations in a shared security organization. The Warsaw Pact and the North Atlantic Treaty Organization are examples.

alliance transition theory—roughly the same logic of power transition theory, but instead of focusing only on a single state's capabilities, it aggregates the capabilities of all states in competing alliance blocs.

alliances—a written and signed agreement between two or more states that identifies their commitments to one another in reference to some security issue.

anarchy—the absence of a single political entity with centralized control, such as a government, as is the case in the international system.

artificial intelligence—a broad metric of machine-based activity from machine learning to systems designed to act as neural networks with decision-making capacity.

autarchic—complete control by the state over all internal politics and economic activity with no external interference.

authority—the "rightful rule" of a dominant state both as central to the hierarchy and deemed legitimate by those whom it rules over.[1]

bilateral trade treaty—an agreement between two states to reduce political trade barriers such as quotas and tariffs.

Brexit—the ongoing political process of the United Kingdom leaving the European Union that began with a referendum in 2016.

capabilities—the tangible material resources necessary to the exercise of power.

capital—goods that are used to produce other goods, such as a factory or financial investment.

causality—the connection between two or more variables that allow for the change in one to affect the other.

censored data—data that extend further into the past (left-censored) or future (right-censored) but are not included due to limits on data collection.

civil wars—a conflict within a state's territorial borders between two parties competing for the position of the legitimate government over that territory wherein one party is the existing government and the other is a rebel faction.[2]

collective security—an alliance that entails mutual defense commitments among all signatories, increasing the security of all members but not necessarily targeting any specific opponent or threat.

comparative advantage—the relative ability of state to produce a good more effectively or efficiently than others.

comparative regionalism—the comparative analysis of regions to understand their unique politics while developing generalizable theories about how subsystems engage one another.

conflict—an event between two states that entails the threat of possible force or actual observed use of force.

contiguous—adjacent across a territorial border.

correlation—relationship between two or more variables that may or may not be causal.

credibility—the perception that a country will abide by treaties and act on threats consistently.

cyber warfare—a developing field of study of the total effects of attacks by states on the computer systems of another.

DARPAnet—the first physical Internet.

democratic peace—the empirical finding in international relations that democracies do not go to war with one another.

dependency theory—a research agenda interested in the study of continued colonial influence sustained by the trade of primary goods such as raw materials for increasingly complex industrial products, creating the expectation of long-term dependence.

diffusion—the observation of political phenomena to be geographically concentrated and their trend of spreading toward nearby spaces.

dyad—a pair of states. Studying dyads may take place in a directed form (state A does X to state B) or nondirected (states A and B have X amount of trade with one another).

enduring rivalries—repeated conflicts between two countries consistently present over time.

European Union—the political and economic organization composed of Austria, Belgium, Bulgaria, Croatia, Cyprus, Czech Republic, Denmark, Estonia, Finland, France, Germany, Greece, Hungary, Ireland, Italy, Latvia, Lithuania, Luxembourg, Malta, Netherlands, Poland, Portugal, Romania, Slovakia, Slovenia, Spain, Sweden, and the United Kingdom. The union subsumes but does not perfectly overlap with the eurozone, or states on the euro currency headquartered in Frankfurt, and the Schengen Agreement of states with shared open borders.

extrastate—beyond either the borders of a state or between two states, such as involving nonstate actors.

geostrategic—features of geography, such as access, resources, or natural features, that may benefit the security of a state.

globalization—the interconnectedness of individuals and groups across borders facilitated by regional and global organizations, technology, trade patterns, and cross-border cooperative engagement.

grand strategy—the coordinated, overarching strategic goals of a state to achieve security to which it applies its political, military, and economic resources.

Great Game—rivalry between the United Kingdom and Russia primarily fought via proxy in Central Asia.

hierarchy—the rank ordering of actors according to some criteria, most often their power, status, role, or capabilities.

Human Development Index—"a summary measure of average achievement in key dimensions of human development: a long and healthy life, being knowledgeable, and have a decent standard of living."[3]

hypothesis—a proposed causal relationship between variables.

income inequality—difference between the wealthiest cohort and poorest. It can also be measured in the amount of total wealth held by 1 percent of the population.

integration—the creation of additional linkages between countries, often economic.

international law—the set of rules that most countries follow when dealing with other countries.

interventionism—the engagement of military forces in the politics within or between other states not directly involving the user.

intrastate—within the borders of a state.

irredentism—a political ideology seeking to unite a group of people, which can be national, ethnic, or religious, under a single state.

isolationism—a foreign policy designed on withdrawal from the international system in all forms of engagement, both militarily and economic.

lender of last resort—a central bank or international organization that lends money to banks or countries in painful financial periods when they cannot borrow from anywhere else.

liberal—the philosophical ideology emphasizing the freedom of the individual in both their person and property.

liberalization—the process of reducing both internal and external barriers to economic activity as well as fostering an increase in both the civil liberties and political rights of individuals.

logrolling—the sharing of support among differing interests within a state to ensure all involved groups achieve their goals.

majoritarian—a system in which the majority will is supreme and not restricted by institutional structures or minority political power.

Marshall Plan—the post–World War II reconstruction policy of the United States primarily in Europe.

massive retaliation—nuclear capacity at the level needed to devastate an opponent's population.

Mercosur—the economic organization in South America intended to promote free trade between members.

middle-income trap—the economic condition where, due to domestic economic and demography variables, a country fails to develop fully.

mutually assured destruction—nuclear weapon arsenals large enough to create near-total population losses between two states.

necessary condition—a cause of some outcome without which that outcome does not occur.

neoconservatism—the advancement of democratic or liberal norms using military force and expansionist foreign policies.

neo-mercantilism—the political view that economic policy decisions should be dictated primarily by security concerns.

norm—a commonly accepted manner of conducting behavior or an ethical criterion for conduct.

North American Free Trade Agreement (NAFTA)—the agreement between the United States, Canada, and Mexico that reduces tariffs.

nuclear triad—deploying nuclear warheads by sea, land, and air. It is most commonly a combination of missile silos, submarines, and short- and long-range tactical missiles and aircraft.

null hypothesis—the absence of the effect between variables in the hypothesis.

offshore balancing—the military support of preferred regional actors to balance rising challengers.

operationalization—the assignment of an empirical, numerical value to a concept.

opportunity cost—the cost of doing something determined by what could have been done alternatively with the same time and resources.

parity—the state at which two or more states perceive their capabilities to be relatively equal.

Philadelphian system—pre–U.S. Civil War concept of a union without clear coercive force from a central authority.

Phoenix Factor—despite the destruction of war, states that lose still recover their power within a matter of a couple of decades.

polarity—the number of uniquely powerful states in the international system, either unipolar for one, bipolar for two, or multipolar for three or more.

political capacity—the ability of a governing institutional structure to extract capabilities for foreign policy use, such as through taxation.

population pyramid—a graphical representation of the total population with gender distribution included. It is used as a method to illustrate the relative size of generations.

power—the ability to force other actors "to do something [they] would not otherwise do."[4]

privatization—the transfer of government owned industries and assets to private owners.

probabilistic—the quality of an outcome not being certain but instead more or less likely to occur.

protectionism—the political position that states should use trade barriers to reduce the domestic competitiveness of goods made in other states to protect domestic industries.

proxy—a third party used to execute some foreign policy goal through policy recommendation and provision of material support by another.

proxy war—a conflict in which one or both sides of a conflict have support from an external third party.

qualitative—an interest in small-scale studies with more in-depth yet still rigorous analysis of cases.

quantifiable—it is possible to create a measurement of a variable and an effect.

quantitative—a mathematically focused method of study with an emphasis on large-scale empirical studies.

reach—the ability to project power across distance away from the base of that power, such as a military installation or a state's capital.

realpolitik—an approach to the conduct of international politics that seeks to maximize the benefits to the state given the system as it is rather than aspiring to alter the norms and rules by which the state operates.

regionalism—the clustering of politics in geographically concentrated places, including attempts at developing international institutions and trading partnerships.

secessionist conflict—a conflict wherein the rebelling group seeks to leave with some portion of territory from an existing state to another existing state or to create a new state.

second strike—a deployed nuclear arsenal large enough to withstand a sudden attack and still have the capacity to retaliate.

shatterbelts—geographic spaces in the international system that are uniquely prone to conflict, typically residing between two uniquely powerful states and offering some geostrategic value.

states—territorially based actors with recognized control over some geographic space with a single government. Recognition as legitimate frequently originates in an international body, such as the United Nations, or from the most powerful state in the system, such as the United States.

status—the recognition of a position in the hierarchy, role, or authority that is both self-ascribed internally as well as attributed by all or some relevant group of states.

status quo—the existing norms and rules that govern the international system and its conduct, shaping expectations of how actors might behave.

strategic rivalries—competition between two states over a substantive strategic issue that may or may not turn violent.

sufficient condition—a variable that guarantees an outcome when present.

supranational law—involving more than one country or having power or authority that is greater than that of single countries.

system services—costs most often born by the dominant power within an organization, for example, the North Atlantic Treaty Organization supported by the United States.

theory—an explanation for the cause of some outcome.

Treaty of Versailles—the event that diplomatically ended World War I. It is thought to have contributed to World War II as it required substantial payments from the defeated to the victors undermining their recovery and causing grievances.

war—a severely violent conflict between two states, typically involving more than 1,000 battle deaths.

Washington Consensus—the set of provisions created by U.S. economic theorists that have become the foundation of much of international developmental aid.

Westphalian System—concept of sovereign states being independent entities. It is no longer centralized by loyalty to individuals such as monarchs but loyalty to the territorial state.

Notes

CHAPTER 1: A HIERARCHICAL APPROACH

1. Robert A. Dahl, "The Concept of Power," *Behavioral Science* 2, no. 3 (1957): 201.

2. J. Patrick Rhamey Jr and Bryan R. Early, "Going for the Gold: Status-Seeking Behavior and Olympic Performance," *International Area Studies Review* 16, no. 3 (2013): 244–261.

3. David A. Lake, "Escape from the State of Nature: Authority and Hierarchy in World Politics," *International Security* 32, no. 1 (2007): 47–79; Thomas J. Volgy, Renato Corbetta, Keith A. Grant, and Ryan G. Baird, eds., *Major Powers and the Quest for Status in International Politics* (New York: Palgrave, 2011).

4. Distinguishing between opportunity and willingness as applied as a framework for state behavior originates with Harvey Starr, "'Opportunity' and 'Willingness' as Ordering Concepts in the Study of War," *International Interactions* 4, no. 4 (1978): 363–387.

5. For this reason, many statistical analyses of international politics focus only on relationships between neighboring states and major powers, as the opportunity for some outcome is considered basically zero if two states are both nonmajor powers and distant from one another. See Douglas Lemke and William Reed. "The Relevance of Politically Relevant Dyads," *Journal of Conflict Resolution* 45, no. 1 (2001):126–44.

6. World Bank National Accounts Data and Organisation for Economic Cooperation and Development National Accounts Data Files. Last accessed July 12, 2019, https://data.worldbank.org.

7. Ali Fisunoglu, Kyungkook Kang, Tadeusz Kugler, and Jacek Kugler, "Absolute Political Capacity Dataset, 1960–2015." Presented at the annual meeting of the International Studies Association, Toronto, Canada, March 27–30, 2019.

8. The formula for scaling a state's power over distance can be found in Bueno de Mesquita, Bruce, *The War Trap* (New Haven, CT: Yale University Press, 1981). See pp. 103–108.

9. See Renato Corbetta, Thomas J. Volgy, and J. Patrick Rhamey, "Major Power Status (In)Consistency and Political Relevance in International Relations Studies," *Peace Economics, Peace Science and Public Policy* 19, no. 3 (2013): 291–307.

10. Charles F. Doran, *Systems in Crisis: New Imperatives of High Politics at Century's End* (Cambridge: Cambridge University Press, 1991); David M. Edelstein, *Over the Horizon: Time, Uncertainty, and the Rise of Great Powers* (Ithaca, NY: Cornell University Press, 2017).

11. For additional discussion of the relationship between role and hierarchical position in the system, see the work on role theory and the corresponding discussion of the United States and Israel in Cameron Thies, *The United States, Israel, and the Search for International Order: Socializing States* (New York: Routledge, 2013).

12. Dale C. Copeland, "Realism and Neorealism in the Study of Regional Conflict," in *International Relations Theory and Regional Transformation*, ed. T. V. Paul (Cambridge: Cambridge University Press, 2012), 49–73.

13. There are hierarchical approaches that are less empirical in their research, such as the English school and World Systems Theory. Barry Buzan, *An Introduction to the English School: The Societal Approach* (Cambridge: Polity, 2014); Immanuel Wallerstein, *World-Systems Analysis: Theory and Methodology* (Beverly Hills, CA: Sage, 1982).

14. Lake, "Escape from the State of Nature," 17.

15. Lake, "Escape from the State of Nature," 41.

16. G. John Ikenberry, *Liberal Leviathan: The Origins, Crisis, and Transformation of the American World Order* (Princeton, NJ: Princeton University Press, 2011).

17. James N. Rosenau, "Pre-Theories and Theories of Foreign Policy," in *The Scientific Study of Foreign Policy*, ed. James N. Rosenau (New York: New York Free Press, 1971), 95–150.

CHAPTER 2: CONCEPTS AND MEASURES

1. Jack S. Levy, 1988. "Domestic Politics and War," *Journal of Interdisciplinary History* 18, no. 4 (1988): 662.

2. See, for example, Douglas M. Gibler, 2012. *The Territorial Peace: Borders, State Development, and International Conflict* (Cambridge: Cambridge University Press, 2012).

3. Edward D. Mansfield and Jack Snyder. 1995. "Democratization and the Danger of War," *International Security* 20, no. 1 (1995): 5–38.

4. Stephen L. Quackenbush, L. 2011. *Understanding General Deterrence: Theory and Application* (New York: Palgrave Macmillan, 2011); Frank C. Zagare and D. Marc Kilgour, *Perfect Deterrence* (Cambridge: Cambridge University Press, 2000).

5. Although challenging, questions related to this issue can be approached empirically. See, for example, Mary Caprioli and Mark A. Boyer, "Gender, Violence, and International Crisis." *Journal of Conflict Resolution* 45, no. 4 (2001): 503–18.

6. For a more detailed discussion, see, for example, Alice H. Eagly and Mary C. Johannesen-Schmidt, "The Leadership Styles of Women and Men," *Journal of Social Issues* 57, no. 4 (2002): 781–97.

7. Central Intelligence Agency, *Soviet Military Power 1985* (Washington, DC: Central Intelligence Agency, 1985).

8. This is not an exact number, but the working estimation of the total production of the T/54/55, including licensed production, is approximately 100,000 units. See Christopher F. Foss, *Jane's Tanks and Combat Vehicles Recognition Guide*, 3rd ed. (New York: Collins, 2003), for details on tank dimensions, although the story of metal circling the Earth is likely apocryphal.

9. This is when taking into account total U.S. military expenditure by state. U.S. Department of Defense, Office of Economic Adjustment, *Defense Spending by State—Fiscal Year 2017*. (Washington, DC: Department of Defense, 2017).

10. Ronald L. Tammen and Jacek Kugler, eds, *The Performance of Nations* (Lanham, MD: Rowman and Littlefield, 2012).

11. See, for example, the use of relative power in the form of capability ratios in many international relations statistical analyses, such as William J. Dixon, "Democracy and the Peaceful Settlement of International Conflict," *American Political Science Review* 88, no. 1 (1994): 14–32.

12. William R Thompson, "Polarity, the Long Cycle, and Global Power Warfare," *Journal of Conflict Resolution* 30 (1986): 587–615.

13. Douglas Lemke, *Regions of War and Peace* (Cambridge: Cambridge University Press, 2002).

14. Jonathan Markowitz, Christopher Fariss, and R. Black McMahan, "Producing Goods and Projecting Power: How What You Make Influences What You Take," *Journal of Conflict Resolution* 63, no. 6 (2019): 1368–402.

CHAPTER 3: INTERNATIONAL CONFLICT

1. Brock F. Tessman and Steve Chan, "Power Cycles, Risk Propensity, and Great-Power Deterrence," *Journal of Conflict Resolution* 48, no. 2 (2004): 131–53.

2. Michelle Benson, "Extending the Bounds of Power Transition Theory," *International Interactions* 33, no. 3 (2007): 211–15.

3. William J. Dixon, "Democracy and the Peaceful Settlement of International Conflict," *American Political Science Review* 88, no. 1 (1994): 14–32.

4. Neta C. Crawford, "Human Cost of the Post-9/11 Wars: Lethality and the Need for Transparency," 2018, Watson Institute, Province, RI.

5. See, for example, Jonathan W. Keller and Dennis M. Foster, "Don't Tread on Me: Constraint-Challenging Presidents and Strategic Conflict Avoidance," *Presidential Studies Quarterly* 46, no. 4 (2016): 756–62.

6. Hans J. Morgenthau, *Politics among Nations: The Struggle for Power and Peace*, 6th ed., rev. by Kenneth W. Thompson (New York: McGraw-Hill, [1948] 1985).

7. Stephen G. Brooks and William C. Wohlforth, *America Abroad: Why the Sole Superpower Should not Pull Back from the World* (Oxford: Oxford University Press, 2016), 13.

8. Douglas Lemke, *Regions of War and Peace* (Cambridge: Cambridge University Press, 2002). See p. 99.

9. See, for example, the graphs of capabilities on pp. 14 and 15 in William C. Wohlforth, "The Stability of a Unipolar World," *International Security* 24, no. 1 (1999): 5–41.

10. See Bueno de Mesquita, *The War Trap* (New Haven, CT: Yale University, 1981) about when states might fight losing wars.

11. David A. Lake 2009. *Hierarchy in International Relations* (Cornell, NY: Cornell University Press, 2009).

12. Peter J. Katzenstein, *A World of Regions: Asia and Europe in the American Imperium* (Ithaca, NY: Cornell University Press, 2005).

13. Dale C. Copeland, "Realism and Neorealism in the Study of Regional Conflict," in *International Relations Theory and Regional Transformation*, ed. T. V. Paul (Cambridge: Cambridge University Press, 2012), 49–73.

14. John J. Mearsheimer, "Back to the Future: Instability in Europe after the Cold War," *International Security* 15, no. 1 (1990): 5–56.

15. Lemke, *Regions of War and Peace*.

16. The loss of strength gradient is first proposed by Kenneth E. Boulding, *Conflict and Defense: A General Theory* (San Francisco, CA: Harper, 1962). The formula that Lemke uses is adapted from Bueno de Mesquita, *The War Trap*.

17. Lemke, *Regions of War and Peace*, 134.

18. J. Patrick Rhamey, Jr., Michael O. Slobodchikoff, and Thomas J. Volgy, "Order and Disorder across Geopolitical Space: The Effect of Declining Dominance on Interstate Conflict," *Journal of International Relations and Development* 18, no. 4 (2015): 383–406.

19. Paul R. Hensel and Paul F. Diehl, "Testing Empirical Propositions about Shatterbelts, 1945–1976," *Political Geography* 13, no. 1 (1994): 33–51.

20. J. Patrick Rhamey, Jr., and Bryan R. Early, "Going for the Gold: Status Seeking Behavior and Olympic Performance," *International and Area Studies Review*, 16, no. 4 (2013): 244–61.

21. Thomas J. Volgy, Renato Corbetta, Keith Grant, and Ryan Baird, eds., *Major Powers and the Quest for Status in International Politics: Global and Regional Perspectives* (London: Palgrave Macmillan, 2011).

22. Zeev Maoz, "Network Polarization, Network Interdependence, and International Conflict, 1816–2002," *Journal of Peace Research* 43, no. 4 (2006): 391–411.

23. Birol A. Yesilada, Jacek Kugler, Gaspare Genna, and Osman Goktug Tanrikulu, *Global Power Transition and the Future of the European Union* (New York: Routledge, 2017).

24. Douglas Lemke and William Reed, "Regime Types and Status Quo Evaluations: Power Transition Theory and the Democratic Peace," *International Interactions* 22, no. 2 (1996): 143–64.

25. Jacek Kugler, Ronald L. Tammen, and John Thomas, "How Political Performance Impacts Conflict and Growth," *The Performance of Nations*, ed. Jacek Kugler and Ronald L. Tammen (Lanham, MD: Rowman and Littlefield), 75–96, 2012. For a detailed discussion of the political economy of the Third Reich and how excessive extraction quickly crippled the economy and therefore military, see Gunter Reimann, *The Vampire Economy: Doing Business under Fascism* (Auburn, AL: Ludwig von Mises Institute, 2011).

26. Renato Corbetta, Thomas J. Volgy, and J. Patrick Rhamey, Jr., "Major Power Status (In)Consistency and Political Relevance in International Relations Studies," *Peace Economics, Peace Science and Public Policy* 19, no. 3 (2013): 291–307.

27. Patricia L. Sullivan and Michael T. Koch. 2011, "MIPS_codebook_Sullivan. pdf," 2011. Replication data for Military Intervention by Powerful States (MIPS), last accessed November 14, 2019. Harvard Dataverse, V1, https://doi.org/10.7910/DVN/KRUFQH/ZDOATU.

28. Lake, *Hierarchies*, 2009.

29. Lake, *Hierarchies*, 2009, 111.

30. Data available at www.volgy.org/projects-and-data. J. Patrick Rhamey, Kirssa Cline, Nicholas Thorne, Jacob Cramer, Jennifer L. Miller, and Thomas J. Volgy, "The Diplomatic Contacts Database v. 3.0" (2012), School of Government and Public Policy, University of Arizona, Tucson.

31. Corbetta, Volgy, and Rhamey, "Major Power Status"; Brian Efird, Jacek Kugler, and Gaspare M. Genna, "From War to Integration: Generalizing Power Transition Theory." *International Interactions* 29, no. 4 (2003): 293–313.

32. Thomas J. Volgy, Kelly Marie Gordell, Paul Bezerra, and J. Patrick Rhamey, Jr., "Conflict, Regions, and Regional Hierarchies," in *Oxford Encyclopedia of Empirical International Relations Theory*, ed. William R. Thompson (Oxford: Oxford University Press, 2017, 335–362).

33. A.F.K. Organski and Jacek Kugler, "The Costs of Major Wars: The Phoenix Factor." *The American Political Science Review* 71, no. 4 (1977): 1347–66; Tadeusz Kugler, Kyungkook Kang, Jacek Kugler, Marina Arbetman-Rabinowitz, and John Thomas, "Demographic and Economic Consequences of Conflict," *International Studies Quarterly* 57, no. 1 (2013): 1–12.

CHAPTER 4: RIVALRIES AND ALLIANCES

1. Brett Ashley Leeds, "Do Alliances Deter Aggression? The Influence of Military Alliances on the Initiation of Militarized Interstate Disputes," *American Journal of Political Science* 47, no. 3 (2003): 427–39.

2. Todd Sandler, "Alliance Formation, Alliance Expansion, and the Core," *Journal of Conflict Resolution* 43, no. 6 (1999): 727–47.

3. Woosang Kim, "Alliance Transitions and Great Power War," *American Journal of Political Science* 35, no. 4 (1991): 833–50.

4. Woosang Kim, "Power, Alliance, and Major Wars, 1816–1975," *Journal of Conflict Resolution* 33, no. 2 (1989): 255–73.

5. Leeds, "Do Alliances Deter Aggression?"

6. See text of the Triple Alliance and details on the ATOP coding sheet for ATOP ID 1350. Brett Ashley Leeds, Jeffrey Ritter, Sara McLaughlin Mitchell, and Andrew G. Long, "ATOP V4.01 Codesheets" (August 28, 2018), last accessed July 12, 2019, www.atopdata.org/documentation.html.

7. Brett Ashley Leeds, "Alliance Treaty Obligations and Provisions (ATOP) Codebook, Version 4.0" (2018), 11, www.atopdata.org/data.html.

8. Bruce Bueno de Mesquita, "Measuring Systemic Polarity," *Journal of Conflict Resolution* 19, no. 2 (1975): 187–216.

9. Hans J. Morgenthau, *Politics Among Nations: The Struggle for Power and Peace*, 6th ed., rev. by Kenneth W. Thompson (New York: McGraw-Hill, [1948] 1985).

10. A. F. K. Organski, *World Politics*, 2nd ed. (New York: Knopf, 1968). See p. 339.

11. Kim, "Alliance Transitions."

12. As with the table in chapter 3, polarity is again determined in extended periods, based on the work of William R. Thompson, "Polarity, the Long Cycle, and Global Power Warfare," *Journal of Conflict Resolution* 30 (1986): 587–615.

13. Barry Buzan and Ole Waever, *Regions and Powers: The Structure of International Security* (Cambridge: Cambridge University Press, 2003).

14. Kentaro Sakuwa, "Regional Alliance Structure and International Conflict," *World Political Science* 15, no. 1 (2019): 55–74.

15. Dale C. Copeland, "Realism and Neorealism in the Study of Regional Conflict," in *International Relations Theory and Regional Transformation*, ed. T. V. Paul (Cambridge: Cambridge University Press, 2012), 49–73.

16. See ATOP alliance ID 5090. Brett Ashley Leeds, Jeffrey M. Ritter, Sara McLaughlin Mitchell, and Andrew G. Long, "Alliance Treaty Obligations and Provisions, 1815–1944," *International Interactions* 28, no. 3 (2002): 237–60.

17. John J. Mearsheimer, "Back to the Future: Instability in Europe after the Cold War," *International Security* 15, no. 1 (1990): 5–56.

18. North Atlantic Treaty Organization. "Lord Ismay," last accessed November 14, 2019, https://www.nato.int/cps/en/natohq/declassified_137930.htm.

19. Stephen G. Brooks and William C. Wohlforth, *America Abroad: Why the Sole Superpower Should Not Pull Back from the World* (Oxford: Oxford University Press, 2016). See pp. 88–102.

20. James P. Klein, Gary Goertz, and Paul F. Diehl, "The New Rivalry Data Set: Procedures and Patterns," *Journal of Peace Research* 43, no. 3 (2006): 331–48.

21. Paul F. Diehl and Gary Goertz, *War and Peace in International Rivalry* (Ann Arbor: University of Michigan Press, 2000).

22. William R. Thompson, "Identifying Rivals and Rivalries in World Politics," *International Studies Quarterly* 45, no. 4 (2001): 557–86.

23. Kentaro Sakuwa and William R. Thompson, "On the Origins, Persistence and Termination of Spatial and Positional Rivalries in World Politics: Elaborating a Two-Issue Theory of Conflict Escalation," *International and Areas Studies Review* (2019), https://doi.org/10.1177/2233865919846729.

24. J. Patrick Rhamey, Jr., Michael O. Slobodchikoff, and Thomas J. Volgy, "Order and Disorder across Geopolitical Space: The Effect of Declining Dominance on Interstate Conflict," *Journal of International Relations and Development* 18, no. 4 (2015): 383–406.

CHAPTER 5: INTRASTATE CONFLICTS

1. At the 2018 meeting of the Peace Science Society (International), an elite conference of scholars that began with a focus on understanding the causes of international conflict, almost half of the papers presented were focused instead on conflicts within states rather than between them.

2. Kristian Skrede Gleditsch, Idean Salehyan, and Kenneth Schultz, "Fighting at Home, Fighting Abroad: How Civil Wars Lead to International Disputes," *Journal of Conflict Resolution* 52, no. 2 (2018): 479–506.

3. Douglas Lemke and Patrick M. Regan, "Interventions as Influence," in *The Scourge of War: New Extension on an Old Problem*, ed. Paul F Diehl (Ann Arbor: University of Michigan Press, 2004), 145–68; Michael G. Findley and Tze Kwang Teo, "Rethinking Third-Party Interventions into Civil Wars: An Actor-Centric Approach," *The Journal of Politics* 68, no. 4 (2006): 828–37.

4. Stephen E. Gent, 2008. "Going in When it Counts: Military Intervention and the Outcome of Civil Conflicts," *International Studies Quarterly* 52, no. 4 (2008): 713–35. Data on civil war interventions from Patrick M. Regan, "Third-Party Interventions and the Duration of Intrastate Conflicts," *Journal of Conflict Resolution* 46, no. 1 (2002): 55–73.

5. Meredith Sarkees and Frank Wayman, *Resort to War: 1816–2007* (Washington, DC: CQ Press, 2010).

6. Barry R. Posen, "Civil Wars and the Structure of World Power," *Daedalus* 146, no. 4 (2017): 167–79.

7. Correlates of War Project, "State System Membership List, v2016" (2017), last accessed November 14, 2019. http://correlatesofwar.org.

8. Paul R. Hensel and Paul F. Diehl, 1994. "Testing Empirical Propositions about Shatterbelts, 1945–1976," *Political Geography* 13, no. 1 (1994): 33–52.

9. Patrick M. Regan, *Civil Wars and Foreign Powers: Outside Interventions and Intrastate Conflict* (Ann Arbor: University of Michigan Press, 2000), 28.

10. Lian Stack, "In Slap at Syria, Turkey Shelters Anti-Assad Fighters," *New York Times*, October 27, 2011, Last Accessed December 4, 2019. www.nytimes.com/2011/10/28/world/europe/turkey-is-sheltering-antigovernment-syrian-militia.html

11. Figures on total deaths from the Syria Observatory for Human Rights at www.syriahr.com/en/?p=120851. Data from the United Nations High Commissioner for Refugees (UNHCR) for Syria, last accessed July 29, 2019, available at https://data2.unhcr.org/en/situations/syria.

12. Paul Collier, Anke Hoeffler, and Mans Soderbom, "On the Duration of Civil War," *Journal of Peace Research* 41, no. 3 (2004): 253–73.

13. Paul Collier and Anke Hoeffler, "Greed and Grievance in Civil War." *Oxford Economic Papers* 56(2004): 563–95.

14. James Fearon and David Laitin, "Ethnicity, Insurgency, and Civil War," *American Political Science Review* 97, no. 1 (2003): 75–90.

15. Douglas Lemke and Jeff Carter, "Birth Legacies, State Making, and War," *The Journal of Politics* 78, no. 2 (2016): 497–511.

16. Karl R. DeRouen, Jr., and David Sobek, "The Dynamics of Civil War Duration and Outcome," *Journal of Peace Research* 41, no. 3 (2004): 303–20.

17. The average value for states in the year before experiencing an intrastate conflict is .26. The average for all states is .39. See Ali Fisunoglu, Kyungkook Kang, Tadeusz Kugler, and Jacek Kugler, "Absolute Political Capacity Dataset, 1960–2015" (presented at the annual meeting of the International Studies Association, Toronto, Canada, March 27–30, 2019). For the list of intrastate conflicts, see Sarkees and Wyman, *Resort to War*.

18. Halvard Buhaug and Scott Gates, "The Geography of Civil War," *Journal of Peace Research* 39, no. 4 (2002): 417–33;, Halvard Buhaug and P. Lujala, "Accounting for Scale: Measuring Geography in Quantitative Studies of Civil War," *Political Geography* 24, no. 4 (2005): 399–418.

19. Kristian Skrede Gleditsch, *All International Politics is Local: The Diffusion of Conflict, Integration, and Democratization* (Ann Arbor: University of Michigan Press, 2002).

20. Douglas Lemke, "Intra-national IR in Africa," *Review of International Studies* 37, no. 1 (2011): 49–70.

21. The description of the American Civil War as a "civil war" is a misnomer. The English Civil War, for example, is accurately a civil war as the two sides, monarchists and parliamentarians, struggled for control of the state itself. In the American Civil War, however, the Confederate States declared their secession from the Union, not a desire to overthrow the government. Making these distinctions is important given the different causes and outcomes we might observe between the two conflicts.

22. Katja Favretto, "Should Peacemakers Take Sides? Major Power Mediation, Coercion, and Bias," *American Political Science Review* 103, no. 2 (2009): 248–63.

23. Troop contributions from United Nations, "Summary of Contribution to UN Peacekeeping by Country, Mission, and Post" (2019), last accessed June 14, 2019, https://peacekeeping.un.org/sites/default/files/3-country_and_mission.pdf.

CHAPTER 6: THE COLD WAR

1. GDP data from the Maddison data set lumps Germany together as a single entity. Using the ratio of East German to West German capabilities from the CINC data, GDP is divided between East and West as an approximation. For military spending, we use the values listed in the CINC data. David Singer, Stuart Bremer, and John Stuckey, "Capability Distribution, Uncertainty, and Major Power War, 1820–1965," in *Peace, War, and Numbers*, ed. Bruce Russet (Beverly Hills, CA: Sage, 1972), 19–48; Jutta Bolt, Robert Inklaar, Herman de Jong, and Jan Luiten van Zanden, "Rebasing 'Maddison': New Income Comparisons and the Shape of Long-Run Economic Development," Maddison Project Working Paper 10, Madison Project Database, last accessed November 14, 2019 (2018) www.rug.nl/ggdc/historicaldevelopment/maddison/releases/maddison-project-database-2018.

2. It would be preferable to adjust the economic capabilities by the capacity of individual states as we have done elsewhere. However, given the secretive and heavily fabricated numbers available on Soviet internal taxation and spending, an accurate measure of capacity is unavailable. Even if we were able to adjust by capacity, and if Soviet capacity were greater than the United States, it is highly unlikely that it would be sufficiently high to bring the Soviet Union to parity with the United States.

3. GDP as a measure is not without its flaws. GDP itself can be manipulated by the policy choices of states, as it contains consumer spending, savings rates, exports less imports, and government spending. The first three can be manipulated by policy choices of states indirectly, but government spending is itself a direct reflection of, rather than being an exhibition of, available resources and could be deficit or inflationary spending. A better measure, although not heavily used in the literature, may be adapting the size of the economy (GDP) by the wealth per person within that economy (GDP per capita, thus GDP times GDP per capita) as has been done by Michael Beckley, "The Power of Nations: Measuring What Matters," *International Security*, 43, no. 2 (2018): 7–44. For an example of using alternative analysis using

market capitalization rather than GDP, see Kirssa Cline, J. Patrick Rhamey Jr., Alex is Henshaw, Alesia Sedziaka, Aakriti Tandon, and Thomas J. Volgy, "Identifying Regional Powers and Their Status," in *Major Powers and the Quest for Status in International Politics*, ed. Thomas J. Volgy, Renato Corbetta, Keith A. Grant, and Ryan G. Baird (New York: Palgrave Macmillan, 2011), 133–57.

4. William C. Wohlforth, "The Stability of a Unipolar World," *International Security* 24, no. 1 (1999): 5–41.

5. Franklyn D. Holzman, "Soviet Military Spending: Assessing the Numbers Game," *International Security* 6, no. 4 (1982): 78–100.

6. Robert Krulwich, "You (and Almost Everyone You Know) Owe Your Life to This Man." *National Geographic*, March 24, 2016, last accessed July 29, 2019, https://news.nationalgeographic.com/2016/03/you-and-almost-everyone-you-know-owe-your-life-to-this-man/.

7. Thomas J. Volgy, Renato Corbetta, Keith A. Grant, and Ryan G. Baird, *Major Powers and the Quest for Status in International Politics* (New York: Palgrave Macmillan, 2011).

8. Stephen G. Brooks and William C. Wohlforth, *America Abroad: Why the Sole Superpower Should not Pull Back from the World* (Oxford: Oxford University Press, 2016).

9. James P. Klein, Gary Goertz, and Paul F. Diehl, "The New Rivalry Data Set: Procedures and Patterns," *Journal of Peace Research* 43, no. 3 (2006): 331–48.

10. Dov H. Levin, "Partisan Electoral Interventions by Great Powers: Introducing the PEIG Dataset," *Conflict Management and Peace Science* 36, no. 1 (2016): 88–106.

11. George F. Kennan [Mr. X], "The Sources of Soviet Conduct," *Foreign Affairs* 25, no.4 (July 1947): 566–82.

12. For an illustration from the year 1960, see J. Patrick Rhamey, Jr., Michael O. Slobodchikoff, and Thomas J. Volgy, "Order and Disorder across Geopolitical Space: The Effect of Declining Dominance on Interstate Conflict," *Journal of International Relations and Development* 18, no. 4 (2015): 383–406. See p. 393.

13. This map was made using historicalmapchart.net, governed by an attribution-sharealike 4.0 international license (CC BY-SA 4.0). Parity line added. Intervention data from Patricia L. Sullivan and Michael T. Koch, "Military Intervention by Powerful States (MIPS) Codebook, Version 2.0" (2008), last accessed June 23, 2019, http://plsullivan.web.unc.edu/files/2011/09/MIPS_codebook_Sullivan.pdf.

CHAPTER 7: ORGANIZATIONAL FORMATION AND EVOLUTION

1. For an exploration of identifying institutional strength and evolution to take on new responsibilities, see Kathy Powers and Gary Goertz, "The Economic-Institutional Construction of Regions: Conceptualisation and Operationalisation," *Review of International Studies* 37, no. 5 (2011): 2387–416.

2. G. John Ikenberry, *Liberal Leviathan: The Origins, Crisis, and Transformation of the American World Order* Princeton, NJ: Princeton University Press, 2011). See p. 5.

3. Robert O. Keohane, *After Hegemony: Cooperation and Discord in the World Political Economy* (Princeton, NJ: Princeton University Press, 1984).

4. Michael J. Gilligan, *Empowering Exporters: Reciprocity, Delegation, and Collective Action in American Trade Policy* (Ann Arbor, MI: University of Michigan Press, 1997).

5. Susan Strange, *States and Markets* (London: Pinter, 1988). See p. 25.

6. Strange, *States and Markets*, 24–25.

7. William. R. Thompson, "Long Waves, Technological Innovation, and Relative Decline," *International Organization* 44, no. 2 (1990): 201–33; George Modelski, 1987. *Long Cycles in World Politics* (Seattle: University of Washington Press, 1987); Jack Goldstone, *Revolution and Rebellion in the Early Modern World* (Berkeley: University of California Press, 1991).

8. Eric Toussaint, "Domination of the United States on the World Bank," *Committee for the Abolition of Third World Debt* (2014), last accessed November 11, 2019, http://cadtm.org/domination-of-the-united-states-on; Randall Stone, *Controlling Institutions: International Organizations and the Global Economy* (New York: Cambridge University Press, 2011).

9. James R. Vreeland and Axel Dreher, *The Political Economy of the United Nations Security Council: Money and Influence* (New York: Cambridge University Press, 2014).

10. Jonathan Kirshner, *Currency and Coercion* (Princeton, NJ: Princeton University Press, 1995).

11. Michael J. Warning, *Transnational Public Governance: Networks, Law, and Legitimacy* (Basingstoke, UK: Palgrave Macmillan, 2009).

12. Relatedly, the large-scale modern war is often considered to be the American Civil War. It was the first major war to make use of mechanized transportation in the form of railroads, steamships, rapid-fire weaponry, and communications technology with the telegraph. All three played pivotal roles in the great world wars that were to follow, increasing in their effectiveness and capacity for destruction.

13. Janet M. Hartley, "Is Russia Part of Europe? Russian Perceptions of Europe in the Reign of Alexander I," *Cahiers du Monde Russia*, 33, no. 4 (1992): 369–85.

14. Deborah Avant and Oliver Westerwinter, eds, *The New Power Politics: Networks and Transnational Security Governance* (New York: Oxford University Press, 2016).

15. C. Randall Henning, *Tangled Governance: International Regime Complexity, the Troika, and the Euro Crisis* (Oxford: Oxford University Press, 2017).

CHAPTER 8: REGIONALIZATION AND TRADE

1. Alexander Morris Carr-Saunders, *World Population: Past Growth and Present Trends* (Oxford: Clarendon Press, 1936); Ronald Inglehart, *Modernization and Postmodernization: Cultural, Economic and Political Change in 43 Societies* (Princeton, NJ: Princeton University Press, 1997); William R. Thompson, *The Emergence of the Global Political Economy* (London: Routledge, 2003); Carla Norrlof, *America's Global Advantage: U.S. Hegemony and International Cooperation* (New York: Cambridge University Press, 2010).

2. Alison Bashford, *Global Population: History, Geopolitics, and Life on Earth* (New York: Columbia University Press, 2014); Jack S. Levy, "Power Transition

Theory and the Rise of China," in *China's Ascent: Power, Security, and the Future of International Politics*, ed. R. S. Ross and Z. Feng (Ithaca, NY: Cornell University Press, 2008), 11–33.

3. Cullen S. Hendrix and Idean Salehyan, "Climate Change, Rainfall, and Social Conflict in Africa," *Journal of Peace Research* 49, no. 1 (2012): 35–50.

4. The one possible exception to this statement is Japan during parts of the 1990s, which spent much of its foreign policy activity beyond its region as a major power. See Kirssa Cline, J. Patrick Rhamey Jr., Thomas J. Volgy, Alexis Henshaw, Alesia Sedziaka, and Aakriti Tandon, "Identifying Regional Powers and Their Status," in *Major Powers and the Quest for Status in International Politics*, ed. Thomas J. Volgy, Renato Corbetta, Keith A. Grant, and Ryan G. Baird (New York: Palgrave MacMillan, 2011), 133–57.

5. Data used to create table 8.1 are available at www.patrickrhamey.com/row. J. Patrick Rhamey, Jr., "Regions of Opportunity and Willingness Data Codebook v3" (2019), last accessed June 30, 2019, www.patrickrhamey.com/row; Thomas J. Volgy, Paul Bezerra, Jacob Cramer, and J. Patrick Rhamey Jr., "The Case for Comparative Regional Analysis in International Politics," *International Studies Review* 19 (2017): 452–80.

6. Rob Picheta, "Nissan Cites Brexit 'Uncertainty' as it Scraps Plans to Build Model in Britain," *CNN*, February 3, 2019, last accessed June 30, 2019, www.cnn.com/2019/02/03/business/nissan-sunderland-scraps-plans-gbr-intl/index.html.

7. Helen Reid, "Brexit Uncertainty Has Cost Britain 600 Million Pounds a Week—Goldman Sachs," *Reuters*, April 1, 2019, last accessed June 30, 2019, www.reuters.com/article/us-britain-eu-goldmansachs/brexit-uncertainty-has-cost-britain-600-million-pounds-a-week-goldman-sachs-idUSKCN1RD25N.

CHAPTER 9: DEVELOPMENT AND GLOBALIZATION

1. Maddison Project Database, version 2018. Jutta Bolt, Robert Inklaar, Herman de Jong, and Jan Luiten van Zanden, "Rebasing 'Maddison': New Income Comparisons and the Shape of Long-Run Economic Development" (2018), Maddison Project Working Paper 10.

2. *Human Development Index (HDI) | Human Development Reports*. Hdr.undp.org, last accessed November 9, 2019, http:hdr.undp.org/en/content/human-development-index-hdi.asp.

3. United Nations, Department of Economic and Social Affairs, Population Division, *World Population Prospects: The 2019 Revision*, DVD Edition (2019), last accessed November 9, 2019, https://population.un.org/wpp/Publications/Files/WPP2019_Highlights.pdf.

4. Robert Solow, "A Contribution to the Theory of Economic Growth," *The Quarterly Journal of Economics* 70, no. 1 (1956): 65. Karl Marx, *Das Kapital, a Critique of Political Economy* (Chicago: H. Regnery, [1818–1883] 1959).

5. Paul M. Romer, "Endogenous Technological Change," *Journal of Political Economy* 98, no. 5 (1990): S71–S102.

6. Bela Balassa, Gerardo M. Bueno, Pedro Pablo Kuczynski, and Mario Henrique Simonsen, *Toward Renewed Economic Growth in Latin America* (Mexico City:

El Colegio de Mexico; Washington: Institute for International Economics, 1986); Daron Acemoglu, Simon Johnson, and James A. Robinson, "The Colonial Origins of Comparative Development: An Empirical Investigation," *American Economic Review* 91, no. 5 (December 2001): 1369–401.

7. Gerard Caprio and Patrick Honohan, *Finance for Growth: Policy Choices in a Volatile World* (Washington, DC: World Bank, 2001).

8. The full list is (1) Fiscal Discipline, (2) Reordering Public Expenditure Priorities, (3) Tax Reform, (4) Liberalization of Interest Rates, (5) Competitive Exchange Rates, (6) Trade Liberalization, (8) Privatization, (9) Deregulation, and (10) Property Rights. See chapter 2 of John Williamson, *Latin American Adjustment: How Much Has Happened?* (Washington, DC: Peterson Institute for International Economics, 1990). For evaluation, see also Nancy Birdsall and Augusto de la Torre, *Washington Contentious: Economic Policies for Social Equity in Latin America* (Washington: Carnegie Endowment for International Peace and Inter-American Dialogue, 2001); John Williamson, "What Should the World Bank Think about the Washington Consensus?" *World Bank Research Observer* 15, no. 2 (August 2000): 251–64.

9. Joseph E. Stiglitz, *Globalization and its Discontents* (New York: Norton, 2002).

10. Hernando De Soto, *The Mystery of Capital: Why Capitalism Triumphs in the West and Fails Everywhere Else* (London: Black Swan, 2000).

11. William Easterly, *The Elusive Quest for Growth: Economists' Adventures and Misadventures in the Tropics* (Boston: MIT Press, 2001).

CHAPTER 10: CONTEMPORARY REGIONAL ORDERS IN THE AMERICAN IMPERIUM

1. Thomas J. Volgy, Paul Bezerra, Jacob Cramer, and J. Patrick Rhamey Jr. "The Case for Comparative Regional Analysis in International Politics," *International Studies Review* 19, no. 3 (2017): 452–80.

2. See, for example, Craig Volden, "States as Policy Laboratories: Emulating Success in Children's Health Insurance Program," *American Journal of Political Science*, 50, no. 2 (2006): 294–312.

3. Volgy et al., "The Case for Comparative Regional Analysis."

4. Regional designations are those from the FIGO data. Thomas J. Volgy, Elizabeth Fausett, Keith A Grant, and Stuart Rodgers, "Identifying Formal Intergovernmental Organizations," *Journal of Peace Research* 45, no. 6 (2008): 849–62, data, last accessed July 27, 2019, are available online at www.u.arizona.edu/~volgy/data.html.

5. Peter J. Katzenstein, *A World of Regions: Asia and Europe in the American Imperium* (Ithaca, NY: Cornell University Press, 2005).

6. Daniel H. Deudney, "The Philadelphian System: Sovereignty, Arms Control, and Balance of Power in the American States-Union, Circa 1787–1861," *International Organization* 49, no. 2 (1995): 191–228.

7. Janet M. Hartley, "Is Russia Part of Europe? Russian Perceptions of Europe in the Reign of Alexander I," *Cahiers du Monde Russia*, 33, no. 4 (1992): 369–85.

8. Colin Ward, "The Anarchist Sociology of Federalism." In *Autonomy, Solidarity, Possibility: The Colin Ward Reader*, ed. D. F. White and C. Wilbert (Oakland, CA: AK Press, 2011), 285–94.

9. For a more detailed examination of the history and decision-making of the European Union, see Michelle Cini and Nieves Pérez-Solórzano Borragán, *European Union Politics*, 5th ed. (Oxford: Oxford University Press, 2016).

10. See for example Winston Churchill, "United States of Europe: September 19, 1946. University of Zurich," 1946, last accessed June 16, 2019. https://winstonchur chill.org/resources/speeches/1946-1963-elder-statesman/united-states-of-europe

11. Thomas Pedersen, "Cooperative Hegemony: Power, Ideas and Institutions in Regional Integration," *Review of International Studies* 28, no. 4 (2002): 677–96.

12. See for more detail Organization of African Unity, *Constitutive Act of the African Union*, last accessed July 27, 2019, https://au.int/sites/default/files/pages/34873-file-constitutiveact_en.pdf.

13. Thomas Kwasi Tieku, "The African Union: Successes and Failures," in *Oxford Research Encyclopedia of Politics* (Oxford: Oxford University Press, 2019), last accessed November 14, 2019, https://oxfordre.com/politics/view/10.1093/acrefore/9780190228637.001.0001/acrefore-9780190228637-e-703.

14. See the decade maps for the ROW data at http://patrickrhamey.com/row. J. Patrick Rhamey, Jr., "Regions of Opportunity and Willingness Data Codebook v3" (2019), last accessed July 28, 2019, www.patrickrhamey.com/row. Volgy et al., "The Case for Comparative Regional Analysis."

15. James J. Hentz, *Into Africa*, Hoover Digest 4 (Palo Alto, CA: Hoover Institution, 2008).

16. Kirssa Cline, J. Patrick Rhamey, Jr., Thomas J. Volgy, Alexis Henshaw, Alesia Sedziaka, and Aakriti Tandon, "Identifying Regional Powers and Their Status," in *Major Powers and the Quest for Status in International Politics*, ed. Thomas J. Volgy, Renato Corbetta, Keith A. Grant, and Ryan G. Baird (New York: Palgrave Macmillan, 2011), 133–57.

17. The regional space where South Africa is a regional power is restricted to only Zambia, Zimbabwe, Mozambique, Lesotho, and Eswatini.

18. For example, see Yasmine Ryan, "Gabon 'Siphoned Funds' to France," *Al-Jazeera*, December 29, 2010, www.aljazeera.com/news/africa/2010/12/20101 22984115531832.html.

19. David Stasavage, "The CFA Franc Zone and Fiscal Discipline," *Journal of African Economies* 6, no. 1 (1997): 132–67.

20. Denis M. Tull, "China's Engagement in Africa: Scope, Significance and Consequences," *Journal of Modern African Studies* 44, no. 3 (2006): 459–79.

21. Douglas Lemke, *Regions of War and Peace* (Cambridge: Cambridge University Press, 2002); Thomas J. Volgy, Kelly Marie Gordell, Paul Bezerra, and J. Patrick Rhamey, Jr., "Conflict, Regions, and Regional Hierarchies," in *Oxford Encyclopedia of Empirical International Relations Theory*, ed. William R. Thompson (Oxford: Oxford University Press, 2017), 335–62.

CHAPTER 11: DETERRENCE AND THE POTENTIAL FOR GREAT-POWER WAR

1. Kenneth Waltz, "The Spread of Nuclear Weapons: More May Better." *Adelphi Papers* 21, no. 171 (1981).

2. Walter Brown Note (Brown, Walter, Excerpts from the "Book"), July 10 to August 3, 1945, Box 2-1, James Byrnes Papers, State Department Material, Clemson: Clemson University Library.

3. Ward Wilson, "The Bomb Did not Beat Japan . . . Stalin Did," *Foreign Policy*, May 30, 2013, last accessed June 25, 2019, https://foreignpolicy.com/2013/05/30/the-bomb-didnt-beat-japan-stalin-did/.

4. *United States Strategic Bombing Survey Summary Report (Pacific War)* (Washington, DC: U.S. Government Printing Office, 1946, July 1), 26, last accessed June 26, 2019, www.anesi.com/ussbs01.htm#jstetw.

5. Kenneth N. Waltz, 1988. "The Origins of War in Neorealist Theory," *Journal of Interdisciplinary History* 18, no. 4 (1988): 615–28. Erik Gartzke and Matthew Kroenig, "Nukes with Numbers: Empirical Research on the Consequences of Nuclear Weapons for International Conflict," *Annual Review of Political Science* 19 (2016): 397–412.

6. Stephen L. Quackenbush, *Understanding General Deterrence: Theory and Application* (New York: Palgrave Macmillan, 2011); Frank C. Zagare and D. Marc Kilgour, *Perfect Deterrence* (Cambridge: Cambridge University Press, 2000).

7. Quackenbush, *Understanding General Deterrence*; Zagare and Kilgour, *Perfect deterrence*.

8. Stephen L. Quackenbush, "Empirical Analyses of Deterrence," in *Oxford Encyclopedia of Empirical International Relations Theory*, ed. William R. Thompson (Oxford: Oxford University Press, 2017), 682–701.

9. Brett V. Benson, "Unpacking Alliances: Deterrent and Compellent Alliances and Their Relationship with Conflict 1816–2000," *Journal of Politics*, 73, no. 4 (2011): 1111–27.

10. Kyungkook Kang and Jacek Kugler, "Assessment of Deterrence and Missile Defense in East Asia: A Power Transition Perspective," *International Area Studies Review* 18, no. 3 (2015): 280–96; Jacek Kugler and Frank Zagare, "The Long-Term Stability of Deterrence," *International Interactions* 15, no. 3/4 (1990): 255–78.

11. Kenneth N. Waltz, "Why Iran Should Get the Bomb: Nuclear Balancing Would Mean Stability," *Foreign Affairs* 91, no. 4 (July/August 2012): 2–5.

12. Carl Sagan, Richard Turco, George W. Rathjens, Ronald H. Siegel, Starley L. Thompson, and Stephen H. Schneider, 1986. "The Nuclear Winter Debate," *Foreign Affairs* 65, no. 1 (Fall 1986): 163–78.

13. Waltz, "The Spread of Nuclear Weapons."

14. Leonard Goldberg (executive producer) and John Badham (director). *WarGames* [Motion Picture] (United States: MGM/UA, 1983).

15. Bernard Brodie, *The Absolute Weapon: Atomic Power and World Order* (New York: Harcourt, Brace and Company, 1946).

16. "New START Treaty Aggregate Numbers of Strategic Offensive Arms," factsheet, January 12 (effective date: March 1, 2019), last accessed November 14, 2019, www.state.gov/new-start-treaty-aggregate-numbers-of-strategic-offensive-arms-10/#_ftn1

17. Ministry of Defense, "UK Nuclear Deterrent" (2019), last accessed November 14, 2019, https://assets.publishing.service.gov.uk/government/uploads/system/uploads/attachment_data/file/510878/Fact_sheet-nuclear_deterrent_FINAL_v15.pdf

18. The best source for constantly updated information on nuclear arsenals is produced by the *Bulletin of the Atomic Scientists*, available online at https://thebulletin.org/nuclear-notebook-multimedia.

CHAPTER 12: LIBERALISM AND THE
DEMOCRATIC PEACE

1. Data from Freedom House code both political and personal freedoms, which begins in 1973. Freedom House, "Freedom in the World Data and Resources" (2019), last accessed June 18, 2018, https://freedomhouse.org/content/freedom-world-data-and-resources. Data coding just democracy is available from the Polity IV data set and date back to 1816. See Monty G. Marshall, Ted Robert Gurr, and Keith Jaggers, *Polity IV Project: Political Regime Characteristics and Transitions, 1800–2017* (Vienna, VA: Center for Systemic Peace, 2018), last accessed July 21, 2019, www.systemicpeace.org/inscrdata.html.

2. For the sake of readability, we restrict democracy to 8 and higher in Polity IV, as the traditional threshold of 6 and higher would greatly increase the number of states in the diagram. Thus, we labeled the democracy category "most democratic." Similarly, we included the top fifteen trading partners, ranging from Switzerland up through China. Microstates not included in the Polity IV data, such as Iceland and Malta, are left out of the diagram despite institutional membership.

3. Peter J. Katzenstein, *A World of Regions: Asia and Europe in the American Imperium* (Ithaca, NY: Cornell University Press, 2005).

4. R. J. Rummel, "Libertarianism and International Violence," *Journal of Conflict Resolution* 27, no. 1 (1983): 27–71; R. J. Rummel, "Libertarian Propositions on Violence within and between Nations: A Test against Published Research Results," *Journal of Conflict Resolution* 29, no. 3 (1985): 419–55.

5. Immanuel Kant, "Perpetual Peace: A Philosophical Sketch," in *Kant: Political Writings*, ed. H. S. Reiss (Cambridge: Cambridge University Press, [1795] 1991), 93–130; See also Bruce Russett, John R. Oneal, and David R. Davis, "The Third Leg of the Kantian Tripod for Peace: International Organizations and Militarized Disputes, 1950–1985," *International Organization* 52, no. 3 (1998): 441–67.

6. John J. Mearsheimer, "The False Promise of International Institutions," *International Security*, 19, no. 3 (1995): 5–49.

7. Robert Axelrod and Robert O. Keohane, "Achieving Cooperation under Anarchy: Strategies and Institutions," *World Politics* 38, no. 1 (1985): 226–54.

8. Jack S. Levy, "Domestic Politics and War," *Journal of Interdisciplinary History* 18, no. 4 (1988): 653–73. See p. 662.

9. William J. Dixon, "Democracy and the Management of International Conflict," *Journal of Conflict Resolution* 37, no. 1 (1993): 42–68.

10. James D. Fearon, "Domestic Political Audiences and the Escalation of International Disputes," *American Political Science Review* 88 (1994): 577–92.

11. Bruce Bueno de Mesquita, James D. Morrow, Randolph M. Siverson, and Alastair Smith, "An Institutional Explanation of the Democratic Peace," *American Political Science Review*, 93, no. 4 (1999): 791–807.

12. For example, see Erik Gartzke, "The Capitalist Peace," *American Journal of Political Science* 51, no.1 (2007): 166–91.

13. Douglas M. Gibler, *The Territorial Peace: Borders, State Development, and International Conflict* (Cambridge: Cambridge University Press, 2012).

14. See, for example, the discussion by William R. Thompson, "Democracy and Peace: Putting the Cart before the Horse?" *International Organization* 50, no. 1 (1996): 141–74.

15. Raymond Cohen, "Pacific Unions: A Reappraisal of the Theory that Democracies Do Not Go to War with Each Other," *Review of International Studies* 20, no. 3 (1994): 207–23.

16. Monty G. Marshall, Ted Robert Gurr, and Keith Jaggers, *Polity IV Project: Political Regime Characteristics and Transitions, 1800–2017* (Vienna, VA: Center for Systemic Peace, 2018), last accessed July 21, 2019, www.systemicpeace.org/inscrdata.html.

17. Michael Coppedge, John Gerring, Carl Henrik Knutsen, Staffan I. Lindberg, Jan Teorell, David Altman, Michael Bernhard, M. Steven Fish, Adam Glynn, Allen Hicken, Anna Lührmann, Kyle L. Marquardt, Kelly McMann, Pamela Paxton, Daniel Pemstein, Brigitte Seim, Rachel Sigman, Svend-Erik Skaaning, Jeffrey Staton, Steven Wilson, Agnes Cornell, Lisa Gastaldi, Haakon Gjerløw, Nina Ilchenko, Joshua Krusell, Laura Maxwell, Valeriya Mechkova, Juraj Medzihorsky, Josefine Pernes, Johannes von Römer, Natalia Stepanova, Aksel Sundström, Eitan Tzelgov, Yi-ting Wang, Tore Wig, and Daniel Ziblatt, "V-Dem [Country-Year/Country-Date] Dataset v9", Varieties of Democracy (V-Dem) Project. https://doi.org/10.23696/vdemcy19. Last Accessed 27 August 2019; Daniel Pemstein, Kyle L. Marquardt, Eitan Tzelgov, Yi-ting Wang, Juraj Medzihorsky, Joshua Krusell, Farhad Miri, and Johannes von Römer, "The V-Dem Measurement Model: Latent Variable Analysis for Cross-National and Cross-Temporal Expert-Coded Data" (2019), V-Dem Working Paper No. 21, 4th ed., Varieties of Democracy Institute, University of Gothenburg.

18. John Högström, "Does the Choice of Democracy Measure Matter? Comparisons between Two Leading Democracy Indices, Freedom House and Polity IV," *Government and Opposition* 48, no. 2 (2013): 201–21.

19. For a more in-depth discussion, see Steve Chan, "In Search of the Democratic Peace: Problems and Promise," *Mershon International Studies Review* 41, no. 1 (1997): 59–91.

20. Ron Mackay, *Britain's Fleet Air Arm in World War Two* (Atglen, PA: Schiffer, 2005), 141.

21. George Modelski, "Evolutionary Paradigm for Global Politics," *International Studies Quarterly* 40, no. 3 (1996): 321–42.

22. For a series of discussions of how system-level effects impact the observation of the democratic peace, see Karen Rasler and William R. Thompson, *Puzzles of the Democratic Peace: Theory, Geopolitics and the Transformation of World Politics* (London: Palgrave Macmillan, 2005).

23. George Modelski, "Long Cycles and International Regimes," *E-International Relations*, October 15, 2012, last accessed July 31, 2019, www.e-ir.info/2012/10/15/long-cycles-and-international-regimes/. See also the idea that the value of democracy is affected by peace at the systemic level in Sara McLaughlin Mitchell, Scott Gates, and Håvard Hegre, "Evolution in Democracy-War Dynamics," *Journal of Conflict Resolution* 43, no. 6 (1999): 771–92.

24. Kristian Skrede Gleditsch, *All International Politics Is Local: The Diffusion of Conflict, Integration, and Democratization* (Ann Arbor: University of Michigan Press, 2002).

25. G. John Ikenberry, *After Victory: Institutions, Strategic Restraint, and the Rebuilding of Order after Major Wars* (Princeton, NJ: Princeton University Press, 2001).

26. Susan Strange, *The Retreat of the State: The Diffusion of Power in the World Economy* (Cambridge: Cambridge University Press, 1996). Ernst B. Haas, *Beyond the Nation State* (Stanford, CA: Stanford University Press, 1964).

27. Daniel H. Deudney, "The Philadelphian System: Sovereignty, Arms Control, and Balance of Power in the American Trans-Union, Circa 1787–1861," *International Organization* 49, no. 2 (1995): 191–228.

28. Douglas Lemke and William Reed, "Regime Types and Status Quo Evaluations: Power Transition Theory and the Democratic Peace," *International Interactions*, 22, no. 2 (1996): 143–64.

CHAPTER 13: LESSONS FOR THE AMERICAN IMPERIUM FROM THE DECLINE OF THE BRITISH EMPIRE

1. H. J. Mackinder, *Democratic Ideals and Reality: A Study in the Politics of Reconstruction* (New York: Henry Holt, 1919), 186.

2. H. J. Mackinder, "The Geographical Pivot of History," *The Geographical Journal* 23, no. 4 (1904): 421–37.

3. For more on the concentration of foreign policy excursions at the beginning of Queen Victoria's reign, often ending in failure, see chapter 1 of Byron Farwell, *Queen Victoria's Little Wars* (New York: W. W. Norton, 1972).

4. David Fromkin, "The Great Game in Asia," *Foreign Affairs* 58, no. 4 (1980): 937–38.

5. Jack Snyder, *Myths of Empire: Domestic Politics and International Ambition* (Ithaca, NY: Cornell University Press, 1991), 4.

6. Snyder, *Myths of Empire*, 49.

7. Snyder, *Myths of Empire*, 170–71.

8. Michael Clodfelter, *Warfare and Armed Conflicts: A Statistical Encyclopedia of Casualty and Other Figures, 1492–2015*, 4th ed. (Jefferson, NC: McFarland, 2017).

9. William Mulligan, "Gladstone and the Primacy of Foreign Policy," in *The Primacy of Foreign Policy in British History, 1660–2000*, ed. William Mulligan and Brendan Simms (London: Palgrave Macmillan, 2010), 181–96.

10. For a more detailed discussion, see Snyder, *Myths of Empire*, chap. 5.

11. Valmai Philips, *Enterprising Australians* (Kensington, New South Wales, Australia: Bay Books, 1984), 22.

12. Jutta Bolt, Robert Inklaar, Herman de Jong and Jan Luiten van Zanden, "Rebasing 'Maddison': New Income Comparisons and the Shape of Long-Run Economic Development" (2018), Maddison Project Database, v 2018, last accessed July 13, 2019, www.ggdc.net/maddison.

13. Christopher Layne, "From Preponderance to Offshore Balancing: America's Future Grand Strategy," *International Security* 22, no. 1 (1997): 86–124.

14. Douglas Lemke, *Regions of War and Peace* (Cambridge: Cambridge University Press, 2002). Thomas J. Volgy, Paul Bezerra, Jacob Cramer, and J. Patrick Rhamey, Jr., "The Case for Comparative Regional Analysis in International Politics," *International Studies Review* 19, no. 3 (2017): 452–80.

15. John J. Mearsheimer, introduction to *American Diplomacy: Sixtieth-Anniversary Expanded Edition* by George F. Kennan (Chicago: University of Chicago Press, 2012), vii–xliv.)

16. Christopher Clark, *The Sleepwalkers: How Europe Went to War in 1914* (New York: Harper Collins, 2012).

17. Rudyard Kipling, "In Aid of Recruiting, Southport," *Southport Guardian*, June 23, 1915.

18. See the text of the German Request for Free Passage through Belgium, August 2, 1914, last accessed November 14, 2019, http://www.nationalarchives.gov.uk/path ways/firstworldwar/first_world_war/p_ultimatum.htm.

19. See, for example, the announcement by the German government, February 14, 1915, last accessed November 14, 2019 https://library.cqpress.com/cqresearcher/document.php?id=cqresrre1939102500.

20. Douglas Carl Peifer, *Choosing War: Presidential Decisions in the* Maine, Lusitania, *and* Panay *Incidents* (Oxford: Oxford University Press, 2016), 88.

21. Diana Preston, Lusitania: *An Epic Tragedy* (New York: Bloomsbury, 2015).

22. Haas, *The Ideological Origins of Great Power Politics, 1789-1989*, 128.

23. George Modelski and William R. Thompson, *Seapower in Global Politics, 1494–1993* (Seattle: University of Washington Press, 1988).

24. Patrick E. Tyler, "China's Military Stumbles Even as Its Power Grows," *New York Times*, December 3, 1996.

25. Reuters, "China Says Its Gender Imbalance 'Most Serious' in the World," January 21, 2015, last accessed July 23, 2019, https://uk.reuters.com/article/uk-china-onechild-idUKKBN0KU0V720150121.

26. David M. Edelstein, *Over the Time Horizon: Time, Uncertainty, and the Rise of Great Powers* (Ithaca, NY: Cornell University Press, 2017).

27. John R. Oneal and Bruce Russett, "Assessing the Liberal Peace with Alternative Specifications: Trade Still Reduces Conflict," *Journal of Peace Research* 36, no. 4 (1999): 423–42.

28. G. John Ikenberry, *Liberal Leviathan: The Origins, Crisis, and Transformation of the American World Order* (Princeton, NJ: Princeton University Press, 2011), 1.

29. Mary Elise Sarotte, "A Broken Promise? What the West Really Told Moscow about NATO Expansion," *Foreign Affairs* 93, no. 5 (September/October 2015): 90–97.

CHAPTER 14: AMERICAN DECLINE, CHINESE RISE, AND THE UNEXPECTED FUTURE

1. Robert Gilpin and William Gilpin, *US Power and the Multinational Corporation* (London: Macmillan, 1975).

2. United Nations, Department of Economic and Social Affairs, Population Division, *World Population Prospects: The 2015 Revision*, DVD Edition (New York: United Nations, Department of Economic and Social Affairs, 2015).

3. Ronald D. Lee and Andrew Mason, "What Is the Demographic Dividend?" *Finance and Development*, 43, no. 3 (2006): 16–17.

4. Tadeusz Kugler and S. Swaminathan, "The Politics of Population," *International Studies Review* 8, no. 4 (2006): 581–96; Kyungkook Kang and Tadeusz Kugler, "International Political Economy and Political Demography: An Interdisciplinary Exploration," in *Interdisciplinary Approaches to International Studies*, ed. Patrick James and Steve Yetiv (London: Palgrave Macmillan, 2006), 263–87; Tadeusz Kugler, "Demography and International Relations: Politics, Economics, Sociology and Public Health," in *Interdisciplinary Approaches to International Studies*, ed. Patrick James and Steve Yetiv (London: Palgrave Macmillan, 2017), 229–61; Tadeusz Kugler, Kyungkook Kang, Jacek Kugler, Marina Arbetman-Rabinowitz, and John Thomas, "Demographic & Economic Consequences of Conflict," *International Studies Quarterly* 57, no. 1 (2013): 1–12.

5. Richard Jackson and Neil Howe, *The Graying of the Great Powers: Demography and the Geopolitics in the 21st Century* (Washington, DC: Center for Strategic and International Studies, 2012).

6. Michael C. Horowitz, "Artificial Intelligence, International Competition, and the Balance of Power," *Texas National Security Review* 1, no. 3 (May 2018): 37–57.

7. Cyberwarfare is a hot topic in policy communities, although some have found that cyber warfare is merely a tool of preexisting espionage techniques; see Brandon Valeriano and Ryan C. Maness, *Cyber War versus Cyber Realities: Cyber Conflict in the International System* (Oxford: Oxford University Press, 2015). However, future AI developments may transition cyber warfare from a hypothetical to a reality.

8. G. John Ikenberry, *Liberal Leviathan: The Origins, Crisis, and Transformation of the American World Order* (Princeton, NJ: Princeton University Press, 2012).

GLOSSARY

1. David A. Lake, "Escape from the State of Nature: Authority and Hierarchy in World Politics," *International Security* 32, no. 1 (2007): 47–79. See p. 50.

2. Erin K. Jenne and Milos Popovic, "Managing Internationalized Civil Wars," in *The Oxford Research Encyclopedia of Empirical International Relations Theory*, vol. 2, ed. William R. Thompson (Oxford: Oxford University Press, 2018), 511–21. See p. 512.

3. This definition is taken from the United Nations Development Programme, "Human Development Index (HDI)," last accessed August 25, 2019, http://hdr.undp.org/en/content/human-development-index-hdi.asp.

4. This most frequently used definition from Robert Dahl does not specify the means, but only that power is used by one to make another do something they believe to be contrary to their interests. See Robert A. Dahl, "The Concept of Power," *Behavioral Science* 2, no. 3 (1957): 201–25. See p. 201.

Bibliography

Acemoglu, Daron, Simon Johnson, and James A. Robinson. 2001. "The Colonial Origins of Comparative Development: An Empirical Investigation." *American Economic Review* 91, no. 5 (December): 1369–401.

Avant, Deborah, and Oliver Westerwinter, eds. 2016. *The New Power Politics: Networks and Transnational Security Governance.* New York: Oxford University Press.

Axelrod, Robert, and Robert O. Keohane. 1985. "Achieving Cooperation under Anarchy: Strategies and Institutions." *World Politics* 38, no. 1:226–54.

Balassa, Bela, Gerardo M. Bueno, Pedro Pablo Kuczynski, and Mario Henrique Simonsen. 1986. *Toward Renewed Economic Growth in Latin America.* Mexico City: El Colegio de Mexico; Washington, DC: Institute for International Economics.

Bashford, Alison. 2014. *Global Population: History, Geopolitics, and Life on Earth.* New York: Columbia University Press.

Beckley, Michael. 2018. "The Power of Nations: Measuring What Matters." *International Security* 43, no. 2:7–44.

Benson, Brett V. 2011. "Unpacking Alliances: Deterrent and Compellent Alliances and their Relationship with Conflict 1816–2000." *Journal of Politics* 73, no. 4:1111–27.

Benson, Michelle. 2007. "Extending the Bounds of Power Transition Theory." *International Interactions* 33, no. 3:211–15.

Birdsall, Nancy, and Augusto de la Torre. 2001. *Washington Contentious: Economic Policies for Social Equity in Latin America.* Washington, DC: Carnegie Endowment for International Peace and Inter-American Dialogue.

Bolt, Jutta, Robert Inklaar, Herman de Jong, and Jan Luiten van Zanden. 2018. "Rebasing 'Maddison': New Income Comparisons and the Shape of Long-Run Economic Development," Maddison Project Working Paper 10, Groningen: University of Groningen.

Boulding, Kenneth E. 1962. *Conflict and Defense: A General Theory*. San Francisco, CA: Harper.

Brodie, Bernard. 1946. *The Absolute Weapon: Atomic Power and World Order*. New York: Harcourt, Brace and Company.

Brooks, Stephen G., and William C. Wohlforth. 2016. *America Abroad: Why the Sole Superpower Should not Pull Back from the World*. Oxford: Oxford University Press.

Bueno de Mesquita, Bruce. 1975. "Measuring Systemic Polarity." *Journal of Conflict Resolution* 19, no. 2:187–216.

Bueno de Mesquita, Bruce. 1981. *The War Trap*. New Haven, CT: Yale University Press.

Bueno de Mesquita, Bruce, James D. Morrow, Randolph M. Siverson, and Alastair Smith. 1999. "An Institutional Explanation of the Democratic Peace." *American Political Science Review* 93, no. 4: 791-807.

Buhaug, Halvard, and P. Lujala 2005. "Accounting for Scale: Measuring Geography in Quantitative Studies of Civil War." *Political Geography* 24, no. 4:399–418.

Buhaug, Halvard, and Scott Gates. 2002. "The Geography of Civil War." *Journal of Peace Research* 39, no. 4:417–33.

Buzan, Barry. 2014. *An Introduction to the English School: The Societal Approach*. Cambridge: Polity.

Buzan, Barry, and Ole Waever. 2003. *Regions and Powers: The Structure of International Security*. Cambridge: Cambridge University Press.

Caprio, Gerard, and Patrick Honohan. 2001. *Finance for Growth: Policy Choices in a Volatile World*. Washington, DC: World Bank.

Caprioli, Mary, and Mark A. Boyer. 2001. "Gender, Violence, and International Crisis." *Journal of Conflict Resolution* 45, no. 4:503–18.

Carr-Saunders, Alexander Morris. 1936. *World Population: Past Growth and Present Trends*. Oxford: Clarendon Press.

Cederman, Lars Erik, Kristian Skrede Gleditsch, and Halvard Buhaug. 2013. *Inequality, Grievances, and Civil War*. Cambridge: Cambridge University Press.

Central Intelligence Agency. 1985. *Soviet Military Power 1985*. Washington, DC: Central Intelligence Agency.

Chan, Steve. 1997. "In Search of the Democratic Peace: Problems and Promise." *Mershon International Studies Review* 41, no. 1:59–91.

Churchill, Winston. 1946. "United States of Europe: September 19, 1946. University of Zurich." Last accessed June 16, 2019. https://winstonchurchill.org/resources/speeches/1946-1963-elder-statesman/united-states-of-europe.

Cini, Michelle, and Nieves Pérez-Solórzano Borragán. 2016. *European Union Politics*. 5th ed. Oxford: Oxford University Press.

Clark, Christopher. 2012. *The Sleepwalkers: How Europe Went to War in 1914*. New York: Harper Collins.

Cline, Kirssa, J. Patrick Rhamey Jr., Alex is Henshaw, Alesia Sedziaka, Aakriti Tandon, and Thomas J. Volgy. 2011. "Identifying Regional Powers and their Status." In *Major Powers and the Quest for Status in International Politics,* edited by Thomas J. Volgy, Renato Corbetta, Keith A. Grant, and Ryan G. Baird, 133–57. New York: Palgrave Macmillan.

Clodfelter, Michael. 2017. *Warfare and Armed Conflicts: A Statistical Encyclopedia of Casualty and Other Figures, 1492–2015.* 4th ed. Jefferson, NC: McFarland.

Cohen, Raymond. 1994. "Pacific Unions: A Reappraisal of the Theory that Democracies Do Not Go to War with Each Other." *Review of International Studies* 20, no. 3:207–23.

Collier, Paul, and Anke Hoeffler. 2004. "Greed and Grievance in Civil War." *Oxford Economic Papers* 56:563–95.

Collier, Paul, Anke Hoeffler, and Mans Soderbom. 2004. "On the Duration of Civil War." *Journal of Peace Research* 41, no. 3:253–73.

Copeland, Dale C. 2012. "Realism and Neorealism in the Study of Regional Conflict." In *International Relations Theory and Regional Transformation*, edited by T. V. Paul, 49–73. Cambridge: Cambridge University Press.

Coppedge, Michael, John Gerring, Carl Henrik Knutsen, Staffan I. Lindberg, Jan Teorell, David Altman, Michael Bernhard, M. Steven Fish, Adam Glynn, Allen Hicken, Anna Lührmann, Kyle L. Marquardt, Kelly McMann, Pamela Paxton, Daniel Pemstein, Brigitte Seim, Rachel Sigman, Svend-Erik Skaaning, Jeffrey Staton, Steven Wilson, Agnes Cornell, Lisa Gastaldi, Haakon Gjerløw, Nina Ilchenko, Joshua Krusell, Laura Maxwell, Valeriya Mechkova, Juraj Medzihorsky, Josefine Pernes, Johannes von Römer, Natalia Stepanova, Aksel Sundström, Eitan Tzelgov, Yi-ting Wang, Tore Wig, and Daniel Ziblatt. 2019. "V-Dem [Country-Year/Country-Date] Dataset v9," Varieties of Democracy (V-Dem), last accessed November 14, 2019, https://www.v-dem.net/en/.

Corbetta, Renato, Thomas J. Volgy, and J. Patrick Rhamey. 2013. "Major Power Status (In)Consistency and Political Relevance in International Relations Studies." *Peace Economics, Peace Science and Public Policy* 19, no. 3:291–307.

Correlates of War Project. 2017. "State System Membership List, v2016," last accessed November 14, 2019. http://correlatesofwar.org.

Crawford, Neta C. 2018. *Human Cost of the Post-9/11 Wars: Lethality and the Need for Transparency.* Providence, RI: Watson Institute.

Dahl, Robert A. 1957. "The Concept of Power." *Behavioral Science* 2, no. 3:201–25.

Deudney, Daniel H. 1995. "The Philadelphian System: Sovereignty, Arms Control, and Balance of Power in the American States-Union, Circa 1787–1861." *International Organization* 49, no. 2:191–228.

DeRouen, Karl R. Jr., and David Sobek. 2004. "The Dynamics of Civil War Duration and Outcome." *Journal of Peace Research* 41, no. 3:303–20.

De Soto, Hernando. 2000. *The Mystery of Capital: Why Capitalism Triumphs in the West and Fails Everywhere Else.* London: Black Swan.

Diehl, Paul F., and Gary Goertz. 2000. *War and Peace in International Rivalry.* Ann Arbor: University of Michigan Press.

Dixon, William J. 1993. "Democracy and the Management of International Conflict." *Journal of Conflict Resolution* 37, no. 1:42–68.

Dixon, William J. 1994. "Democracy and the Peaceful Settlement of International Conflict." *American Political Science Review* 88, no. 1:14–32.

Doran, Charles F. 1991. *Systems in Crisis: New Imperatives of High Politics at Century's End.* Cambridge: Cambridge University Press.

Eagly, Alice H., and Mary C. Johannesen-Schmidt. 2002. "The Leadership Styles of Women and Men." *Journal of Social Issues* 57, no. 4:781–97.

Easterly, William R. 2002. *The Elusive Quest for Growth: Economists' Adventures and Misadventures in the Tropics.* Cambridge, MA: MIT Press.

Edelstein, David M. 2017. *Over the Time Horizon: Time, Uncertainty, and the Rise of Great Powers.* Cornell, NY: Cornell University Press.

Efird, Brian, Jacek Kugler, and Gaspare M. Genna. 2003. "From War to Integration: Generalizing Power Transition Theory." *International Interactions* 29, no. 4:293–313.

Farwell, Byron. 1972. *Queen Victoria's Little Wars.* New York: W. W. Norton.

Favretto, Katja. 2009. "Should Peacemakers Take Sides? Major Power Mediation, Coercion, and Bias." *American Political Science Review* 103, no. 2: 248–63.

Fearon, James D. 1994. "Domestic Political Audiences and the Escalation of International Disputes." *American Political Science Review* 88:577–92.

Fearon, James. 1995. "Rationalist Explanations for War." *International Organization* 49, no. 3:379–414.

Fearon, James, and David Laitin. 2003. "Ethnicity, Insurgency, and Civil War." *American Political Science Review* 97, no. 1:75–90.

Findley, Michael G., and Tze Kwang Teo. 2006. "Rethinking Third-Party Interventions into Civil Wars: An Actor-Centric Approach." *The Journal of Politics* 68, no. 4:828–37.

Fisunoglu, Ali, Kyungkook Kang, Tadeusz Kugler, and Jacek Kugler. 2019. "Absolute Political Capacity Dataset, 1960–2015." Presented at the annual meeting of the International Studies Association, Toronto, Canada.

Foss, Christopher F. 2003. *Jane's Tanks and Combat Vehicles Recognition Guide.* 3rd ed. New York: Collins.

Freedom House. 2019. "Freedom in the World Data and Resources." Last accessed June 18, 2019. https://freedomhouse.org/content/freedom-world-data-and-resources.

Fromkin, David. 1980. "The Great Game in Asia." *Foreign Affairs* 58, no. 4:937–38.

Gartzke, Erik. 2007. "The Capitalist Peace." *American Journal of Political Science* 51, no. 1:166–91.

Gartzke, Erik, and Matthew Kroenig. 2016. "Nukes with Numbers: Empirical Research on the Consequences of Nuclear Weapons for International Conflict." *Annual Review of Political Science* 19:397–412.

Gent, Stephen E. 2008. "Going in When it Counts: Military Intervention and the outcome of Civil Conflicts." *International Studies Quarterly* 52, no. 4:713–35.

Gibler, Douglas M. 2012. *The Territorial Peace: Borders, State Development, and International Conflict.* Cambridge: Cambridge University Press.

Gilligan, Michael. J. 1997. *Empowering Exporters: Reciprocity, Delegation, and Collective Action in American Trade Policy.* Ann Arbor: University of Michigan Press.

Gilpin, Robert. 1987. *The Political Economy of International Relations.* Princeton, NJ: Princeton University Press.

Gilpin, Robert, and William Gilpin. 1975. *US Power and the Multinational Corporation.* London: Macmillan.

Gleditsch, Kristian Skrede. 2002. *All International Politics Is Local: The Diffusion of Conflict, Integration, and Democratization.* Ann Arbor: University of Michigan Press.

Gleditsch, Kristian Skrede, Idean Salehyan, and K. Schultz. 2008. "Fighting at Home, Fighting Abroad: How Civil Wars Lead to International Disputes." *Journal of Conflict Resolution* 52, no. 2:479–506.

Goldberg, Leonard (Executive Producer) and John Badham (Director). 1983. *WarGames* [Motion Picture]. United States: MGM/UA.

Goldstone, Jack. 1991. *Revolution and Rebellion in the Early Modern World.* Berkeley: University of California Press.

Haas, Ernst B. 1964. *Beyond the Nation State.* Stanford, CA: Stanford University Press.

Haas, Mark L. 2005. *The Ideological Origins of Great Power Politics, 1789-1989.* Ithaca, NY: Cornell University Press.

Hartley, Janet M. 1992. "Is Russia Part of Europe? Russian Perceptions of Europe in the Reign of Alexander I." *Cahiers du Monde Russia*, 33, no. 4: 369–85.

Hdr.undp.org. *Human Development Index (HDI) | Human Development Reports.* Last accessed November 9, 2019. http:hdr.undp.org/en/content/human-development-index-hdi.asp.

Hendrix, Cullen S., and Idean Salehyan. 2012. "Climate Change, Rainfall, and Social Conflict in Africa." *Journal of Peace Research* 49, no. 1:35–50.

Henning, C. Randall. 2017. *Tangled Governance: International Regime Complexity, the Troika, and the Euro Crisis.* Oxford: Oxford University Press.

Hensel, Paul R., and Paul F. Diehl. 1994. "Testing Empirical Propositions about Shatterbelts, 1945–1976." *Political Geography* 13, no. 1:33–51.

Hentz, James J. 2005. *South Africa and the Logic of Regional Cooperation.* Bloomington: Indiana University Press.

Hentz, James J. 2008. *Into Africa.* Hoover Digest No. 4. Palo Alto, CA: Hoover Institution.

Högström, John. 2013. "Does the Choice of Democracy Measure Matter? Comparisons between Two Leading Democracy Indices, Freedom House and Polity IV." *Government and Opposition* 48, no. 2:201–21.

Holzman, Franklyn D. 1982. "Soviet Military Spending: Assessing the Numbers Game." *International Security* 6, no. 4:78–100.

Horowitz, Michael C. 2018. "Artificial Intelligence, International Competition, and the Balance of Power." *Texas National Security Review* 1, no. 3 (May): 37–57.

Ikenberry, G. John. 2001. *After Victory: Institutions, Strategic Restraint, and the Rebuilding of Order After Major Wars*. Princeton, NJ: Princeton University Press.

Ikenberry, G. John. 2011. *Liberal Leviathan: The Origins, Crisis, and Transformation of the American World Order*. Princeton, NJ: Princeton University Press.

Inglehart, Ronald. 1997. *Modernization and Postmodernization: Cultural, Economic and Political Change in 43 Societies*. Princeton, NJ: Princeton University Press.

Jackson, Richard, and Neil Howe. 2012. *The Graying of the Great Powers: Demography and the Geopolitics in the 21st Century*. Washington, DC: Center for Strategic and International Studies.

Jenne, Erin K., and Milos Popovic. 2018. "Managing Internationalized Civil Wars." In *The Oxford Research Encyclopedia of Empirical International Relations Theory*, vol. 2, edited by William R. Thompson, 511–21. Oxford: Oxford University Press.

Jervis, Robert. 1982–1983. "Deterrence and Perception." *International Security*, 7, no. 3:3–30.

Kang, Kyungkook, and Jacek Kugler. 2015. "Assessment of Deterrence and Missile Defense in East Asia: A Power Transition Perspective." *International Area Studies Review* 18, no. 3:280–96.

Kang, Kyungkook, and Tadeusz Kugler. 2017. "International Political Economy and Political Demography: An Interdisciplinary Exploration." In *Interdisciplinary Approaches to International Studies*, edited by Patrick James and Steve Yetiv, 263–87. London: Palgrave Macmillan.

Kant, Immanuel. (1795) 1991. "Perpetual Peace: A Philosophical Sketch." In *Kant: Political Writings*, edited by H. S. Reiss. Cambridge: Cambridge University Press, 93–130.

Katzenstein, Peter J. 2005. *A World of Regions: Asia and Europe in the American Imperium*. Ithaca, NY: Cornell University Press.

Keller, Jonathan W., and Dennis M. Foster. 2016. "Don't Tread on Me: Constraint-Challenging Presidents and Strategic Conflict Avoidance." *Presidential Studies Quarterly* 46, no. 4:756–62.

Kennan, George F. [Mr. X]. 1947. "The Sources of Soviet Conduct." *Foreign Affairs* 25, no. 4 (July): 566–82.

Keohane, Robert O. 1984. *After Hegemony: Cooperation and Discord in the World Political Economy*. Princeton, NJ: Princeton University Press.

Keohane, Robert O., and Joseph S. Nye. 1977. *Power and Interdependence: World Politics in Transition*. Boston, MA: Little, Brown.

Kim, Woosang. 1989. "Power, Alliance, and Major Wars, 1816–1975." *Journal of Conflict Resolution* 33, no. 2:255–73.

Kim, Woosang. 1991. "Alliance Transitions and Great Power War." *American Journal of Political Science* 35, no. 4:833–50.

Kindleberger, Charles P. 1973. *The World in Depression 1929–1939*. Berkeley: University of California Press.

King, Gary, Robert O. Keohane, and Sidney Verba. 1994. *Designing Social Inquiry: Scientific Inference in Qualitative Research*. Princeton, NJ: Princeton University Press.

Kipling, Rudyard. 1915. "In Aid of Recruiting, Southport." *Southport Guardian*, June 23.

Kirshner, Jonathan. 1995. *Currency and Coercion*. Princeton, NJ: Princeton University Press.

Klein, James P., Gary Goertz, and Paul F. Diehl. 2006. "The New Rivalry Data Set: Procedures and Patterns." *Journal of Peace Research* 43, no. 3:331–48.

Krugman, Paul. 1991. "Increasing Returns and Economic Geography." *Journal of Political Economy* 99, no. 3:483–99.

Krulwich, Robert. 2016. "You (and Almost Everyone You Know) Owe Your Life to This Man." *National Geographic*, March 24. Last accessed July 29, 2019. https://news.nationalgeographic.com/2016/03/you-and-almost-everyone-you-know-owe-your-life-to-this-man.

Kugler, Jacek, and Frank Zagare. 1990. "The Long-Term Stability of Deterrence." *International Interactions* 15:255–78.

Kugler, Jacek, and William Domke. 1986. "Comparing the Strength of Nations." *Comparative Political Studies* 19, no. 1:39–69.

Kugler, Jacek, Ronald L. Tammen, and John Thomas. 2012. "How Political Performance Impacts Conflict and Growth." In *The Performance of Nations*, edited by Jacek Kugler and Ronald L. Tammen, 75–96. Lanham, MD: Rowman and Littlefield.

Kugler, Tadeusz. 2017. "Demography and International Relations: Politics, Economics, Sociology and Public Health." In *Interdisciplinary Approaches to International Studies*, edited by Patrick James and Steve Yetiv, 229–61. London: Palgrave Macmillan.

Kugler, Tadeusz, and S. Swaminathan, S. 2006. "The Politics of Population." *International Studies Review* 8, no. 4:581–96.

Kugler, Tadeusz, Kyungkook Kang, Jacek Kugler, Marina Arbetman-Rabinowitz, and John Thomas. 2013. "Demographic & Economic Consequences of Conflict." *International Studies Quarterly* 57, no. 1:1–12.

Lake, David A. 2006. "American Hegemony and the Future of East–West Relations." *International Studies Perspectives* 7, no. 1:23–30.

Lake, David A. 2007. "Escape from the State of Nature: Authority and Hierarchy in World Politics." *International Security* 32, no. 1:47–79.

Lake, David A. 2009. *Hierarchies in International Relations*. Ithaca, NY: Cornell University Press.

Larson, Deborah, T. V. Paul, and William C. Wohlforth. 2014. *Status in World Politics*. Cambridge: Cambridge University Press.

Layne, Christopher. 1997. "From Preponderance to Offshore Balancing: America's Future Grand Strategy." *International Security* 22, no. 1:86–124.

Lee, Ronald D., and Andrew Mason. 2006. "What Is the Demographic Dividend?" *Finance and Development* 43, no. 3:16–17.

Leeds, Brett Ashley. 2003. "Do Alliances Deter Aggression? The Influence of Military Alliances on the Initiation of Militarized Interstate Disputes." *American Journal of Political Science* 47, no. 3:427–39.

Leeds, Brett Ashley. 2018. "Alliance Treaty Obligations and Provisions (ATOP) Codebook, Version 4.0," last accessed November 14, 2019, www.atopdata.org/data.html.

Leeds, Brett Ashley, Jeffrey M. Ritter, Sara McLaughlin Mitchell, and Andrew G. Long. 2002. "Alliance Treaty Obligations and Provisions, 1815–1944." *International Interactions* 28:237–60.

Leeds, Brett Ashley, Jeffrey Ritter, Sara McLaughlin Mitchell, and Andrew G. Long. 2018. "ATOP V4.01 Codesheets." Last accessed July 12, 2019. www.atopdata.org/documentation.html.

Lemke, Douglas. 2002. *Regions of War and Peace*. Cambridge: Cambridge University Press.

Lemke, Douglas. 2011. "Intra-National IR in Africa." *Review of International Studies* 37, no. 1:49–70.

Lemke, Douglas, and Jeff Carter. 2016. "Birth Legacies, State Making, and War." *The Journal of Politics,* 78, no.2: 497–511.

Lemke, Douglas, and Patrick M. Regan. 2004. "Interventions as Influence." In *The Scourge of War: New Extension on an Old Problem*, edited by Paul F. Diehl, 145–68. Ann Arbor: University of Michigan Press.

Lemke, Douglas, and William Reed. 1996. "Regime Types and Status Quo Evaluations: Power Transition Theory and the Democratic Peace." *International Interactions* 22, no. 2:143–64.

Lemke, Douglas, and William Reed. 2001. "The Relevance of Politically Relevant Dyads." *Journal of Conflict Resolution* 45, no. 1:126–44.

Levin, Dov H. "Partisan Electoral Interventions by Great Powers: Introducing the PEIG Dataset." *Conflict Management and Peace Science* 36, no. 1:88–106.

Levy, Jack S. 1988. "Domestic Politics and War." *Journal of Interdisciplinary History* 18, no. 4:653–73.

Levy, Jack S. 2008. "Power Transition Theory and the Rise of China." In *China's Ascent: Power, Security, and the Future of International Politics*, edited by R. S. Ross and Z. Feng, 11–33. Ithaca, NY: Cornell University Press.

Mackay, Ron. 2005. *Britain's Fleet Air Arm in World War Two*. Atglen, PA: Schiffer.

Mackinder, H. J. 1904. "The Geographical Pivot of History." *The Geographical Journal* 23, no. 4:421–37.

Mackinder, H. J. 1919. *Democratic Ideals and Reality: A Study in the Politics of Reconstruction*. New York: Henry Holt.

Mansfield, Edward D., and Jack Snyder. 1995. "Democratization and the Danger of War." *International Security* 20, no. 1:5–38.

Maoz, Zeev. 2006. "Network Polarization, Network Interdependence, and International Conflict, 1816–2002." *Journal of Peace Research* 43, no. 4:391–411.

Markowitz, Jonathan, Christopher Fariss, and R. Black McMahan. 2019. "Producing Goods and Projecting Power: How What You Make Influences What You Take." *Journal of Conflict Resolution* 63, no. 6: 1368–402.

Marshall, Monty G., Ted Robert Gurr, and Keith Jaggers. 2018. *Polity IV Project: Political Regime Characteristics and Transitions, 1800–2017*. Vienna, VA: Center for Systemic Peace, last accessed July 31, 2019. www.systemicpeace.org/inscrdata.html.

Marx, Karl. (1818–1883) 1959. *Das Kapital, a Critique of Political Economy*. Chicago, IL: H. Regnery.

Mearsheimer, John J. 1990. "Back to the Future: Instability in Europe after the Cold War." *International Security* 15, no. 1:5–56.

Mearsheimer, John J. 1995. "The False Promise of International Institutions." *International Security* 19, no. 3:5–49.

Mearsheimer, John J. 2012. Introduction to *American Diplomacy: Sixtieth-Anniversary Expanded Edition*, by George F. Kennan. Chicago: University of Chicago Press, vii–xliv.

Ministry of Defence. 2019. "UK Nuclear Deterrent." Last accessed November 14, 2019. https://assets.publishing.service.gov.uk/government/uploads/system/uploads/attachment_data/file/510878/Fact_sheet-nuclear_deterrent_FINAL_v15.pdf.

Mitchell, Sara McLaughlin, Scott Gates, and Håvard Hegre. 1999. "Evolution in Democracy-War Dynamics." *Journal of Conflict Resolution* 43, no. 6:771–92.

Modelski, George. 1987. *Long Cycles in World Politics*. Seattle: University of Washington Press.

Modelski, George. 1996. "Evolutionary Paradigm for Global Politics." *International Studies Quarterly* 40, no. 3:321–42.

Modelski, George. 2012. "Long Cycles and International Regimes." *E-International Relations*, October 15. Last accessed July 31, 2019. www.e-ir.info/2012/10/15/long-cycles-and-international-regimes.

Modelski, George, and William R. Thompson. 1988. *Seapower in Global Politics, 1494–1993*. Seattle: University of Washington Press.

Modelski, George, Tessaleno Devezas, and William R. Thompson, eds. 2008. *Globalization as Evolutionary Process: Modeling Global Change*. New York: Routledge.

Morgenthau, Hans J. (1948) 1985. *Politics Among Nations: The Struggle for Power and Peace*. 6th ed. Revised by Kenneth W. Thompson. New York: McGraw-Hill.

Mulligan, William. 2010. "Gladstone and the Primacy of Foreign Policy." In *The Primacy of Foreign Policy in British History, 1660–2000*, edited by William Mulligan and Brendan Simms. London: Palgrave Macmillan, 181-196.

Norrlof, Carla. 2010. *America's Global Advantage: U.S. Hegemony and International Cooperation*. New York: Cambridge University Press.

North Atlantic Treaty Organization. "Lord Ismay," Last accessed November 14, 2019, https://www.nato.int/cps/en/natohq/declassified_137930.htm.

Oneal, John R., and Bruce Russett. 1999. "Assessing the Liberal Peace with Alternative Specifications: Trade Still Reduces Conflict." *Journal of Peace Research* 36, no. 4:423–42.

Organization of African Unity. 2000. *Constitutive Act of the African Union*. Last accessed July 27, 2019. https://au.int/sites/default/files/pages/34873-file-constitutiveact_en.pdf.

Organski, A. F. K. 1968. *World Politics*, 2nd ed. New York: Alfred A. Knopf.

Organski, A. F. K., and Jacek Kugler. 1977. "The Costs of Major Wars: The Phoenix Factor." *The American Political Science Review* 71, no. 4:1347–66.

Palmer, Glenn, Vito D'Orazio, Michael R. Kenwick, and Roseanne W. McManus. Forthcoming. "Updating the Militarized Interstate Dispute Data: A Response to Gibler, Miller, and Little." *International Studies Quarterly*. Last accessed July 31, 2019. https://doi.org/10.1093/isq/sqz045.

Pedersen, Thomas. 2002. "Cooperative Hegemony: Power, Ideas and Institutions in Regional Integration." *Review of International Studies* 28, no. 4:677–96.

Peifer, Douglas Carl. 2016. *Choosing War: Presidential Decisions in the* Maine, Lusitania, *and Panay Incidents.* Oxford: Oxford University Press.

Pemstein, Daniel, Kyle L. Marquardt, Eitan Tzelgov, Yi-ting Wang, Juraj Medzihorsky, Joshua Krusell, Farhad Miri, and Johannes von Römer. 2019. "The V-Dem Measurement Model: Latent Variable Analysis for Cross-National and Cross-Temporal Expert-Coded Data." V-Dem Working Paper No. 21, 4th ed., Varieties of Democracy Institute, University of Gothenburg.

Philips, Valmai. 1984. *Enterprising Australians.* Kensington, New South Wales, Australia: Bay Books.

Picheta, Rob. 2019. "Nissan Cites Brexit 'Uncertainty' as it Scraps Plans to Build Model in Britain." *CNN,* February 3. Last accessed June 30, 2019. www.cnn.com/2019/02/03/business/nissan-sunderland-scraps-plans-gbr-intl/index.html.

Posen, Barry R. 2017. "Civil Wars and the Structure of World Power." *Daedalus* 146, no. 4:167–79.

Powers, Kathy, and Gary Goertz. 2011. "The Economic-Institutional Construction of Regions: Conceptualisation and Operationalisation." *Review of International Studies* 37. No. 5: 2387–416.

Preston, Diana. 2015. Lusitania: *An Epic Tragedy.* New York: Bloomsbury.

Quackenbush, Stephen. L. 2011. *Understanding General Deterrence: Theory and Application.* New York: Palgrave Macmillan.

Quackenbush, Stephen L. 2017. "Empirical Analyses of Deterrence." In *Oxford Encyclopedia of Empirical International Relations Theory,* edited by William R. Thompson. Oxford: Oxford University Press, 682–701.

Rasler, Karen, and William R. Thompson. 2005. *Puzzles of the Democratic Peace: Theory, Geopolitics and the Transformation of World Politics.* London: Palgrave Macmillan.

Ray, James Lee. 1995. *Democracy and International Conflict: An Evaluation of the Democratic Peace Proposition.* Columbia: University of South Carolina Press.

Regan, Patrick M. 2000. *Civil Wars and Foreign Powers: Outside Interventions and Intrastate Conflict.* Ann Arbor: University of Michigan Press.

Regan, Patrick M. 2002. "Third-Party Interventions and the Duration of Intrastate Conflicts." *Journal of Conflict Resolution* 46, no. 1:55–73.

Reid, Helen. 2019. "Brexit Uncertainty Has Cost Britain 600 Million Pounds a Week—Goldman Sachs." Reuters, April 1. Last accessed June 30, 2019. www.reuters.com/article/us-britain-eu-goldmansachs/brexit-uncertainty-has-cost-britain-600-million-pounds-a-week-goldman-sachs-idUSKCN1RD25N.

Reimann, Gunter. 2011. *The Vampire Economy: Doing Business under Fascism.* Auburn, AL: Ludwig von Mises Institute.

Reuters. 2015. "China Says its Gender Imbalance 'Most Serious' in the World." January 21. Last accessed July 2, 2019. https://uk.reuters.com/article/uk-china-onechild-idUKKBN0KU0V720150121.

Rhamey, J. Patrick Jr. 2019. "Regions of Opportunity and Willingness Data Codebook v3." Last accessed June 30, 2019. www.patrickrhamey.com/row.

Rhamey Jr, J. Patrick, and Bryan R. Early. 2013. "Going for the Gold: Status-Seeking Behavior and Olympic Performance." *International Area Studies Review* 16, no. 3:244–61.

Rhamey, J. Patrick Jr., Michael O. Slobodchikoff, and Thomas J. Volgy. 2015. "Order and Disorder across Geopolitical Space: The Effect of Declining Dominance on Interstate Conflict." *Journal of International Relations and Development* 18, no. 4: 383–406.

Rhamey, J. Patrick, Kirssa Cline, Nicholas Thorne, Jacob Cramer, Jennifer L. Miller, and Thomas J. Volgy. 2012. "The Diplomatic Contacts Database v. 3.0." School of Government and Public Policy, University of Arizona, Tucson. Last accessed November 14, 2019. http://www.u.arizona.edu/~volgy/data.html.

Romer, Paul M. 1990. "Endogenous Technological Change." *Journal of Political Economy* 98, no. 5:S71–S102.

Rosenau, James N. 1971. "Pre-Theories and Theories of Foreign Policy." In *The Scientific Study of Foreign Policy*, edited by James N. Rosenau, 95–150. New York: New York Free Press.

Rummel, R. J. 1983. "Libertarianism and International Violence." *Journal of Conflict Resolution* 27, no. 1:27–71.

Rummel, R. J. 1985. "Libertarian Propositions on Violence within and between Nations: A Test Against Published Research Results." *Journal of Conflict Resolution* 29, no. 3:419–55.

Russett, Bruce, John R. Oneal, and David R. Davis. 1998. "The Third Leg of the Kantian Tripod for Peace: International Organizations and Militarized Disputes, 1950–1985." *International Organization* 52, no. 3:441–67.

Ryan, Yasmine. 2010. "Gabon 'Siphoned Funds' to France." *Al-Jazeera*, December 29. Last Accessed November 14, 2019. www.aljazeera.com/news/africa/2010/12/2010122984115531832.html.

Sagan, Carl, Richard Turco, George W. Rathjens, Ronald H. Siegel, Starley L. Thompson, and Stephen H. Schneider. 1986. "The Nuclear Winter Debate." *Foreign Affairs* 65, no. 1 (Fall): 163–78.

Sakuwa, Kentaro. 2019. "Regional Alliance Structure and International Conflict." *World Political Science* 15, no. 1:55–74.

Sakuwa, Kentaro, and William R. Thompson. 2019. "On the Origins, Persistence and Termination of Spatial and Positional Rivalries in World Politics: Elaborating a Two-Issue Theory of Conflict Escalation." *International and Areas Studies Review*. https://doi.org/10.1177/2233865919846729.

Sandler, Todd. 1999. "Alliance Formation, Alliance Expansion, and the Core." *Journal of Conflict Resolution* 43, no. 6:727–47.

Sarkees, Meredith, and Frank Wayman. 2010. *Resort to War: 1816–2007*. Washington, DC: CQ Press.

Sarotte, Mary Elise. 2014. "A Broken Promise? What the West Really Told Moscow about NATO Expansion." *Foreign Affairs* 93, no. 5 (September/October): 90–97.

Singer, J. David, Stuart Bremer, and John Stuckey. 1972. "Capability Distribution, Uncertainty, and Major Power War, 1820–1965." In *Peace, War, and Numbers*, edited by Bruce Russet, 19–48. Beverly Hills, CA: Sage.

Snyder, Jack. 1991. *Myths of Empire: Domestic Politics and International Ambition*. Ithaca, NY: Cornell University Press.

Snyder, Jack. 2004. "One World, Rival Theories." *Foreign Policy* 145 (November/December): 52–62.

Solow, Robert. 1956. "A Contribution to the Theory of Economic Growth." *The Quarterly Journal of Economics* 70, no. 1:65–94.

Stack, Lian. 2011. "In Slap at Syria, Turkey Shelters Anti-Assad Fighters." *New York Times*, October 27. Last accessed November 14, 2019. https://www.nytimes.com/2011/10/28/world/europe/turkey-is-sheltering-antigovernment-syrian-militia.html

Starr, Harvey. 1978. "'Opportunity' and 'Willingness' as Ordering Concepts in the Study of War." *International Interactions* 4, no. 4:363–87.

Stasavage, David. 1997. "The CFA Franc Zone and Fiscal Discipline." *Journal of African Economies* 6, no. 1:132–67.

State Department. 2019. "New START Treaty Aggregate Numbers of Strategic Offensive Arms." Fact sheet, January 12 (effective date: March 1, 2019). www.state.gov/new-start-treaty-aggregate-numbers-of-strategic-offensive-arms-10/#_ftn1.

Stiglitz, Joseph E. 2003. *Globalization and its Discontents*. New York: W. W. Norton.

Stone, Randall W. 2011. *Controlling Institutions: International Organizations and the Global Economy*. New York: Cambridge University Press.

Strange, Susan. 1988. *States and Markets*. London: Pinter.

Strange, Susan. 1996. *The Retreat of the State: The Diffusion of Power in the World Economy*. Cambridge: Cambridge University Press.

Sullivan, Patricia L., and Michael T. Koch. 2008. "Military Intervention by Powerful States (MIPS) Codebook, Version 2.0." Last accessed June 23, 2019. http://plsullivan.web.unc.edu/files/2011/09/MIPS_codebook_Sullivan.pdf.

Sullivan, Patricia L., and Michael T. Koch. 2011. "MIPS_codebook_Sullivan.pdf." Replication data for Military Intervention by Powerful States (MIPS), last accessed June 23, 2019, Harvard Dataverse, V1. https://doi.org/10.7910/DVN/KRUFQH/ZDOATU.

Tammen, Ronald L., and Jacek Kugler, eds. 2012. *The Performance of Nations*. Lanham, MD: Rowman and Littlefield.

Tessman, Brock F., and Steve Chan. 2004. "Power Cycles, Risk Propensity, and Great-Power Deterrence." *Journal of Conflict Resolution* 48, no. 2:131–53.

Thies, Cameron. 2013. *The United States, Israel, and the Search for International Order: Socializing States*. New York: Routledge.

Thompson, William R. 1986. "Polarity, the Long Cycle, and Global Power Warfare." *Journal of Conflict Resolution* 30:587–615.

Thompson, William. R. 1990. "Long Waves, Technological Innovation, and Relative Decline." *International Organization* 44, no. 2:201–33.

Thompson, William R. 1996. "Democracy and Peace: Putting the Cart before the Horse?" *International Organization* 50, no. 1:141–74.

Thompson, William R. 2001. "Identifying Rivals and Rivalries in World Politics." *International Studies Quarterly* 45, no. 4:557–86.

Thompson, William. R. 2003. *The Emergence of the Global Political Economy*. London: Routledge.

Thompson, William R., ed. 2018. *The Oxford Encyclopedia of Empirical International Relations Theory*. Oxford: Oxford University Press.

Tieku, Thomas Kwasi. 2019. "The African Union: Successes and Failures." In *Oxford Research Encyclopedia of Politics*. Oxford: Oxford University Press, last accessed November 14, 2019, https://oxfordre.com/politics/view/10.1093/acrefore/9780190228637.001.0001/acrefore-9780190228637-e-703.

Toussaint, Eric. 2014. "Domination of the United States on the World Bank." *Committee for the Abolition of Third World Debt*. Last accessed November 11, 2019. http://cadtm.org/domination-of-the-united-states-on.

Tull, Denis M. 2006. "China's Engagement in Africa: Scope, Significance and Consequences." *Journal of Modern African Studies* 44, no. 3:459–79.

Tyler, Patrick E. 1996. "China's Military Stumbles Even as Its Power Grows." *New York Times*, December 3.

United Nations. 2019. "Summary of Contribution to UN Peacekeeping by Country, Mission, and Post." Last accessed June 14, 2019. https://peacekeeping.un.org/sites/default/files/3-country_and_mission.pdf.

United Nations, Department of Economic and Social Affairs, Population Division. 2015. *World Population Prospects: The 2015 Revision*. DVD Edition. New York: Department of Economic and Social Affairs, United Nations.

United Nations, Department of Economic and Social Affairs, Population Division. 2019. *World Population Prospects: The 2019 Revision*. DVD Edition. New York: Department of Economic and Social Affairs, United Nations.

United Nations High Commissioner for Refugees. "Syria Observatory for Human Rights." www.syriahr.com/en/?p=120851. Data, last accessed July 29, 2019, from the for Syria available at https://data2.unhcr.org/en/situations/syria.

United States Strategic Bombing Survey Summary Report (Pacific War). 1946, July 1. Washington, DC: U.S. Government Printing Office. Last accessed June 26, 2019. www.anesi.com/ussbs01.htm#jstetw.

U.S. Department of Defense, Office of Economic Adjustment. 2017. *Defense Spending by State—Fiscal Year 2017*. Washington, DC: Department of Defense.

Valeriano, Brandon, and Ryan C. Maness. 2015. *Cyber War versus Cyber Realities: Cyber Conflict in the International System*. Oxford: Oxford University Press.

Volden, Craig. 2006. "States as Policy Laboratories: Emulating Success in Children's Health Insurance Program." *American Journal of Political Science* 50, no. 2:294–312.

Volgy, Thomas J. 1974. "Reducing Conflict in International Politics: The Impact of Structural Variables." *International Studies Quarterly* 18, no. 2:179–210.

Volgy, Thomas J., Elizabeth Fausett, Keith A. Grant, and Stuart Rodgers. 2008. "Identifying Formal Intergovernmental Organizations." Journal of Peace Research 45, no. 6:849–62. Data, last accessed July 27, 2019, are available at www.u.arizona.edu/~volgy/data.html.

Volgy, Thomas J., Kelly Marie Gordell, Paul Bezerra, and J. Patrick Rhamey Jr. 2017. "Conflict, Regions, and Regional Hierarchies." In Oxford Encyclopedia of Empirical International Relations Theory, edited by William R. Thompson. Oxford: Oxford University Press, 335–62.

Volgy, Thomas J., Paul Bezerra, Jacob Cramer, and J. Patrick Rhamey Jr. 2017. "The Case for Comparative Regional Analysis in International Politics." *International Studies Review* 19:452–80.

Volgy, Thomas J., Renato Corbetta, Keith A. Grant, and Ryan G. Baird, eds. 2011. *Major Powers and the Quest for Status in International Politics*. New York: Palgrave.

Vreeland, James R., and Axel Dreher. 2014. *The Political Economy of the United Nations Security Council: Money and Influence*. New York: Cambridge University Press.

Wallerstein, Immanuel. 1982. *World-Systems Analysis: Theory and Methodology*. Beverly Hills, CA: Sage.

Walter Brown Note (Brown, Walter, Excerpts from the "Book"), July 10, 1945 to August 3, 1945, Box 2–1, State Department Material, James Byrnes Papers, Clemson University Library.

Waltz, Kenneth N. 1979. *Theory of International Politics*. New York: McGraw-Hill.

Waltz, Kenneth N. 1981. "The Spread of Nuclear Weapons: More May Better." *Adelphi Papers* 21, no. 171.

Waltz, Kenneth. N. 1988. "The Origins of War in Neorealist Theory." *Journal of Interdisciplinary History* 18, no. 4:615–28.

Waltz, Kenneth N. 2012. "Why Iran Should Get the Bomb: Nuclear Balancing Would Mean Stability." *Foreign Affairs* 91, no. 4 (July/August): 2–5.

Ward, Colin. 2011. "The Anarchist Sociology of Federalism." In *Autonomy, Solidarity, Possibility: The Colin Ward Reader*, edited by D. F. White and C Wilbert, 285–94. Oakland, CA: AK Press.

Warning, Michael J. 2009. *Transnational Public Governance: Networks, Law, and Legitimacy*. Basingstoke, UK: Palgrave Macmillan.

Wendt, Alexander. 1999. *Social Theory of International Politics*. Cambridge: Cambridge University Press.

Williamson, John. 1990. *Latin American Adjustment: How Much Has Happened?* Washington, DC: Peterson Institute for International Economics.

Williamson, John. 2000. "What Should the World Bank Think about the Washington Consensus?" *World Bank Research Observer* 15, no. 2 (August): 251–64.

Wilson, Ward. 2013. "The Bomb Did not Beat Japan . . . Stalin Did." *Foreign Policy*, May 30. Last accessed June 25, 2019. https://foreignpolicy.com/2013/05/30/the-bomb-didnt-beat-japan-stalin-did.

Wohlforth, William C. 1999. "The Stability of a Unipolar World." *International Security* 24, no. 1:5–41.

World Bank National Accounts Data and Organisation for Economic Co-operation and Development National Accounts Data Files. 2019. The World Bank. Last accessed November 14, 2019. https://data.worldbank.org.

The World Factbook. 2019. Washington, DC: Central Intelligence Agency. Last accessed August 1, 2019. www.cia.gov/library/publications/the-world-factbook.

Yesilada, Birol A., Jacek Kugler, Gaspare Genna, and Osman Goktug Tanrikulu. 2017. *Global Power Transition and the Future of the European Union*. New York: Routledge.

Zagare, Frank C., and D. Marc Kilgour. 2000. *Perfect Deterrence*. Cambridge: Cambridge University Press.

Index

Note: Page references for figures are *italicized* and tables are **bold**.